STRIVE FOR A 5

STRIVE FOR A 5

Preparing for the AP✦ United States History Exam

Colleen Shanley Kyle
Lakeside School, Seattle, Washington

Jonathan M. Chu
University of Massachusetts, Boston

Ellen W. Parisi
Williamsville East High School and D'Youville College

AMERICA'S HISTORY
Seventh Edition

James A. Henretta
Rebecca Edwards
Robert O. Self

Bedford/St. Martin's

Boston ◆ New York

For Bedford/St. Martin's

Publisher for History: Mary Dougherty
Executive Editor for History: Traci Mueller Crowell
Director of Development for History: Jane Knetzger
Senior Editor: Heidi Hood
Developmental Editor: Adrianne Hiltz
Assistant Production Editor: Lidia MacDonald
Production Supervisor: Andrew Ensor
Marketing Manager, U.S. History: Paul Stillitano
Senior Marketing Manager for High School: Daniel McDonough
Copyeditor: Susan Moore
Permissions Manager: Kalina Ingham Hintz
Photo Research: Carole Frohlich, The Visual Connection Image Research, Inc.
Cover Design: Billy Boardman
Cartography: Mapping Specialists, Ltd.
Text Design and Composition: DeNee Reiton Skipper
Printing and Binding: RR Donnelley and Sons

President: Joan E. Feinberg
Editorial Director: Denise B. Wydra
Director of Marketing: Karen R. Soeltz
Director of Production: Susan W. Brown
Associate Director, Editorial Production: Elise S. Kaiser
Managing Editor: Elizabeth M. Schaaf

Manufactured in the United States of America.

2 3 4 5 6 15 14 13 12

For information, write: Bedford/St. Martin's, 75 Arlington Street, Boston, MA 02116 (617-399-4000)

ISBN: 978-0-312-66195-3

Acknowledgments

Acknowledgments and copyrights can be found at the back of the book on page 265, which constitutes an extension of the copyright page.

Brief Contents

Contents

Preface for Teachers

Strive for a 5: Preparing for the AP U.S. History Exam is a student prep guide, designed to provide students with a thorough review of the course material while practicing AP test-taking skills that will stand them in good stead for the AP U.S. History (APEH) Exam. Designed to pair seamlessly with *America's History,* Seventh Edition, by James A. Henretta, Rebecca Edwards, and Robert O. Self, *Strive for a 5* applies a strong AP-specific framework to the text's narrative and offers extended attention to the College Board exam format and test-taking strategies. Either assigned as a core component of your test preparation coursework or recommended to students as an independently navigable review and practice tool, *Strive for a 5* is designed to familiarize students with the APUSH Exam format, thematically organize and review the key concepts, and provide level-appropriate practice exam questions and answer explanations. For students who are striving for a five, there is no better preparation guide.

The College Board is currently in the process of revising the exam structure of the APUSH and other AP exams. The revised exam emphasizes conceptual understanding and primary source analysis. Students will find ample and relevant practice of these skills within the pages of *Strive for a 5.*

Features of this Prep Guide

The **Strategies for the AP Exam** section serves as an introduction to the College Board's AP United States History Exam, complete with a breakdown of the scoring system, an overview of the different question forms, and essay-writing instruction.

In the **Review** section, **period overviews** follow the textbook's structure and group the course material into seven broad chronological periods, each with its own narrative summary and thematic timeline from *America's History.* Within each period, **Essential Questions** and conceptual **Review Exercises** guide students in organizing and summarizing the major developments of each era through graphic organizers, maps, and other conceptual review tools. Each of the seven parts include period-specific **Practice Questions**, including 15 multiple choice questions, one DBQ, and a few free-response essay questions, followed by an answer key with explanations and page references to *America's History,* Seventh Edition, for further review.

Two full-length AP-style practice exams conclude the volume. With 80 multiple-choice questions, a DBQ, and six free-response essay questions each, these practice exams offer students the chance to measure their progress and areas in need of further review before the College Board exam. Each practice exam comes with model answers and explanations keyed to *America's History,* Seventh Edition. Students will become increasingly comfortable with the AP style while completing a comprehensive review of the textbook material.

Acknowledgments

I am grateful to all who read and contributed to this work. Jonathan Chu and Ellen Parisi contributed to the discussion of document-based questions and scoring, as well to the selection of document-based and free-response questions. At Bedford/St. Martin's Director of Development for History, Jane Knetzger, gave me the opportunity to write this supplement, Editorial Assistant Adrianne Hiltz provided patience and nurturing support early in the writing process, and Senior Editor Heidi Hood skillfully saw the development of the book through to completion. I would like to thank my colleagues and students at Lakeside School and Deerfield Academy; my husband, Booth; my children, Aidan and Devin; and my own AP U.S. History teacher, Dr. Margaret Crocco, now of Teachers College, who set me on this path and continues to inspire me.

Colleen Shanley Kyle

About the Authors

Colleen Shanley Kyle holds a B.A. in history from Connecticut College and an M.A. from Middlebury College's Bread Loaf School of English. She teaches advanced courses in American studies and World History and a course on revolutions and insurgencies at Lakeside School in Seattle, Washington. She previously taught advanced U.S. History at Deerfield Academy in Deerfield, Massachusetts, where she was awarded the Distinguished Young Teacher's Chair. Colleen participated in an NEH Summer Institute on American women reformers at the University of Massachusetts; presented papers at the World History Association national conference and the Northwest World History Association conference; and is currently a World Affairs Council Fellow in Seattle. Earlier in her career, Colleen worked for Houghton Mifflin's College Division, managing its U.S. history list.

Jonathan M. Chu is associate professor of history at the University of Massachusetts-Boston. He has served as chair of the test development committees of the Advanced Placement U.S. History and College Level Equivalent examinations. In 2011, he assumed the chair of the Academic Advisory Council of the College Board and became a member of its Board of Trustees. He has also served as a reader and standard-setter for the exam since 1992. Chu has conducted professional development workshops for Texas Christian and Fitchburg State universities and for the Boston and Saugus (MA) public schools. The New England representative to the Academic Advisory Committee of the College Board, he has addressed the Organization of American Historians, the American Historical Association, the National Council of Social Studies (OAH-AHA-NCSS) Joint Conference and the College Board on various subjects including the teaching of American history and the Advanced Placement Program.

Ellen W. Parisi has taught the AP U.S. History course at Williamsville Central Schools in Amherst, NY, for over twenty-five years and has been involved with the AP exam in various capacities, as a reader, table, leader, and standard-setter, since 1985. She served on the AP U.S. History Test Development Committee from 1999 to 2003. Since 1998, she has been a College Board consultant, giving presentations at AP U.S. History workshops on teaching AP U.S. History and qualifying future teacher-trainers. She also gave a presentation to the New York State Board of Regents and the NCSS on the relevance of the AP U.S. History Exam.

STRIVE FOR A 5

SECTION 1
Strategies for the AP✦ Exam

✦AP and Advanced Placement Program are registered trademarks of the College Board, which was not involved in the production of and does not endorse this product

Preparing for the AP U.S. History Exam

The African American author James Baldwin once observed, "American history is longer, larger, more various, more beautiful, and more terrible than anything anyone has ever said about it." You have begun your in-depth examination of the story of the United States, and perhaps you've already discovered some beautiful and terrible truths that were new to you. You are also learning how historians examine and write about the past: how to "do" history.

A rigorous historical study of the nation is both challenging and rewarding. The AP Examination in May can serve as a culminating experience, the chance for you to demonstrate your mastery in one three-hour-and-five-minute-long testing period. Though the challenges of the course and test may feel overwhelming from time to time, rest assured that with a little advanced planning and effort, you can enter the examination room confidently. *Strive for a 5* will help you get there!

What's in This Book?

Preparation is the key to success in the AP U.S. History course. Your teacher has already helped you by selecting *America's History*, Seventh Edition, by James Henretta, Rebecca Edwards, and Robert O. Self, as the course textbook. Along with *Strive for a 5,* you have all the tools you need to earn a top score.

Section 1 (which you're reading right now) covers some important information about how to register for the exam, how to set up a review plan for yourself, and what skills and content are tested in the three-hour-and-five-minute test. Here you will also find explanations and examples of the three different types of questions on the AP Exam: multiple-choice questions, document-based questions, and free-response questions. Section 1 also explains how exams are scored so that you will have an idea how well you need to perform in order to achieve a top score.

Section 2 is the longest part of this preparation guide and follows the organization of *America's History*, which is divided into seven chronological parts. Within each part, you will find a thematic timeline and overview essay (both of which appear in the textbook, too), conceptual exercises to review content, and practice questions, including 15 multiple-choice questions, 1 document-based question (DBQ), and 2 or 3 free-response questions (FRQs). Prompts and hints are provided to guide your thinking and responses. At the end of each part, answers for the practice questions are provided with page references to *America's History,* Seventh Edition, to facilitate your review.

Section 3 consists of two full-length AP-style practice exams that require you to put all of your preparation into action. There are no hints this time; these are designed to follow the AP format closely to prepare you for the real thing. You will find extensive answer keys for both practice tests at the end of Section 3.

Overview of the Course

The AP U.S. History course is a comprehensive history of the country from the Columbian Exchange—that's the term for the exchange of peoples, microbes, plants, animals, and commodities around the Atlantic world following 1492—to the present. Your teacher and textbook authors will cover political, cultural, social, economic, and diplomatic history. You will need to be geographically literate, have an excellent grasp of chronology, and understand historical "point of view."

You will also learn how to analyze and interpret primary source materials, connect issues of one time period with those of another, and write clearly and succinctly in order to support a thesis. Thus there's a balance of historical content and skills that you will master as you strive for a 5.

Registering for the Exam

Your teacher and school are likely facilitating your exam registration, but if not, make sure that you do not miss the registration deadline (this usually falls in February). If you are taking this course on your own and are unaffiliated with a school, check with the College Board to find the name of an AP Coordinator for your area. If you are anxious about other registration issues, consult the College Board's Web site (**www.collegeboard.com**) and locate the main AP page. Here you can access a page for students and parents where you will find the *Bulletin for AP Students and Parents* as well as contact information for further inquiries.

Setting Up a Review Schedule

Your teacher has factored the testing date into his or her course planning; she or he may also offer review sessions that are specifically applicable to the AP test. Beyond what your teacher offers, be sure to set up your own review schedule, allowing time to review each of the seven sections of the text, to take and then review the two practice tests, and to review concepts that seem challenging, based on your practice test results.

The spring term at any high school tends to be hectic. Adding AP Exam preparation to your weekly academic goals a few months prior to the exam, particularly if you are taking exams in more than one topic, is essential. You should allow one week each for reviewing the seven textbook sections as outlined in Section 2 of this guide, plus a week each for taking and reviewing the practice tests. Cramming the night before is not a good idea. Your priority the evening before the test is to get a good night's sleep!

How Exams Are Scored

Scoring of the examination is weighted 50 percent to the multiple-choice questions, just over 25 percent to the standard essay questions, and just under 25 percent for the DBQ. The scoring of the multiple-choice questions is measured through a quantitative formula that can be found on the College Board's Web site.

As of 2011, the College Board has changed its method of scoring the multiple-choice section of this and all its AP Exams. In the past, partial credit was deducted for incorrect responses, but starting with the 2011 exam, you no longer lose points for wrong answers:

you simply earn points with correct answers. An incorrect answer affects your score the same as a skipped question would: it does not add or detract from the total score.

This means that you want to answer as many questions correctly as possible—and that making an educated guess on each and every question should be your goal. It is not a good idea to leave any multiple-choice question blank: even random guessing means that you have a one-in-five chance of earning a correct response. Yet you can only be confident of earning a high score by reviewing American history and familiarizing yourself with the College Board's style of questioning.

A critical element in the scoring of the free-response portion of the exam is ensuring that the essays, particularly the DBQs, are evaluated in a statistically valid way—or, that each year the administration of the exam is statistically comparable to the previous year. Each year, over one thousand faculty consultants, or "readers," gather in early June to rank the essays. Unlike a single teacher evaluating his or her own students' work, readers cannot make individual adjustments to compensate for a reasonable or unanticipated misinterpretation of a question. Evaluators must share a broad base of consensus regarding what each question is seeking and use clearly defined standards to guide them.

To provide each student with a fair assessment, rubrics are constructed for readers to use in applying uniform evaluation criteria for the free-response sections. Rubrics for the document-based question and standard essays are constructed by a small committee of experienced faculty consultants or readers known as "exam leaders." Each question has its own committee of exam leaders. Drawing from a general rubric, the exam leaders, selected from a cross section of senior table leaders (themselves highly experienced readers) and of school and college faculty, read through a large, random selection of exams to determine how students responded to the given question. This first read is done collectively; the exam leaders then compare their expectations of student performance to samples of actual performance and determine what elements create criteria for separating categories of answers.

AP readers then use these preliminary criteria to determine how the sample essays would rank across the nine-point scale, identifying what distinguishes strong essays from weak ones and drafting a specific rubric to assess future essays on this scale. The exam leaders in turn consult with table leaders, who review the samples selected to illustrate the spectrum of rankings and to help clarify and refine the rubric. Together, the table and exam leaders arrange sample packets of essays together with the final rubric, which serves to instruct others in the rankings and standardize the assessment of the essays. These packets are distributed to the remaining readers.

Over 350,000 students took the AP U.S. History Exam in 2009—so the exam readers needed to score over one million essays! Because the readers have so many exams to score, **your essays stand a much better likelihood of receiving a good score if they follow a clear essay structure of thesis, supporting evidence, and strong conclusion.**

In other words, you **must** be clear on what the question asks and respond to it as directly as possible. Begin most essentially with a clear and forthright thesis statement. Substantiate that thesis with relevant factual information from the documents (for DBQs) and from relevant background historical knowledge (for DBQs and FRQs). Finally, convey those thoughts through a well-structured, clearly worded essay with a logical conclusion.

Successful Historical Writing

Over two-thirds of the time you spend taking the test will be spent planning and writing the three essays. Framing and responding to analytical questions is an essential part of what historians do; in fact, poet W. H. Auden once noted, "History is, strictly speaking, the study of questions." The essay questions that you see on the AP Exam are designed so that there is more than one way to answer "correctly." As you respond to questions posed to you by your teachers and by the AP Exam writers, always think strategically about how you will frame your argument.

Effective historical writing differs from simple expression of opinion: you must use evidence to back up your generalizations and specific historical data to support your points. Effective historical essay writing starts with a clearly articulated thesis and should build upon a coherent organization.

What does it mean to organize your ideas effectively? Try this exercise. The following sentences are in scrambled order. Read them carefully and figure out how you can order them for maximum clarity. *Hint: which sentence establishes an idea that unifies all of the other information? That one should come first.*

(A) The southern terrain and climate lent itself to farming large tracks of land for cash crops.
(B) Over time, southern planters came to view themselves as akin to landed gentry and shaped a patriarchal social structure that reinforced their authority.
(C) Geographic, economic, and social factors all played a part in advancing the South's dependence on slavery.
(D) The most affordable means of tending to the plantations' cash crops was using slaves.
(E) Slavery was an integral part of southern colonial society.

Write the corresponding letters for each sentence how you think they should be ordered here: ✦ __________ ✦ __________ ✦ __________ ✦ __________ ✦ __________

Now that you've attempted to re-order the sentences, can you figure out what question was being asked?

Here is the question: How did economic, geographic, and social factors encourage the growth of slavery as an important part of the economy of the southern colonies between 1607 and 1775?

Here is how the paragraph can best be organized:

Slavery was an integral part of southern colonial society (E). Geographic, economic, and social factors all played a part in advancing the South's dependence on slavery (C). The southern terrain and climate lent itself to farming large tracks of land for cash crops (A). The most affordable means of tending to the plantations' cash crops was using slaves (D). Over time, southern planters came to view themselves as akin to landed gentry and shaped a patriarchal social structure that reinforced their authority (B).

Note the paragraph's underlying logic: the thesis, or topic sentence, addresses the three factors that influenced the southern development of slavery. Those three factors are then addressed in the order they are first mentioned in the first sentence. Chronology is suggested in the last sentence, which begins, "Over time . . ."

Besides ordering your information thoughtfully, you should always structure your response in a way that responds precisely to the question posed. After you have read a free-response or document-based question, ask yourself: "What is the question asking?" "How many paragraphs should my response have?" "What should the first paragraph include?" Be strategic. Be focused. Remember how many essays the AP readers need to get through in a very short period of time. Clarity and directness are essential qualities of highly scored responses.

Thus bound by the specific guardrails of the question posed, draft your thesis. Establish how many paragraphs you will need, and sketch out an outline that includes the examples you will use as evidence to support your thesis. As you begin to write your supporting paragraphs, remember that sentences need to be clear and coherent, as do entire paragraphs. Each paragraph's topic sentence serves as the thesis for that paragraph; in addition, each paragraph should act as a building block toward proving the essay's main thesis. Keeping the essay's main thesis in mind throughout the writing process will ensure that the composition stays on topic.

Another key to excellent historical writing is continuity or narrative flow, which can be achieved by connecting each paragraph to the ones before and after by means of transitional words and phrases or a linking sentence. When you are reviewing and revising your own essays, ask yourself: "Does this paragraph logically follow from the preceding one?" "Does it add something significant to the thesis announced in the opening paragraph?" "Does it transition smoothly to the next paragraph?" Paying attention to the transitions between your supporting paragraphs will set your writing apart.

Finally, an effective essay must have a conclusion that summarizes its main points and explains how those points interconnect. It is not the place to introduce new information. The conclusion should do more than merely restate the essay's original thesis; it is where you will validate your opinion. Avoid addressing the reader directly or using crutches like "in conclusion" or "in summary"—the content of the concluding paragraph alone should make its purpose clear.

Correlation Guide: AP U.S. History and *America's History,* Seventh Edition

The following topic outline is taken from the 2010 Advanced Placement Program Course Description. While your teacher may choose to emphasize some topics over others, it's important for you to be able to identify and understand these events and trends. The column on the right shows you where to find the topic explained in *America's History,* Seventh Edition.

TOPICS FROM THE COLLEGE BOARD'S U.S. HISTORY	WHERE YOU'LL FIND IT IN *AMERICA'S HISTORY,* SEVENTH EDITION
1. Pre-Columbian Societies Early inhabitants of the Americas American Indian empires in Mesoamerica, the Southwest, and the Mississippi Valley American Indian cultures of North America at the time of European contact	Chapter 1
2. Transatlantic Encounters and Colonial Beginnings, 1492–1690 First European contacts with American Indians Spain's empire in North America French colonization of Canada English settlement of New England, the Mid-Atlantic region, and the South From servitude to slavery in the Chesapeake region Religious diversity in the American colonies Resistance to colonial authority: Bacon's Rebellion, the Glorious Revolution, and the Pueblo Revolt	Chapters 1, 2, & 3

TOPICS FROM THE COLLEGE BOARD'S U.S. HISTORY	WHERE YOU'LL FIND IT IN *AMERICA'S HISTORY*, SEVENTH EDITION
3. Colonial North America, 1690–1754 Population growth and immigration Transatlantic trade and the growth of seaports The eighteenth-century backcountry Growth of plantation economies and slave societies The Enlightenment and the Great Awakening Colonial governments and imperial policy in British North America	Chapters 3 & 4
4. The American Revolutionary Era, 1754–1789 The French and Indian War The Imperial Crisis and resistance to Britain The War for Independence State constitutions and the Articles of Confederation The federal Constitution	Chapters 5 & 6
5. The Early Republic, 1789–1815 Washington, Hamilton, and the shaping of the national government Emergence of political parties: Federalist and Republicans Republican motherhood and education for women Beginnings of the Second Great Awakening Significance of Jefferson's presidency Expansion into the trans-Appalachian West; American Indian resistance Growth of slavery and free Black communities The War of 1812 and its consequences	Chapters 7 & 8
6. Transformation of the Economy and Society in Antebellum America The transportation revolution and creation of a national market economy Beginnings of industrialization and changes in social and class structures Immigration and nativist reaction Planters, yeoman farmers, and slaves in the cotton South	Chapters 9 & 12
7. The Transformation of Politics in Antebellum America Emergence of the second party system Federal authority and its opponents: judicial federalism, the Bank War, tariff controversy, and states' rights debates Jacksonian democracy and its successes and limitations	Chapter 10

TOPICS FROM THE COLLEGE BOARD'S U.S. HISTORY	WHERE YOU'LL FIND IT IN *AMERICA'S HISTORY,* SEVENTH EDITION
8. Religion, Reform, and Renaissance in Antebellum America Evangelical Protestant revivalism Social reforms Ideals of domesticity Transcendentalism and utopian communities American Renaissance: literary and artistic expressions	Chapter 11
9. Territorial Expansion and Manifest Destiny Forced removal of American Indians to the trans-Mississippi West Western migration and cultural interactions Territorial acquisitions Early U.S. imperialism: the Mexican War	Chapter 10 & 13
10. The Crisis of the Union Pro- and antislavery arguments and conflicts Compromise of 1850 and popular sovereignty The Kansas-Nebraska Act and the emergence of the Republican Party Abraham Lincoln, the election of 1860, and secession	Chapter 13
11. Civil War Two societies at war: mobilization, resources, and internal dissent Military strategies and foreign diplomacy Emancipation and the role of African Americans in the war Social, political, and economic effects of war in the North, South, and West	Chapter 14
12. Reconstruction Presidential and Radical Reconstruction Southern state governments: aspirations, achievements, failures Role of African Americans in politics, education, and the economy Compromise of 1877 Impact of Reconstruction	Chapter 15
13. The Origins of the New South Reconfiguration of southern agriculture: sharecropping and crop-lien system Expansion of manufacturing and industrialization The politics of segregation: Jim Crow and disfranchisement	Chapters 15 & 20

TOPICS FROM THE COLLEGE BOARD'S U.S. HISTORY	WHERE YOU'LL FIND IT IN *AMERICA'S HISTORY*, SEVENTH EDITION
14. Development of the West in the Late Nineteenth Century Expansion and development of western railroads Competitors for the West: miners, ranchers, homesteaders, and American Indians Government policy toward American Indians Gender, race, and ethnicity in the far West Environmental impacts of western settlement	Chapter 16
15. Industrial America in the Late Nineteenth Century Corporate consolidation of industry Effects of technological development on the worker and workplace Labor and unions National politics and influence of corporate power Migration and immigration: the changing face of the nation Proponents and opponents of the new order, e.g., Social Darwinism and Social Gospel	Chapters 17 & 18
16. Urban Society in the Late Nineteenth Century Urbanization and the lure of the city City problems and machine politics Intellectual and cultural movements and popular entertainment	Chapter 19
17. Populism and Progressivism Agrarian discontent and political issues of the late nineteenth century Origins of Progressive reform: municipal, state, and national Roosevelt, Taft, and Wilson as Progressive presidents Women's roles: family, workplace, education, politics, and reform Black America: urban migration and civil rights initiatives	Chapter 20
18. The Emergence of America as a World Power American imperialism: political and economic expansion War in Europe and American neutrality The First World War at home and abroad Treaty of Versailles Society and economy in the postwar years	Chapter 21

TOPICS FROM THE COLLEGE BOARD'S U.S. HISTORY	WHERE YOU'LL FIND IT IN *AMERICA'S HISTORY,* SEVENTH EDITION
19. The New Era: 1920s The business of America and the consumer economy Republican politics: Harding, Coolidge, and Hoover The culture of Modernism: science, the arts, and entertainment Responses to Modernism: religious fundamentalism, nativism, and Prohibition The ongoing struggle for equality: African Americans and women	Chapter 22
20. The Great Depression and the New Deal Causes of the Great Depression The Hoover administration's response Franklin Delano Roosevelt and the New Deal Labor and union recognition The New Deal coalition and its critics from the Right and the Left Surviving hard times: American society during the Great Depression	Chapter 23
21. The Second World War The rise of fascism and militarism in Japan, Italy, and Germany Prelude to war: policy of neutrality The attack on Pearl Harbor and United States declaration of war Fighting a multifront war Diplomacy, war aims, and wartime conferences The United States as a global power in the Atomic Age	Chapter 24
22. The Home Front During the War Wartime mobilization of the economy Urban migration and demographic changes Women, work, and family during the war Civil liberties and civil rights during wartime War and regional development Expansion of government power	Chapter 24

TOPICS FROM THE COLLEGE BOARD'S U.S. HISTORY	WHERE YOU'LL FIND IT IN *AMERICA'S HISTORY*, SEVENTH EDITION
23. The United States and the Early Cold War Origins of the Cold War Truman and containment The Cold War in Asia: China, Korea, Vietnam, and Japan Diplomatic strategies and policies of the Eisenhower and Kennedy administrations The Red Scare and McCarthyism Impact of the Cold War on American Society	Chapter 25
24. The 1950s Emergence of the modern civil rights movement The affluent society and "the other America" Consensus and conformity: suburbia and middle-class America Social critics, nonconformists, and cultural rebels Impact of changes in science, technology, and medicine	Chapters 26 & 27
25. The Turbulent 1960s From the New Frontier to the Great Society Expanding movements for civil rights Cold War confrontations: Asia, Latin America, and Europe Beginning of Détente The antiwar movement and the counterculture	Chapters 26, 27, & 28
26. Politics and Economics at the End of the Twentieth Century The election of 1968 and the "Silent Majority" Nixon's challenges: Vietnam, China, and Watergate Changes in the American economy: the energy crisis, deindustrialization, and the service economy The New Right and the Reagan revolution End of the Cold War	Chapters 28, 29, & 30
27. Society and Culture at the End of the Twentieth Century Demographic changes: surge of immigration after 1965, Sunbelt migration, and the graying of America Revolutions in biotechnology, mass communication, and computers Politics in a multicultural society	Chapters 29, 30, & 31

TOPICS FROM THE COLLEGE BOARD'S U.S. HISTORY	WHERE YOU'LL FIND IT IN *AMERICA'S HISTORY,* SEVENTH EDITION
28. The United States in the Post–Cold War World Globalization and the American economy Unilateralism vs. multilateralism in foreign policy Domestic and foreign terrorism Environmental issues in a global context	Chapter 31

Taking The AP U.S. History Exam

This section will provide an outline of the test's three sections. You will learn some basic strategies for tackling AP questions successfully. All three types of AP questions are designed to test your mastery of both historical content and skills.

When starting the AP U.S. History course, many students ask, "Are we going to have to memorize dates?" Here is the answer from the College Board: "Although there is little to be gained by rote memorization of names and dates in an encyclopedic manner, a student must be able to draw upon a reservoir of systematic factual knowledge in order to exercise analytic skills intelligently."[1] So in other words: you're going to have to know your material. Here is how you will be tested.

The AP U.S. History Exam is three hours and five minutes long and consists of two sections: a 55-minute, 80-question multiple-choice section and a 130-minute free-response essay section. The free-response essay section is divided into three parts. Part A is the document-based essay question (the DBQ). Parts B and C consist of two standard essay questions; you will get to choose one to answer. Also included in the 130-minute free-response section is a 15-minute reading period during which students plan their essays and then read and analyze the documents for Part A. Plan on spending 45 minutes writing the DBQ essay in Part A, and 70 minutes planning and writing both essays for Parts B and C.

Approximately 20 percent of the 80 multiple-choice questions cover material through 1789, 45 percent represent the period from 1790 to 1914, and 35 percent cover the period from 1915 to the present (only a few of those questions address the period after 1980). Political history accounts for approximately 35 percent of the questions; social, cultural, and intellectual history another 40 percent; diplomacy and international relations 15 percent; and economic developments approximately 10 percent.

Strategies for the Multiple-Choice Section

The multiple-choice questions on the examination are styled in such a way that they usually require skills beyond simple recognition and recall. Some multiple-choice questions are based on historical evidence (quotations, maps, charts, graphs, cartoons, or photographs) that you must analyze before making an answer choice; others compare topics across time periods, requiring you to draw on your full comprehension of the historical issues underlying the question. Still others demand the ability to discern subtle distinctions between several possible answers to determine which choice is the most correct. There are five possible answers provided for each question.

One of the most difficult things for you to do when answering multiple-choice questions is to overcome your preconceptions. Too often a student reads the question's stem and thinks she knows the answer, yet can't find it among the choices given. That is because the

[1]CollegeBoard AP, *United States History Course Description, May 2010, May 2011.* The College Board, 2009.

questions are usually written in a way that asks you to think differently about a subject or to know the information within a different context. The AP Exam writers aren't likely to frame a fact exactly the way the authors of *America's History* (or any single textbook) do.

The multiple-choice questions generally ask you to connect individual events to a broader historical context. For example, rather than asking, "What journal did Margaret Fuller edit?" and providing the answer choice "*The Dial,* " the question might instead read, "What makes Margaret Fuller significant in American history?" with the answer choice, "She edited a Transcendentalist journal." This is a simple example, but it illustrates the point that you need to know something about Margaret Fuller—namely, that she was a Transcendentalist. Even if you know that Fuller edited *The Dial,* you also need to know what kind of journal it was.

In this way, AP-question writers tend to emphasize the significance and connections of individual events to broader historical themes rather than the memorization of rote details. That being said, you must develop some competence with the details in order to be highly successful.

Another type of question requires you to note the subtle differences between answer choices. Below is an example of a typical multiple-choice question on the AP Exam:

The Compromise of 1850 did which of the following?

(A) Divided all land west of the Mississippi into territories and let the settlers decide whether to allow slavery
(B) Abolished the slave trade in the District of Columbia
(C) Created the Republic of Texas
(D) Stopped states from counting three-fifths of their slave population when determining representation in Congress
(E) Enabled Maine to join the Union as a free state

You will learn in your AP course that choice (C) can be eliminated fairly quickly, but choice (D) requires you to know that the Compromise of 1850 did no such thing. Choice (A) should be immediately mistrusted because of the word "all." Keep an eye out for such definitive words (*all, finally, never, most, none,* etc.) and be cautious when you see them. Choice (E) could also be confusing, but remember that it was the 1820 Missouri Compromise that allowed Maine into the Union as a free state, balancing Missouri's entry as a slave state.

The correct answer is (B): one of the 1850 Compromise's provisions designed to appease opponents of slavery was its abolition within the nation's capital—even though the District of Columbia was surrounded by two slave states (Virginia and Maryland).[2] **Remember: make sure you read all choices carefully, and beware of absolutes.**

[2] The most controversial element of the Compromise of 1850 was its fugitive slave law. Read about it in *America's History,* Seventh Edition, in Chapter 13, "Expansion, War, and Sectional Crisis, 1844–1860."

Here is an example of a question that asks to you analyze evidence before answering:

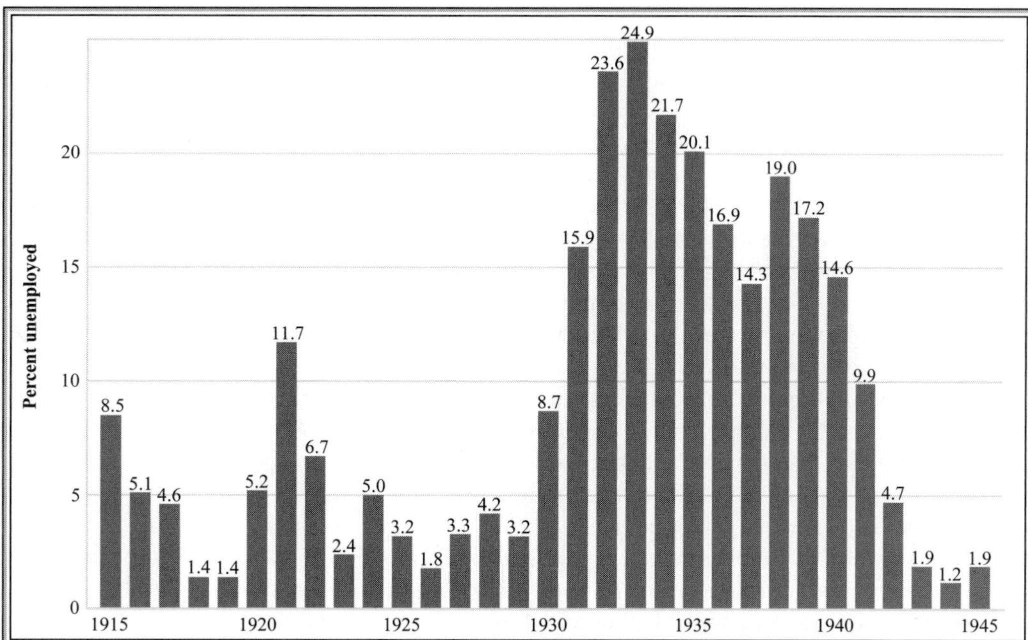

The graph above <u>refutes</u> which of the following statements?

(A) Unemployment decreased every year Franklin Roosevelt was in office.
(B) Unemployment in the United States from 1915 to 1945 reached its peak in 1933.
(C) Unemployment was worse in the eastern United States than it was in the West.
(D) Herbert Hoover was an extremely ineffective president.
(E) The unemployment rate declined during World War I and World War II.

You should first note the question's underlined word—the AP test writers underlined or put words in capitals like EXCEPT to alert you to the most important word in the sentence. *Refute* means to challenge or prove false. (This is an example of a *negative* question; more on that below.)

Next, look carefully at the graph to note the information presented: in this case it shows you the annual rate of unemployment from 1915 to 1945. You can thus easily eliminate the suggested answers that are supported, not refuted, by the information in the graph: (B), because the data for 1933 do show the highest rate of unemployment at 24.9 percent; and (E), because the graph shows the lowest unemployment rate during the two wars. You can also eliminate answers that address information outside the scope of the given data, such as (C), because you aren't given any geographical information. The answer for (D) includes one of those qualitative words—*extremely*—that you should doubt. Besides, historians draw on many different sources before making such an argument; using one measure alone is not responsible analysis.

The correct answer is (A). Why is this information important? Many economists and historians believe that Roosevelt made a mistake in 1937 by responding to fears about the federal deficit and slashing the budget before the economy was sufficiently stable. Besides the increase in unemployment shown on the graph for 1938, the stock market also dropped precipitously. This "Roosevelt recession" was a blow to his presidency. You can read more about it in Chapter 23 of *America's History*.

In terms of tackling the overall section, remember that due to the change in scoring effective starting in 2011, you will not lose points for incorrect responses. Therefore it makes no sense to leave any question blank. This does not mean that random guessing is recommended: be smart, and be strategic! If you can eliminate one or more of the choices for any question, go ahead and choose one the remaining answers.

Another thing to know about the multiple-choice section is that questions get harder as you progress through the section. Expect that the first third of the section will include the easiest questions; the middle third will be more difficult; and the last third will be the most difficult. In the past, questions used to follow a chronological rhythm, but that is no longer the case.

Finally, many AP questions are what we call negative questions: those that have words like NOT or EXCEPT. Your brain works differently when it is figuring out these types of questions; be on the lookout for them and read what's being asked carefully.

In general, work calmly and swiftly through the section, realizing that you have 55 minutes for 80 questions (thus just over 40 seconds per question). The answers go on a generic AP fill-in-the-ovals sheet with many more spaces than you need for the U.S. History exam, so be sure to keep careful track of question numbers and responses, especially if you skip questions to return to them later.

The multiple-choice section takes less than a third of the full time allotted for the AP U.S. History Exam, yet it is worth 50 percent of your final score. The purpose is to test your overall grasp of concepts, trends, and events in American history, as well as your ability to think analytically about them. There is no magic to mastering the multiple-choice questions: your best bet is to practice, practice, *practice*. You will find 15 sample questions for each of the seven sections of *America's History* in Section 2, along with two full 80-question sections in the practice tests in Section 3. Answering about 60 of the 80 multiple-choice questions correctly gives you your best shot at a 4 or 5.

Tips for Answering Multiple-Choice Questions

- Read each question carefully, looking out for negative words such as EXCEPT, NOT, and FALSE.
- Read all possible answers and cross out those you feel are incorrect; narrowing down your choices gives you the chance to make an educated guess.
- Be cautious of words indicating absolutes, like *most, least, all,* and *none.*
- Connect the specific information of the question to broader trends and themes.
- In questions that provide you with evidence, assess the information carefully and eliminate answers that go beyond the bounds of the evidence given.
- Make a habit of checking your answer sheet frequently throughout the testing time to ensure that you are filling in the correct ovals—especially if you skip questions or leave some to come back to later.

The Document-Based Question Essay

The document-based question essay (DBQ) of exam Part A is the hallmark exercise of the AP U.S. History Exam for the College Board and Educational Testing Service. DBQs, which can be drawn from any historical period, ask you to connect relevant evidence from multiple sources and use those connections to construct an analytical or interpretative essay response. In asking you to place the evidence in context and then using it to explain a cause and/or to substantiate a thesis, the AP Exam is, in effect, asking you to perform the central creative act of the historian's craft.

In DBQs, the defense of a thesis is even more critical to success than in a standard essay question, since the documents in effect give part of the answer. The general subject of the question is in some ways irrelevant to whether a student does well on the DBQ. What matters most is the extent to which you have been trained to read and analyze unfamiliar documents, and to explain why and how things came to be a certain way.

Frequently, DBQ documents will contradict each other or be ambiguous. Strong students see in these contradictions or ambiguities opportunities to develop complex responses or theses that in turn lead to the use of the evidence in sophisticated ways. Thus the documents themselves provide important keys needed to answer the question. You are not required to use all the documents accompanying the DBQ—only a "substantial number" of them (interpret this as "more than half")—to demonstrate your ability to weigh the relevance of evidence provided, sort through their complexities, and use those complexities in support of your thesis.

The DBQ also requires the use of outside information that tests your ability to integrate your general background knowledge of the DBQ topic. Students who have not included in their answer factual knowledge clearly outside the purview of the documents provided cannot score higher than a fair grade (4 of 9). Students who are able to select information from the documents and connect them to outside facts generally demonstrate analytical skills that produce stronger essays. Ample use of outside material may also help an exam reader determine that you have used a "substantial number" of the DBQ documents.

One of the most difficult things for a first-time AP student to learn is how to decipher a DBQ. In Section 2 of *Strive for a 5,* you will find a practice DBQ for each of the seven parts of the textbook, along with specific learning objectives, a brief description of how and why the documents provide an answer to the question posed, and directed exercises that will lead you to increasingly more complex analyses.

If you have written a research paper or prepared an evidence-based essay in class, you have already practiced the process of writing a DBQ. The purpose of the essay is to prove a point, using your own knowledge of history and the evidence put before you to arrive at a historical narrative or explanation. The difficult part for many is the need to analyze and assess historical written, quantitative, and visual materials and then synthesize them with their own knowledge of history. Breaking the process down into multiple steps helps you master the process of answering DBQs.

As an example, let's look at the 1990 AP Exam's DBQ on Andrew Jackson. For the purposes of this example, we'll assume that the DBQ had eight accompanying documents (A–H) for you to consider. The first step is to read the question carefully so that you know precisely how to focus your response. Here's the question:

> *Jacksonian Democrats viewed themselves as the guardians of the United States Constitution, political democracy, individual liberty, and equality of economic opportunity. In light of the following documents and your knowledge of the 1820s and 1830s, to what extent do you agree with the Jacksonians' view of themselves?*

Reading this question should prompt some questions of your own, including:

1. What is the question asking?
2. How many topics is the question asking me to address?
3. How many paragraphs will the essay most likely have?
4. What will be the topic order for the paragraphs?

Creating a quick chart can help answer these questions and provide an informal outline for the essay. A good format for this particular essay would include an introduction, a conclusion, and four body paragraphs—one for each of the ideals the Jacksonian Democrats felt they preserved—so the chart below has four columns. Then, as you consider where each document fits into your answer, you can note how some documents apply to more than one paragraph and link them according to the topics they address. In this way, you should see the need to answer the question using the documents as vehicles to prove your thesis, rather than constructing your thesis around the documents.

(Note: This chart is for illustrative purposes only. On exam day, sketching a simple table like this can be extremely valuable as you organize your essay response.)

Jacksonian Ideal	**Guardians of Constitution**	**Political Democracy**	**Individual Liberty**	**Equality of Economic Opportunity**
Documents Supporting Each Ideal	A B G F	A	D E F G	B C E H

Note that we have generated one column for each of the four ideals in the question. Once you have made order out of the documents, you can add to your list of outside information that fits into each category. It may help to write down everything pertinent you know that occurred during the time period. In the case of the 1990 DBQ, students would list everything they know about the Jacksonian era from 1820 to 1840 and then determine what applies to their charts. Armed with this additional information, students will be prepared to develop a thesis that answers the multiple-part document-based question.

Here is how some pieces of outside information could fit into your existing organizational table of documents:

Jacksonian Ideal	**Guardians of Constitution**	**Political Democracy**	**Individual Liberty**	**Equality of Economic Opportunity**
Documents and Outside Information Supporting Each Ideal	A B G F Force Bill Webster-Hayne Debate Jefferson Day Dinner Jackson Response to *Worcester v. Georgia*	A Women's Rights = nonexistent Political Party Conventions End to Voice Voting End Property Qualifica-tions for Voting Spoils system Kitchen Cabinet	D E F G Women's Rights = nonexistent *Worcester v. Georgia* Cherokee Trail of Tears Abolition William Lloyd Garrison and *The Liberator* Dorothea Dix Prison Reform	B C E H Women's Rights = nonexisten Tariff of Abominations Compromise Tariff South Carolina Exposition Protest No Irish Need Apply Kitchen Cabinet

Again, note that some pieces of historical background information are applicable to multiple ideals. This should help you make connections between and among documents, allowing for a more complex analysis.

A strong DBQ response is well organized and establishes a thesis using the documents and outside information. Paragraphs will cohere around a clear topic sentence and idea. Assertions will be supported with relevant selections from the evidence provided.

With practice, you should be able to analyze and digest each document, determine its relevance, and use it in support of a thesis. The very best essays, like good historical writing, focus only on those elements of the documents that serve the thesis. Therefore, do not waste time and space extensively quoting or summarizing the documents; learn how to distinguish pertinent from extraneous material.

What's the best way to cite the documents? Avoid stating "Document A says . . ." in an essay. Imagine that your essay can be read on its own, without that packet of documents attached. It's best to cite the source in the least disruptive manner possible so the essay flows well. Parenthetical citations can work, but it is smoothest to identify the quote within your own sentences, like this: "As Thomas Jefferson wrote in the Declaration of Independence in 1776, 'All men are created equal . . .'."

Tips for Answering Document-Based Questions

- Read the question carefully to determine exactly what is being asked of you.
- Determine how each individual document relates to the question at hand.
- Find sentences in the document excerpts that contain key terms and ideas mentioned in the question.
- Determine the extent to which different document excerpts are similar or contradictory.
- Analyze any maps or visual documents in order to determine relevance to the topic.
- Be sure to include as many pertinent details as possible in support of your DBQ thesis, but don't feel compelled to include extraneous detail.

The Free-Response Question Essays

In Parts B and C of the exam, students choose from one of two standard essay questions from two categories—generally, but not always, divided chronologically at the Civil War. These types of free-response essay questions are included to measure your ability to think critically, recall pertinent information, and write a well-conceived essay that proves your thesis. Answers to these two questions result in just over 25 percent of your overall score. Following the general guidelines for historical writing in the previous section will help you to succeed on the free-response questions.

Tips for Answering Free-Response Questions

- Read all of the questions and determine which ones you can answer most successfully.
- Sketch out a brief outline, recording facts and examples that you remember and organizing them in a sensible way. Each section of the outline should generate a supporting paragraph for your essay. Remember to use clues from the question to structure your essay when possible.
- Develop a thesis that takes a clear stand on the question posed. Be sure to state it in your introductory paragraph.
- Begin each supporting paragraph with a clear topic sentence.
- Consider transitions between paragraphs.
- Conclude by restating your thesis in a fresh way, perhaps by making a connection to another moment in American history.
- Keep in mind the volume of essays the exam readers must plow through. Clarity and organization are key.

General Essay Rubric

Given the massive number of essays the AP readers must assess in a very short period of time, the test developers have developed a rubric to score each essay on a scale of 1 to 9, with 9 being the highest score. The list below shows the ranking, scale, and characteristics of essays that fall in each range.

8–9 (Superior)

Has a clear thesis that reflects a complex understanding of the question.
Analyzes and integrates the documents provided with other sources to provide substantial and relevant evidence supporting the thesis.
Uses a range of evidence to cover the chronological period effectively in support of the thesis.
Contains no major errors. (Note: A major error is defined as a factual or interpretative error that detracts from the thesis.)
Is written clearly and is well organized.

5–7 (Good)

Has a thesis that responds to the question but is imbalanced or one-sided in its descriptions or analyses of positions.
Analyzes a few of the documents and outside information but is mostly descriptive in nature.
May have a few major errors.
Is written clearly.

2–4 (Poor to Fair)

Has a limited or confused thesis.
Mentions some documents but does not apply them effectively in support of a thesis statement.
Has little outside evidence that is relevant to the thesis.
Has major errors that detract from the thesis statement.
Is poorly written and/or not well organized.

0–1 (Off Task or Unresponsive)

Lacks a thesis, does not respond to the question, or is confused.
Has no evidence, or provides evidence that is irrelevant or unrelated to the question.
Has major errors.
Contains severe problems in clarity and/or organization.

Use this rubric like a checklist as you complete the practice questions in this study guide, and aim for essays that score in the 7–9 range. Remember: a clear thesis, ample supporting evidence, and logical organization are the keys to writing successful historical essays.

SECTION 2
A Review of AP U.S. History

PART 1
The Creation of American Society, 1450–1763

This part covers the following chapters in Henretta et al., *America's History,* Seventh Edition:

Chapter 1 The New Global World, 1450–1620

Chapter 2 The Invasion and Settlement of North America, 1550–1700

Chapter 3 Creating a British Empire in America, 1660–1750

Chapter 4 Growth and Crisis in Colonial Society, 1720–1765

Essential Questions

After studying the chapters in Part 1, you should know how to answer the following questions:

1. What were the main characteristics of early modern European society, and how successfully did European settlers replicate those characteristics in America?
2. How did the Columbian Exchange affect the lives of Europeans and American Indians?
3. How did Europeans, American Indians, and Africans interact in the Atlantic world socially and economically?
4. How did European colonists organize themselves politically in America?
5. How did family roles, immigrants, and new religious and intellectual currents affect the emergence of a new American identity?

Resources for Review

In the following pages, you'll find the Thematic Timeline and Essay for Part 1 from *America's History,* exercises to review your knowledge of the period, and AP-style questions that address the time period covered: 15 practice multiple-choice questions, 1 document-based question, and 3 free-response questions. Answers with page references to *America's History* can be found in the Answer Key at the end of this Part 1 review.

Thematic Timeline and Part Essay

The Creation of American Society, 1450–1763

	ECONOMY	SOCIETY	GOVERNMENT	RELIGION	CULTURE
1450	Native American subsistence economy Europeans fish off North American coast	Sporadic warfare among Indian peoples Spanish conquest of Mexico and Peru (1519–1535)	Rise of monarchical nation-states in Europe English monarchs adopt mercantilist policies	Protestant Reformation (1517) sparks century of religious warfare Henry VIII creates Church of England	Diverse Native American cultures in eastern woodlands
1600	First staple export crops: furs and tobacco Subsistence farms in New England	First set of English-Indian wars African servitude begins in Virginia (1619)	James I claims divine right to rule England Virginia House of Burgesses (1619)	Persecuted English Puritans and Catholics migrate to America	Puritans implant Calvinism, education, and freehold ideal
1640	South Atlantic System on sugar islands Mercantilist regulation: first Navigation Act (1651)	White indentured servitude shapes Chesapeake society Indians retreat inland; Africans lose rights (1670s)	English Puritan Revolution Stuart restoration (1660) Bacon's Rebellion in Virginia (1675)	Established churches set up in Puritan New England and Anglican Virginia Dissenters settle in Rhode Island	Aristocratic aspirtions in Chesapeake region
1680	Tobacco trade stagnates Rice cultivation in South Carolina Britain dominates slave trade	Indian wars and slavery grow in the Carolinas Major influx of Africans creates "slave societies"	Central control: Dominion of New England Revolutions in England and colonies (1688–1689)	Rise of tolerance among colonial Protestants Wars with Catholic France in Europe and America	Quaker influence in Pennsylvania Africans create new African American languages and cultures

	ECONOMY	SOCIETY	GOVERNMENT	RELIGION	CULTURE
1720	Mature yeoman farm economy in north 1740s: Imports from Britain increase	Large Scots-Irish and German migration Inequality grows among whites in rural and urban areas	Salutary Neglect allows rise of the colonial assemblies British state supports commercial expansion in Atlantic and India	German and Scots-Irish Pietists in Middle Atlantic region Great Awakening revives religion and splits churches	Expansion of colleges, newspapers, and magazines Franklin and the American Enlightenment
1760	End of British military aid sparks postwar recession	Uprisings by tenants and backcountry farmers	Britain vanquishes France in Great War for Empire (1757–1763)	Rise of evangelical Baptists in Virginia	First signs of a distinct American identity within the Atlantic world

Historians know that societies are the creation of decades, even centuries, of human endeavor and experience. Historians also know that the first Americans were hunters and gatherers who migrated to the Western Hemisphere from Asia. Over many generations, these migrants—the Native Americans—came to live in a wide variety of environments and cultures. In much of North America, they developed kinship-based societies that relied on farming and hunting. But in the lower Mississippi River Valley around 900 A.D., Native Americans fashioned a hierarchical social order similar to those of the impressive civilizations of the Aztecs, Mayas, and Incas.

In Part 1, we describe how Europeans, with their steel weapons, attractive trade goods, and diseases, shredded the fabric of many Native American cultures. Throughout the Western Hemisphere, men and women of European origin—the Spanish in Mesoamerica and South America, the French in Canada, the English along the Atlantic coast of North America—gradually achieved domination over the native peoples.

Our story focuses on the Europeans who settled in the English mainland colonies. They expected to transplant their traditional societies, cultures, and religious beliefs in the soil of the New World. But things did not work out exactly as planned. In learning to live in the new land, English, Germans, and Scots-Irish created societies that differed from those of their homelands in their economic life, social character, political systems, religions, and cultures. Here, in brief, is the story of that transformation as we explain it in Part 1.

Economy: From Subsistence to Staple Crops to Diversification Britain's American colonies were a great economic success as part of an expanding commercial empire. Traditional Europe consisted of poor, overcrowded, and unequal societies that periodically suffered devastating famines. But with few people and bountiful resources, the settlers in North America created a bustling economy in what British and German migrants called "the best poor man's country." Communities of independent farm families produced crops that merchants sold in Europe and the West Indian sugar islands, which were the driving force of the Atlantic economy.

Society: Changing Class, Racial, and Ethnic Conflicts Simultaneously, some European settlements became places of oppressive captivity for Africans, with profound consequences for America's social development. As the supply of white indentured servants from Europe dwindled after 1680, planters in the Chesapeake region imported enslaved African workers to grow tobacco. Spurred by profits in the sugar trade, British slave traders procured hundreds of thousands of slaves from African traders and rulers transported them to West Indian sugar plantations. Slowly and with great effort, the slaves and their descendants created a variety of African American cultures within the European-dominated societies in which they labored.

Government: From Imperial Control to Local Autonomy The first English migrants transplanted authoritarian institutions to America and, beginning around 1650, the home government intervened frequently in their affairs. But after the Glorious Revolution of 1688, white settlers in the English mainland colonies devised an increasingly free and competitive political system. Thereafter, local governments and representative assemblies became more powerful and created a tradition of self-rule that would spark demands for political autonomy after the Great War for Empire ended in 1763.

Religion: From Established Churches to Pluralism The American experience profoundly changed religious institutions and values. Many migrants fled from Europe because of government persecution and conflicts among rival Christian churches. For the most part, they practiced their religions in America without interference. Religion became more prominent in colonial life after the evangelical revivals of the 1740s, and the churches became less dogmatic. Americans increasingly rejected the harshest tenets of Calvinism (a strict version of Protestantism); and a significant minority of educated colonists embraced the rational outlook of the European Enlightenment. As a result, American Protestant Christianity became increasingly tolerant, democratic, and optimistic.

Culture: The Creation of American Identities The new American society witnessed changes in family and community life. The first English settlers lived in patriarchal families ruled by dominant fathers and in communities controlled by men of high status. However, by 1750, many American fathers no longer strictly managed their children's lives and, because of widespread property ownership, many men and some women enjoyed greater personal independence. This new American society was pluralistic, composed of migrants from many European ethnic groups—English, Scots, Scots-Irish, Dutch, and Germans—as well as enslaved Africans and Native American peoples. Distinct regional cultures developed in New England, the Middle Atlantic colonies, the Chesapeake, and the Carolinas. Consequently, an overarching American identity based on the English language, English legal and political institutions, and shared experiences emerged very slowly.

The story of the colonial experience is both depressing and uplifting. Europeans and their diseases destroyed many Native American peoples and European planters held tens of thousands of Africans in bondage. However, white migrants enjoyed unprecedented opportunities for economic security, political freedom, and spiritual fulfillment. This contradictory experience—of native decline, black bondage, and white opportunity—would continue far into the American future.

Essential Questions Review Exercises

Using the guidelines, grids, maps, and schematics that follow, gather evidence that helps you to review concepts and themes from the period 1450 to 1763. Consult *America's History*, Seventh Edition, as well as any relevant materials your teacher has provided to review the information.

1. **What were the main characteristics of early modern European society, and how successfully did European settlers replicate those characteristics in America?**

   A Venn diagram can be helpful for reviewing this kind of material. In the figure below, note the shared characteristics of both European and American colonial societies in the overlapping space in the middle. On the left, record characteristics of European society that were not adopted in the American colonies; on the right, note characteristics of American colonial societies that were uniquely American.

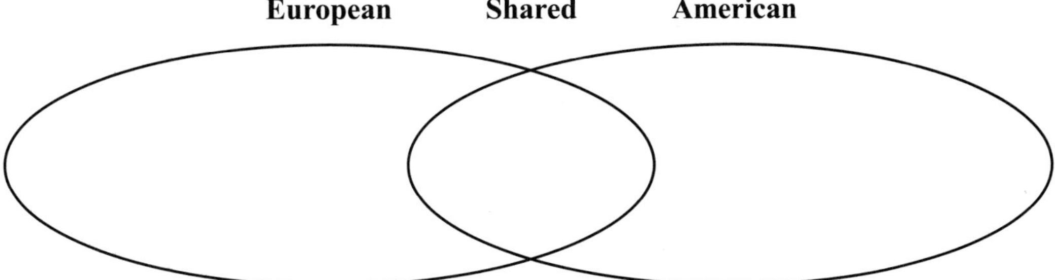

2. **How did the Columbian Exchange affect the lives of Europeans and American Indians?**

   Taking your notes directly on a map for this kind of information is a helpful way of reviewing. Using the blank map of the northern Atlantic world, write in the commodities, peoples, microbes, plants, and animals that made up what historians now call the "Columbian Exchange." Be sure to indicate the origins of items and people as well as where they ended up.

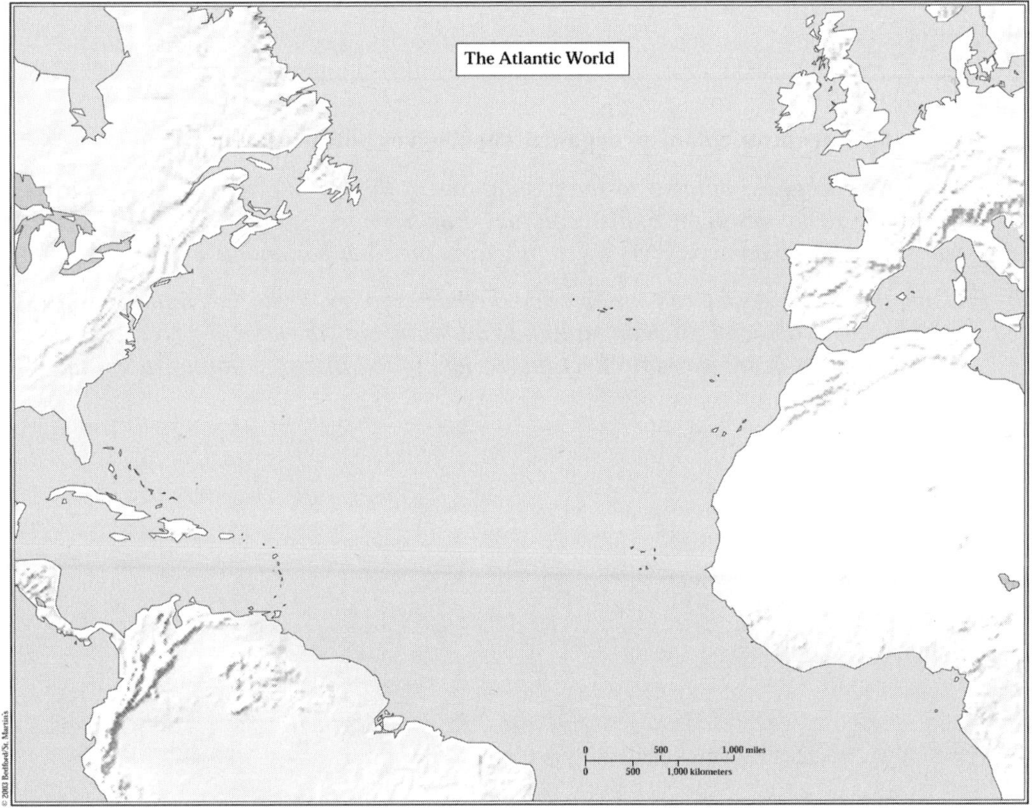

3. **How did Europeans, American Indians, and Africans interact in the Atlantic world socially and economically?**

   Use the table below to record significant interactions among these three groups of peoples in the colonial era.

INTERACTIONS IN THE COLONIAL AMERICAS		
	Social	**Economic**
American Indians	With Africans:	With Africans:
	With Europeans:	With Europeans:
Africans	With Europeans:	With Europeans:

4. **How did European colonists organize themselves politically in America?**

   From New England villages to the plantations of the Carolinas, there were different governing structures in the British colonies. Furthermore, Spanish, French, and Dutch colonies were all administered differently from their mother countries.

   Using the map of eastern North America on the next page, draw the boundaries for the regions ruled by each European nation. In addition, note the kind of governance found in each region, being sure to reflect the variety of the British colonies along the seacoast.

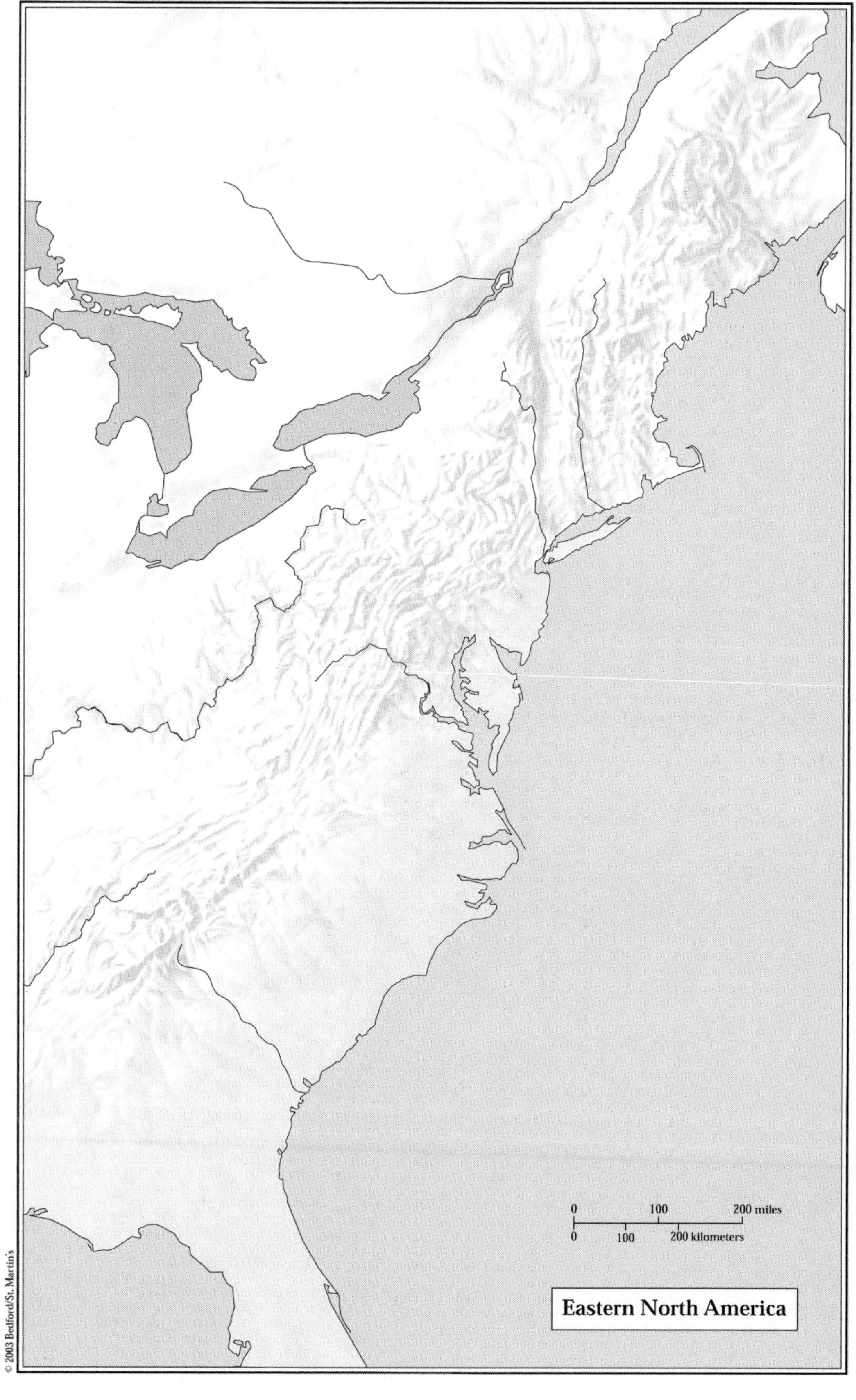
0
100
200 miles
0
100
200 kilometers
Eastern North America

5. **How did family roles, immigrants, and new religious and intellectual currents affect the emergence of a new American identity?**

   Using the table below, record some of the changes that contributed to the formation of a uniquely American culture. Consider family roles, immigrants, religion, and intellectual trends. When relevant, include dates and locations.

A NEW AMERICAN IDENTITY: INFLUENCES AND EVENTS			
Family roles	**Immigrants**	**Religious trends**	**Intellectual currents**

Practice Questions

The following sections allow you to test your knowledge of Part 1. The Directions are verbatim instructions from the College Board's AP Exam; the Hints offer strategies for tackling each type of AP question. Answers to all of the Part 1 practice questions follow.

Multiple-Choice Questions

Directions: Each of the questions or incomplete statements below is followed by five suggested answers or completions. Select the one that is best in each case.

Hints:

- Read each question carefully, looking out for negative words such as EXCEPT, NOT, and FALSE.
- Read all possible answers and cross out those you feel are incorrect; narrowing down your choices gives you the chance to make an educated guess.
- Be cautious of words indicating absolutes, like *most, least, all,* and *none.*
- Connect the specific information of the question to broader trends and themes.
- In questions that provide you with evidence, assess the information carefully and eliminate answers that go beyond the bounds of the evidence given.

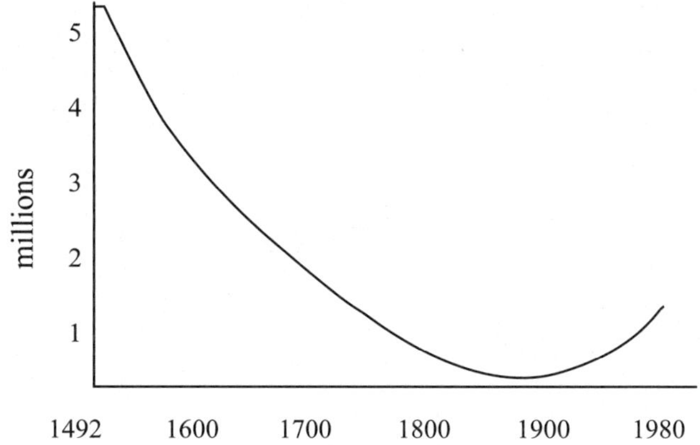

American Indian Population Decline and Recovery in the United States Area, 1492–1980

1. What was the most significant cause for the situation from 1492–1700 shown on the graph above?
   (A) European warfare
   (B) Native American wars over territory
   (C) Disease
   (D) Famine
   (E) Religious wars

2. English, Spanish, and French North American colonies were most alike in that they all
   (A) discouraged feudalistic landholding policies
   (B) served as asylums for people fleeing religious persecution
   (C) had elected representative assemblies
   (D) were subjected to mercantilist policies
   (E) were created by trading companies

3. A similarity among traditional European, Mayan, and Aztec civilizations was that
   (A) hierarchy, authority, and bureaucracy were integral components
   (B) serfdom prevailed
   (C) heresies were harshly punished
   (D) a matrilineal inheritance system existed
   (E) farming was less important to the economy than trade

4. During the Age of Exploration, trade routes shifted from the
   (A) Atlantic to the Pacific Ocean
   (B) Atlantic to the Indian Ocean
   (C) Mediterranean Sea to the Atlantic Ocean
   (D) Indian to the Atlantic Ocean
   (E) Mediterranean Sea to the Indian Ocean

5. An example of mercantilism is
   (A) the Proclamation of 1763
   (B) the Navigation Acts
   (C) the Dominion of New England
   (D) Leisler's Rebellion
   (E) the Albany Plan

6. A result of the Great Awakening was
   (A) a decline in the importance of higher education
   (B) an increased admiration for the growing business community
   (C) an increase in intolerance
   (D) a consolidation of churches
   (E) the growth of a democratic spirit

7. "The strangers' bodies are completely covered, so that only their faces can be seen. Their skin is white, as if it were made of lime. They have yellow hair, though some of them have black. [Soon] a great plague broke out. The illness was so dreadful that no one could walk or move."
   The above quotation is most likely
   (A) an Aztec observation on the disease-ridden Spanish conquest
   (B) a missionary's description of the devastation created by the Black Plague in Europe
   (C) Squanto expressing shock at first seeing the Pilgrims
   (D) Powhatan's description of John Smith's invasion party
   (E) Cortés's first impression of Native Americans

8. An American conception that was a re-creation of a European institution was
   (A) the town meeting
   (B) women's suffrage
   (C) the plantation system
   (D) chattel slavery
   (E) separation of church and state

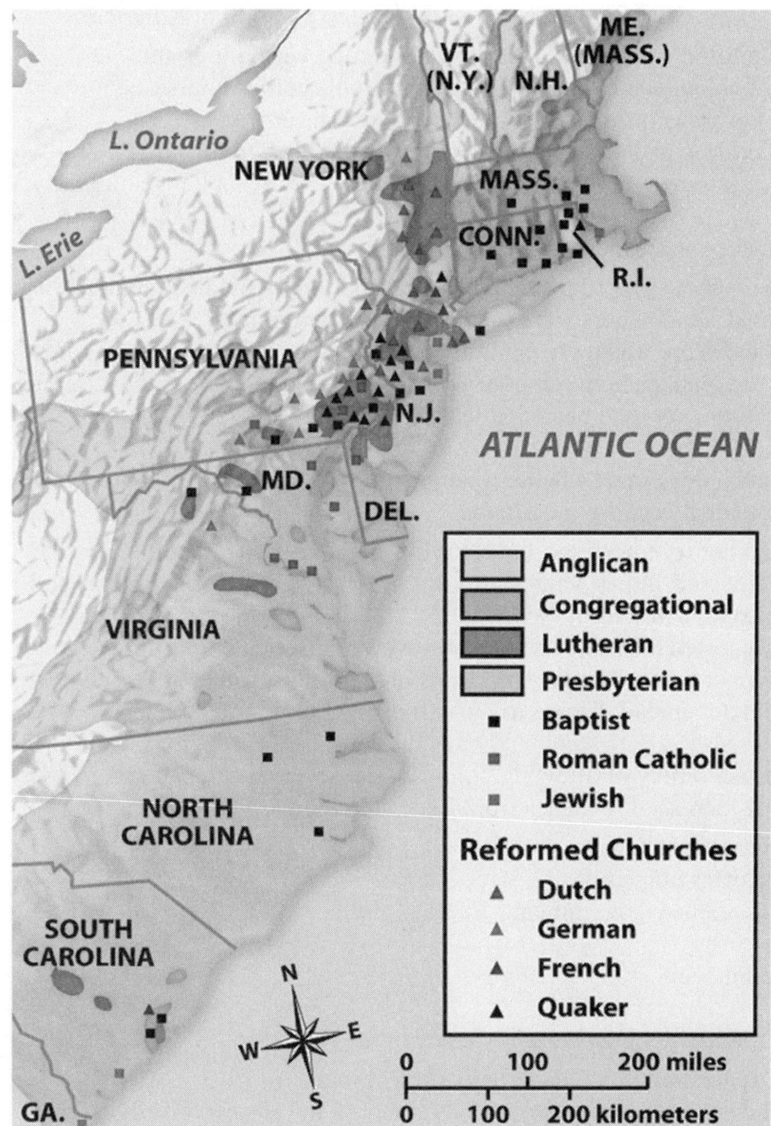

Religious Distribution in the Colonies

9. According to the map above, the colonies most inclined toward religious toleration were
   (A) the Carolinas and Delaware
   (B) Massachusetts, Connecticut, and New Hampshire
   (C) New York, New Jersey, and Pennsylvania
   (D) Virginia, North Carolina, and Maryland
   (E) North Carolina, Rhode Island, and Massachusetts

10 Which of the following colonial settlements established a yeoman society unprecedented in European society?
   (A) The Chesapeake
   (B) New Netherlands
   (C) New England
   (D) New France
   (E) St. Augustine

11. Which of the following is true of child rearing in colonial America?
    (A) Children's formal education was deemed very important.
    (B) Much emphasis was placed on children's cultural pursuits.
    (C) There was little time for idleness and amusement.
    (D) Children had chores to do, but they were sheltered from the really hard work.
    (E) Children were raised to be free thinkers and to challenge authority.

12. In the slave-based societies of the South
    (A) only about 5 to 10 percent of the population dominated the republican institutions
    (B) small landowners were the heart of the community
    (C) the culture was more egalitarian than that of the northern colonies
    (D) relationships between poor whites and freed blacks were encouraged
    (E) nearly everyone owned at least several slaves

13. The French developed a better relationship with the Indians than did either the English or the Spanish because the French
    (A) did not try to convert the Native Americans to Christianity
    (B) respected Indian values, did not use natives for forced labor, and tried to keep alcohol away from them
    (C) supported the Iroquois in their move to consolidate fur trapping under their control
    (D) supported the Native Americans in their quest to free themselves from the Dutch
    (E) did not spread disease to the native peoples

14. The British policy of allowing colonists the ability to manage their own affairs while enjoying increased revenues from trade is known as
    (A) mercantilism
    (B) salutary neglect
    (C) proprietary government
    (D) pietism
    (E) capitalism

15. Bacon's Rebellion inadvertently contributed to
    (A) the decline of the planter elite in Virginia
    (B) the end of representative government in the House of Burgesses
    (C) the expansion of African slavery
    (D) the growth of a commercial economy
    (E) better relations with local Indian tribes

Document-Based Question

Directions: The following question requires you to construct a coherent essay that integrates your interpretation of Documents A–E and your knowledge of the period referred to in the question. High scores are earned only by essays that cite key pieces of evidence from the documents *and* draw on outside knowledge of the period.

Assess the extent to which New England Puritans translated religious ideals into practice.

Use the documents and your knowledge of the years 1630–1700 to construct your response.

Background Reading: *America'sHistory,* Seventh Edition, Chapter 2

Hints:

- With document-based questions, remember to move beyond the specific facts in the documents to seek their more interpretive or analytical aspects. As you read through the documents, underline key passages, jot notes in the margins, and record outside examples and facts that come to mind as you read.
- This is a "to what extent" question, meaning you are determining how successful the Puritans were at translating their religious principles into the organization of their communities. Visual aids can help with questions like these. Determine where on the continuum below you would place your own interpretation:

  VERY SUCCESSFUL ←——————————→ UNSUCCESSFUL
- After reading through the documents, categorize them into groups to generate a paragraph structure for your response. Creating groups based on authorship, time period, geographical region, and document type can often be effective.
- Keep in mind the volume of essays the exam readers must plow through. Clarity and organization are key.

Document A

Source: John Winthrop, "A Model of Christian Charity," 1630.

God Almighty in His most holy and wise providence hath so disposed of the condition of mankind, as in all times some must be rich, some poor, some high and eminent in power and dignity, others mean and in subjection.

The Reason Hereof

First, to hold conformity with the rest of his works, being delighted to show forth the glory of his wisdom in the variety and difference of the creatures; and the glory of his power, in ordering all these differences for the preservation and good of the whole; and the glory of his greatness, ...

Secondly, that he might have the more occasion to manifest the work of his spirit: first upon the wicked in moderating and restraining them, so that the rich and mighty should not eat up the poor, nor the poor and despised rise up against their superiors and shake off their yoke; secondly in the regenerate, in exercising his graces in them, as in the great ones, their love, mercy, gentleness, temperance, etc.; in the poor and inferior sort, their faith, patience, obedience, etc.

Thirdly, that every man might have need of other, and from hence they might be all knit more nearly together in the bonds of brotherly affection. From hence it appears plainly that no man is made more honorable than another or more wealthy, etc., out of any particular and singular respect to himself, but for the glory of his creator and the common good of the creature, man. . . . All men being thus (by divine providence) ranked into two sorts, rich and poor; under the first are comprehended all such as are able to live comfortably by their own means duly improved; and all others are poor according to the former distribution. . . .

. . . for the work we have in hand [, it] is by a mutual consent, through a special overvaluing providence and a more than ordinary approbation of the churches of Christ, to seek out a place of cohabitation and consortship under a due form of government both civil and ecclesiastical. In such cases as this, the care of the public must oversway all private respects, by which not only conscience but mere civil policy doth bind us. . . .

. . . therefore we must not content our selves with usual ordinary means. Whatsoever we did or ought to have done when we lived in England, the same must we do, and more also, where we go. . . .

Now the only way to avoid this shipwreck, and to provide for our posterity, is to follow the counsel of Micah, to do justly, to love mercy, to walk humbly with our God. For this end, we must be knit together in this work as one man. We must entertain each other in brotherly affection, we must be willing to abridge ourselves of our superfluities, for the supply of others' necessities. We must uphold a familiar commerce together in all meekness, gentleness, patience, and liberality. We must delight in each other, make others' conditions our own, rejoice together, mourn together, labor and suffer together, always having before our eyes our commission and community in the work, our community as members of the same body. So shall we keep the unity of the spirit in the bond of peace.... We shall find that the God of Israel is among us, when ten of us shall be able to resist a thousand of our enemies; when he shall make us a praise and glory that men shall say of succeeding plantations, "the Lord make it like that of New England." For we must consider that we shall be as a city upon a hill. The eyes of all people are upon us, so that if we shall deal falsely with our God in this work we have undertaken, and so cause him to withdraw his present help from us, we shall be made a story and a by-word through the world.

Document B

Source: Transcript of the Examination of Anne Hutchinson, 1637.

November 1637,

The Examination of Mrs. Ann[e] Hutchinson at the court at Newtown.

Mr. Winthrop, governor: Mrs. Hutchinson, you are called here as one of those that have troubled the peace of the commonwealth and the churches here; you are known to be a woman that hath had a great share in the promoting and divulging of those opinions that are the cause of this trouble, and to be nearly joined not only in affinity and affection with some of those the court had taken notice of and passed censure upon, but you have spoken divers things as we have been informed, very prejudicial to the honour of the churches and ministers thereof, and you have maintained a meeting and an assembly in your house that hath been condemned by the general assembly as a thing not tolerable nor comely in the sight of God nor fitting for your sex, . . .

Mrs. H. . . . Now if you do condemn me for speaking what in my conscience I know to be truth I must commit myself unto the Lord.

Mr. Nowell. How do you know that was the spirit?

Mrs. H. How did Abraham know that it was God that bid him offer his son, being a breach of the sixth commandment [Thou shalt not kill]?

Deputy Gov. By an immediate voice.

Mrs. H. So to me by an immediate revelation.

Deputy Gov. How! an immediate revelation.

Mrs. H. By the voice of his own spirit to my soul. . . .

Gov. The court hath already declared themselves satisfied concerning the things you hear, and concerning the troublesomeness of her spirit and the danger of her course amongst us, which is not to be suffered. Therefore if it be the mind of the court that Mrs. Hutchinson for these things that appear before us is unfit for our society, and if it be the mind of the court that she shall be banished out of our liberties and imprisoned till she be sent away, let them hold up their hands.

Document C

Settlement Patterns within New England Towns, 1630–1700
Andover, 1650–1692
Nucleated to dispersed in fifty years
New houses
By 1650
By 1692
Meeting House
0 2 4 miles
Merrimack River
Meeting House
(after Vaughn)
0 10 20 miles
0 10 20 kilometers
Village types
Nucleated
Initially nucleated, dispersed by 1700
Dispersed
Continuous English settlements by 1700
Roads
Field boundaries
ATLANTIC OCEAN
BERKSHIRE MOUNTAINS
MASSACHUSETTS
CONNECTICUT
RHODE ISLAND
Hampton
Haverhill
Ipswich
Andover
Manchester
Salem
Newton
Sudbury
Dedham
Worcester
Oxford
Medfield
Plymouth
Barnstable
Greenfield
Northfield
Deerfield
Sunderland
Hatfield
Hadley
Westfield
Woodstock
Windsor
Hartford
Farmington
Wethersfield
Waterbury
Wallingford
Newtown
Guilford
Derby
Housatonic River
Connecticut River
Merrimack River
Long Island
(after Wood)
Wethersfield, 1640
0 0.5 1 mile
Meeting House
(after Andrews)

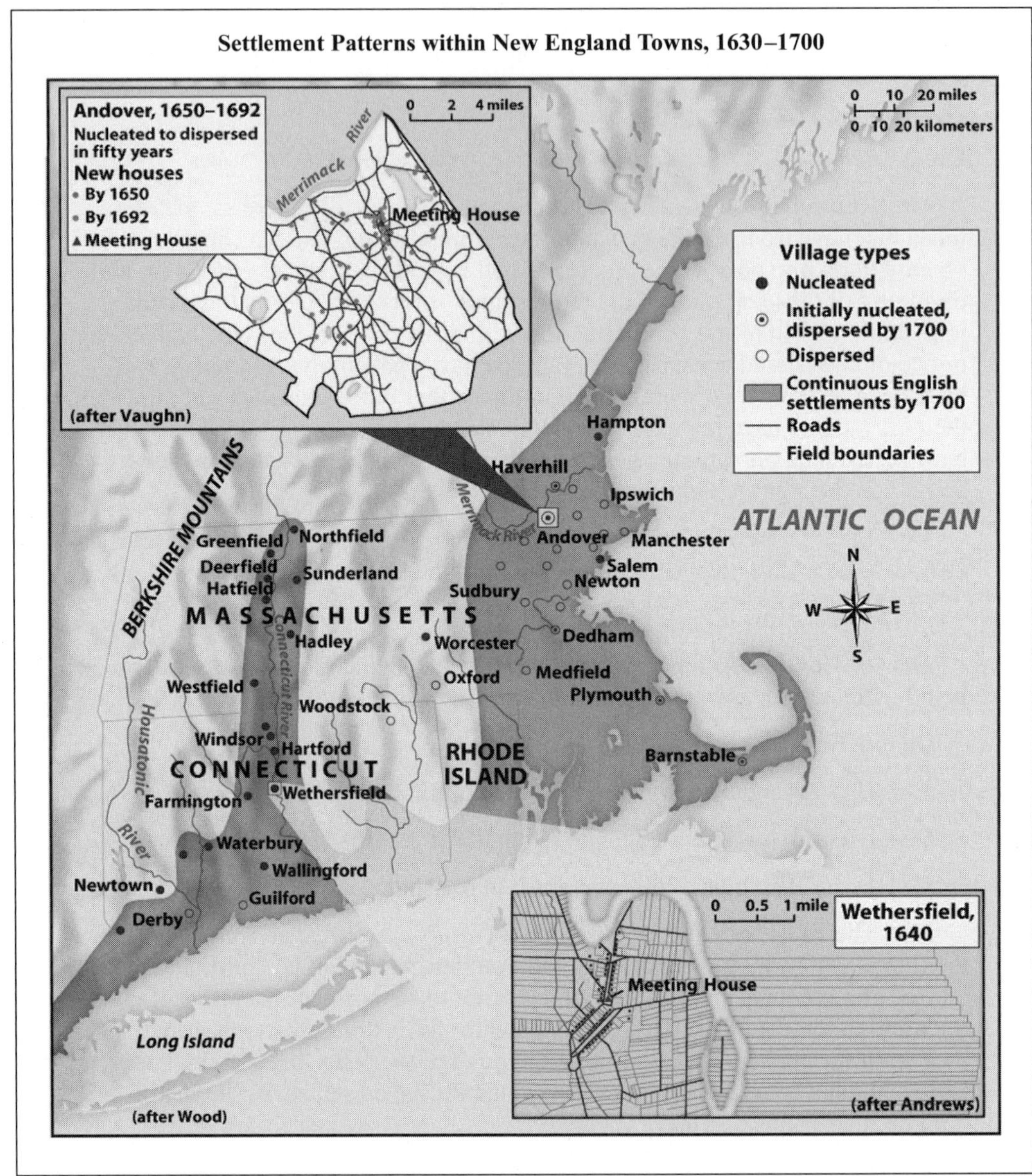

Document D

Source: The Records of the First Church in Salem (1660).

We whose names are here under written, members of the present Church of Christ in Salem, having found by sad experience how dangerous it is to sit loose to the Covenant we make with our God: and how apt we are to wander into by paths, even to the losing of our first aims in entering into Church fellowship: Do therefore, solemnly in the presence of the Eternal God both for our own comforts and those which shall or may be joined unto us renew that Church covenant we find this Church bound unto at their first beginning. . . .

We give ourselves to the Lord Jesus Christ, and the word of his grace, for the teaching, ruling and sanctifying of us in matters of worship, and conversation resolving to cleave to him alone for life and glory; and oppose all contrary ways, canons and constitutions of men in his worship.

We promise to walk with our brethren and sisters in the Congregation with all watchfulness, and tenderness avoiding all jealousies, suspicions, backbitings, conjurings, provokings, secret risings of spirit against them, but in all offences to follow the rule of the Lord Jesus, and to bear and forbear, give and forgive as he hath taught us.

In public or private, we will willingly do nothing to the offence of the Church but will be willing to take advice for ourselves and ours as occasion shall be presented. . . .

We hereby promise to carry ourselves in all lawful obedience, to those that are over us in Church or Commonweal, knowing how well pleasing it will be to the Lord, that they should have encouragement in their places, by our not grieving their spirits through our irregularities. . . .

This Covenant was renewed by the church on a solemn day of Humiliation 6 of 1 month 1660 [March 6, 1661].

Document E

Source: Suffolk County Court Records, 1671–1673.

Robert Marshall . . . [was] accused by Walter Barefoote [of] being an Atheist[;] the Court ordered him the said Marshall to be committed to prison, except he put in bond of two hundred pounds to Appear at the next Court of Assistance to be held at Boston. Accordingly the said Robert Marshall in one hundred pounds as principal…to the Treasurer of the County of Suffolk on condition that the said Marshall shall appear at the next Court of Assistance to answer what shall be alleged against him as to his being an Atheist and that . . . in the mean time be of good behavior. . . .

Brian Murphey, presented for being a common drunkard, which be owned in Court, and also for striking Elinor Shearne that was with Child, and other misdemeanors[.] The Court Sentenced him to be whipped with fifteen Stripes paying fees of Court and prison, Standing committed 'til the Sentence be performed.

Free-Response Questions

Directions: For the following questions, you are advised to spend five minutes planning and thirty minutes writing your answer. Cite relevant historical evidence in support of your generalizations and present your arguments clearly and logically.

Hints:

- Sketch out a brief outline, recording facts and examples that you remember and organizing them in a sensible way. Each section of the outline should generate a supporting paragraph for your essay.
- Develop a thesis that takes a clear stand on the question posed. Be sure to state it clearly in your introductory paragraph.
- Begin each supporting paragraph with a clear topic sentence.
- Consider transitions between paragraphs.
- Conclude by restating your thesis in a fresh way, perhaps by making a connection to another moment in American history.
- Keep in mind the volume of essays the exam readers must plow through. Clarity and organization are key.
- Question-specific hints follow the sample questions below.

1. **"The Great Awakening changed America." Assess the validity of this statement, including social, political, and cultural effects.**

   Thesis development and organization: Did the Great Awakening change America? To what extent? For whom? "Social, political, and cultural effects" gives you a strong suggestion for the topic sentences of three supporting paragraphs.

2. **Analyze the impact of the Columbian Exchange on both the New and Old Worlds.**

   Thesis development and organization: Be careful not to simply report the effects of the Exchange on both worlds. Analyze *means to take a stand. Was the Old World affected more dramatically than the New World was, or vice versa? Once you decide on your thesis, figure out the best way to organize your examples. Among possible categories for comparison, you will definitely want to consider social and economic effects.*

3. **During the seventeenth and eighteenth centuries, people emigrated to the American colonies for a better economic life. Evaluate the extent to which this statement is true with respect to three of the following groups:**

   English in Massachusetts
   Scots-Irish in the Chesapeake
   Quakers in Pennsylvania
   Dutch in New York
   Africans in the southern colonies

   Thesis development and organization: The AP Exam almost always includes a question that allows you to choose from a short selection of topics. The first objective is to choose the topics you can recall most clearly; next, you must shape the comparison into a plausible thesis. To what extent were these groups motivated by economic factors?

What other factors affected their decisions? If you decide that different groups had different motivations, your thesis should reflect this. An example of a strong thesis would be: "While [group 1] and [group 2] were primarily motivated by the promise of economic success, [group 3] was primarily seeking [other goal besides better economy]."

A simple organization will have supporting paragraphs that cohere around each chosen group. Alternatively, you could choose a thematic organization; for example, separate each of the three groups' motivations into economic, political, and cultural reasons.

Answer Key to Part 1 Practice Questions

Multiple-Choice Questions

1. **Answer (C) disease.** Although warfare, food scarcity, and other calamities also befell Native Americans after Europeans arrived, the most devastating event was the arrival of diseases, especially smallpox, in the Americas that had never been there before. (*America's History,* Seventh Edition, Chapter 1, pp. 1–28)

2. **Answer (D) were subjected to mercantilist policies.** Each of these answers does apply to at least one of the main European colonizers. However, only one applies to all, and that is mercantilism, which is defined in Chapter 1 and refers to a system of political economy based on government regulation. (*America's History,* Seventh Edition, Chapter 1, pp. 1–37)

3. **Answer (A) hierarchy, authority, and bureaucracy were integral components.** Be careful to note that the question is not asking you to compare American societies in general with European societies—only the more centralized states, those of the Mayas and Aztecs, described on pp. 10–12. In these places, hierarchy and bureaucracy were essential to maintaining authority, although their contours differed between Europeans and the American states. (*America's History,* Seventh Edition, Chapter 1, pp. 10–12)

4. **Answer (C) Mediterranean Sea to the Atlantic Ocean.** The process of elimination is helpful here: in early American history, clearly the Atlantic Ocean becomes the focus for European explorers and traders, so answers A, B, and E can be eliminated. Although some European traders were involved in the Indian Ocean trade, it was the Mediterranean that was the connector for Europeans to the trade routes of North Africa and Asia, and the focus of European trading for centuries before the Atlantic Ocean was successfully navigated. (*America's History,* Seventh Edition, Chapter 1, pp. 1–19)

5. **Answer (B) the Navigation Acts.** The Navigation Acts are the best example of British mercantilism in practice because they specifically focused on economic activity and increasing revenue for the crown. Leisler's Rebellion has nothing to do with mercantilism, and the 1763 Proclamation and Dominion of New England address political and military decisions by English authorities. (*America's History,* Seventh Edition, Chapter 3, p. 76)

6. **Answer (E) the growth of a democratic spirit.** The Great Awakening was a religious movement that affected many aspects of American life—but none of the first four answers apply. Because preachers stressed the individual's relationship with God, the Great Awakening inspired Americans of all classes to question authority—not only in matters of religion, ultimately. (*America's History,* Seventh Edition, Chapter 4, pp. 122–123)

7. **Answer (A) an Aztec observation on the disease-ridden Spanish conquest.** This answer can be interpreted by the clues in the document: "a great sickness, a plague" is key, as is the author's observation of the invaders' white skin and fair hair. Do not be discouraged by a primary source quote that you do not recognize: no one expects you to have read all of the sources that may appear on the AP test in any given year (nor have most teachers). Just read carefully and look for clues. (*America's History,* Seventh Edition, Chapter 1, p. 29, "Comparing American Voices")

8. **Answer (C) the plantation system.** Through the process of elimination, you should be able to rule out all of the other answers; all of them were developments unique to the United States. Plantation slavery was based on the feudal model in which powerful

nobles governed landless serfs. Europeans first established plantations on islands like Madeira off the coast of North Africa, and then in the West Indies. (*America's History,* Seventh Edition, Chapter 3, p. 82)

9. **Answer (C) New York, New Jersey, and Pennsylvania.** In other words, the Mid-Atlantic colonies. These were the most tolerant of different religions and attracted settlers from many different European places and classes. Pennsylvania was guided by William Penn's Quaker beliefs and his Frame of Government that ensured religious freedom. (*America's History,* Seventh Edition, Chapter 3, p. 76)

10. **Answer (C) New England.** The self-governing communities of New England were made up of yeoman farmers—farmers who owned their own land. They organized their towns in a way that most adult males participated in the town meeting and thus enjoyed fairly equal political influence. (*America's History,* Seventh Edition, Chapter 2, p. 63; Chapter 4, p. 106)

11. **Answer (C) There was little time for idleness and amusement.** Although children were highly esteemed by New England families, and parents fretted over what land they would be able to bequeath to their children, there was no time for anyone to be idle. (*America's History,* Seventh Edition, Chapter 4, pp. 107–108)

12. **Answer (A) only about 5 to 10 percent of the population dominated the republican institutions.** The white planter elite wielded unlimited power over their slaves, and held the lion's share of political power in the colonies. It was anything but an egalitarian society. It is not true that "nearly everyone had at least several slaves"; but on the eve of Revolution in the Chesapeake, 60 percent of white families did have at least one slave. (*America's History,* Seventh Edition, Chapter 3, pp. 92–93)

13. **Answer (B) respected Indian values, did not use natives for forced labor, and tried to keep alcohol away from them.** The French did engage in missionary work, and they did spread disease. However, their missionaries (mostly Jesuits, known as the Black Robes in the Americas) made an effort to learn native languages and did accommodate some native practices. (*America's History,* Seventh Edition, Chapter 2, pp. 44–47)

14. **Answer (B) salutary neglect.** Salutary neglect was a term of praise used by British political philosopher Edmund Burke in 1775, referring to the policies of Whig leader Robert Walpole. During this time, Great Britain enjoyed trade revenues from its North American colonies while allowing for a good deal of self-rule for the colonists—arguably contributing to their later bid for independence. (*America's History,* Seventh Edition, Chapter 3, pp. 97–98)

15. **Answer (C) the expansion of African slavery.** Bacon's rebellion was both a frontier and a class conflict. To avoid further troubles, the planter elite passed a number of laws to appease poorer white colonists, excluding the removal of Indian tribes. They also began to turn from white indentured servitude to African slavery. (*America's History,* Seventh Edition, Chapter 2, pp. 56–57).

Document-Based Question

Assess the extent to which New England Puritans translated religious ideals into practice.

This question asks you to judge whether or not the Puritans' overall project—their intention to build a cohesive community based solely on religious principles—was successful. There is an undeniable idealism within the earlier documents that is challenged by the realities of human society. To some extent, it would be hard to defend the idea that the Puritan founders' intentions matched the reality of New England life a few generations later. But it is easy to credit the Puritans for their extraordinary successes and the profound influence they would have on the United States.

Look for connections between Winthrop's utopianism and orthodoxy (Document A) and the evolution of Puritan society reflected in the rest of the documents. In this regard, the trial of Anne Hutchinson (Document B) provides an early example of dissent against the orthodoxy of the Puritan community, while the Salem Church's restatement of its Covenant in 1660 (Document D) reasserts its commitment to it. The map of settlement patterns within New England towns (Document C) and the Suffolk County Court Records (Document E) also suggest the effect population growth and ordinary social conflict had upon the capacity of Puritans to live up to the ideals of Winthrop or the church members of Salem.

For the strongest response possible, be sure to bring other facts learned from class or the textbook to your DBQ essay; examples would include the exclusive nature of church membership, the difficulty of becoming a church member, or the Salem Witch Trials. To review the Puritans, see Chapter 2 of the textbook.

Free-Response Questions

1. **"The Great Awakening changed America." Assess the validity of this statement, including social, political, and cultural effects.**

   Your essay should touch on the following aspects of the Great Awakening, and should reasonably conclude that the Great Awakening did change America.

   Political Effects:

   - The Great Awakening spurred a strong interest in democratization. If the people were equal in the eyes of God (with no more predestination or clergy hierarchical authority), then they should be equal before the law.
   - If the people were capable of making their own religious decisions without relying on the higher authority of ministers, they could make their own political decisions without deferring to the authority of the great landowners and merchants, or the king or his royal governors.

   Social Effects:

   - Manners and morals were emphasized. If we are all God's children we should treat each other with respect.

   Cultural Effects:

   - Emotionalism became a major part of religious services. Ministers lost some of their former authority among those who read the Bible at home.
   - Religious diversity led to religious toleration. The American colonies were the most religiously tolerant people in the world.

2. **Analyze the impact of the Columbian Exchange on both the New and Old Worlds.**

The Columbian Exchange affected the New World (Western Hemisphere) in these ways:

- New foods—onions, olives, grapes, bananas, coffee beans, peaches, pears, sugar cane, honey, wheat, rice, barley, oats—meant a more varied diet
- New domesticated animals—cattle, sheep, pigs, horses—meant changing lifestyles.
- Disease—smallpox, influenza, typhus, measles, malaria, diphtheria, and whooping cough—made subjugation of the Indians easier for Europeans.

The Columbian Exchange affected on the Old World (Europe, Africa, and Asia) in these ways:

- New foods were brought back from the New World: squash, sweet potatoes, avocados, peppers, pineapple, cocoa beans, peanuts, potatoes, tomatoes, beans, vanilla, corn, pumpkin, turkey, and quinine.
- Gold and silver brought great wealth to Spain and other European nations and launched a commercial revolution of new business and trade practices.

3. **During the seventeenth and eighteenth centuries, people emigrated to the American colonies for a better economic life. Evaluate the extent to which this statement is true with respect to three of the following groups:**

English in Massachusetts
Scots-Irish in the Chesapeake
Quakers in Pennsylvania
Dutch in New York
Africans in the southern colonies

"Extent to which" questions mean that you should choose whether the reasons for emigration were purely economic, not at all economic, or a combination of factors. Your choice of which groups to compare will obviously shape your overall thesis. Below is a brief outline of some of the reasons each group chose to emigrate.

English in Massachusetts:

(Most students will choose the Puritans in New England, though the more sophisticated responses will include the Pilgrims as well.)

- Puritans stated that they came for religious "freedom," but their theocracy and demands for orthodoxy after arriving in the New World indicate differently.
- Puritans had problems with the Anglican Church and Bishop Laud.
- New English laws threatened Puritan economic livelihood.
- King James I threatened to kick Puritans out of England—or worse.
- The Pilgrims had left England for Holland, but moved further abroad in order to maintain English identity.
- Mayflower Compact adopted Puritan religious organization as the model for political structure.
- Winthrop left England in search of religious freedom and land. He and his associates formed a joint-stock company supported by sympathetic merchants but restricted participation to Puritans.

Scots-Irish in the Chesapeake:

(Savvy students will note that the Scots-Irish originally settled in Pennsylvania before moving south.)

- Irish Test Act of 1704 restricted voting rights to Anglicans; Scots-Irish were largely Presbyterian.
- They faced discrimination and economic regulation at home.
- They were unable to hold public offices in Britain.
- They faced heavy taxes and duties at home: English duties on woolens woven by Scots-Irish, taxes for Scots-Irish farmers.

Quakers in Pennsylvania:

- They faced persecution in England for refusing to serve in the army or pay taxes to the Church of England.
- William Penn founded Pennsylvania as a refuge for Quakers.
- Penn promised cheap land and religious freedom, which attracted middling farmers from northwestern England and Germans.
- Penn's Frame of Government applied Quaker principles to politics.
- All property-owning men could vote and hold office.

Dutch in New York:

- New Netherland (which later became New York) was founded by Henry Hudson for the Dutch East India Company, and the Dutch West India Company later took over.
- The motives of the Dutch were economic. Fur trading became the primary motivation for colonizing the region.
- Patronships encouraging broader settlement by the Dutch failed.

Africans in the southern colonies:

- They were brought as slaves or indentured servants; they did not choose to emigrate.
- The economy of south depended on their labor.
- Their presence in the southern colonies was part of an economic venture by slave traders.

PART 2
The New Republic, 1763–1820

This part covers the following chapters in Henretta et al., *America's History,* Seventh Edition:

Chapter 5 Toward Independence: Years of Decision, 1763–1776

Chapter 6 Making War and Republican Governments, 1776–1789

Chapter 7 Politics and Society in the New Republic, 1787–1820

Chapter 8 Creating a Republican Culture, 1790–1820

Essential Questions

After studying the chapters in Part 2, you should know how to answer the following questions:

1. Why did the British North American colonies revolt against Great Britain?
2. How did the United States defeat Great Britain during the American Revolution?
3. How and why did Americans craft a new government founded on republican ideals and institutions? To what extent were those ideals achieved for all Americans in this period?
4. How did European political events of the 1790s and early 1800s influence the political development of the United States?
5. Why did the War of 1812 take place, and what was its impact in the Americas and Europe?
6. How did the contest for power between the Federalist and Republican parties affect the newly constituted federal government?
7. In what ways did Americans seek to build a Democratic Republican society and culture?

These four chapters span the Revolution, the creation of the United States, and its political and economic foundations. You'll want to pay careful attention to the events leading up to the Revolution, its causes and effects, and the ideas that animated the creation of institutions that, for better or worse, guided all that came after. These concepts feature prominently on the AP test and establish patterns and tensions that echo throughout the remainder of the nation's history.

Resources for Review

In the following pages, you'll find the Thematic Timeline and Essay for Part 2 from *America's History*, exercises to review your knowledge of the period, and AP-style questions that address the time period covered: 15 practice multiple-choice questions, 1 document-based question, and 3 free-response questions. Answers with page references to *America's History* can be found in the Answer Key at the end of this Part 2 review.

Thematic Timeline and Part Essay

The New Republic, 1763–1820

	GOVERNMENT	DIPLOMACY	ECONOMY	SOCIETY	CULTURE
1763	Stamp Act Congress (1765) Committees of correspondence First Continental Congress (1774)	Treaty of Paris (1763) gives Britain control of Canada, Florida, and parts of India	Merchants defy Sugar and Stamp Acts Boycotts spur Patriot women to make textiles	Artisans win political influence Quebec Act (1774) allows Catholicism	Patriots call for American unity Concept of popular sovereignty takes hold
1775	Second Continental Congress (1775) States institute republican constitutions	Independence declared (1776) French provide secret aid to Patriots Treaty of Alliance with France (1778)	Manufacturing expands during war Cut off of trade and severe inflation threaten economy War debt grows	Judith Sargent Murray writes *On the Equality of the Sexes* (1779) Emancipation of slaves begins in the North	Thomas Paine's *Common Sense* (1776) calls for a republic Fall in European migration (1775–1820) enhances American identity

	GOVERNMENT	DIPLOMACY	ECONOMY	SOCIETY	CULTURE
1780	Articles of Confederation ratified (1781) Legislatures emerge as supreme in states Philadelphia convention drafts U.S. Constitution (1787)	Treaty of Paris (1783) Britain restricts U.S. trade with West Indies U.S. government signs treaties with Indian peoples	Bank of North America founded (1781) Commercial recession (1783–1789) Land speculation increases in West	Virginia enacts religious freedom legislation (1786) Politicians and ministers deny vote to women; praise republican motherhood	Noah Webster defines American English State cessions and land ordinances create national domain in West Many German settlers keep own language
1790	Conflict over Alexander Hamilton's economic policies First national parties: Federalists and Republicans	Wars between France and Britain Jay Treaty, Pinckney Treaty (both 1795) Undeclared war with France (1798)	First Bank of the United States (1792–1811) States charter business corporations Outwork system grows	Bill of Rights ratified (1791) Creation of French Republic (1793) sparks ideological debate Sedition Act limits freedom of press (1798)	Indians form Western Confederacy (1790) Second Great Awakening (1790–1860) Political divisions emerge between South and North
1800	Jefferson's "Revolution of 1800" reduces activism of national government Chief Justice Marshall asserts federal judicial powers	Napoleonic Wars (1802–1815) Haitian rebellion and independence Louisiana Purchase (1803) Embargo Act (1807)	Cotton output and demand for African labor expands Farm productivity improves Embargo encourages U.S. manufacturing	New Jersey retracts suffrage for propertied women (1807) Atlantic slave trade legally ends (1808)	Tenskwatawa and Tecumseh revive Western Indian Confederacy Free blacks enhance sense of African American identity

	GOVERNMENT	DIPLOMACY	ECONOMY	SOCIETY	CULTURE
1810	Triumph of Republican Party and end of Federalist Party State constitutions democratized	War of 1812 (1812–1815) J. Q. Adams makes border treaties Monroe Doctrine (1823)	Second Bank of the United States chartered (1816–1836) Supreme Court guards property Emergence of a national economy	Suffrage for white men expands American Colonization Society (1817) Missouri Compromise (1819–1821)	War of 1812 tests national unity Religious benevolence engenders social reform movements

"The American war is over," Philadelphia Patriot Benjamin Rush declared in 1787, "but this is far from being the case with the American Revolution. On the contrary, nothing but the first act of the great drama is closed. It remains yet to establish and perfect our new forms of government." As we will suggest in Part 2, the job was even greater than Rush imagined. The republican revolution that began with the Patriot resistance movement of 1765 and took shape with the Declaration of Independence in 1776 reached far beyond politics. It challenged many of the values and institutions of the colonial social order and forced Americans to consider fundamental changes in their economic, religious, and cultural practices. Here, in summary, are the main themes of our discussion of America's emerging political and social order.

Government: Creating Republican Institutions Once Americans had repudiated their allegiance to Britain and its monarch, they had to create new systems of government. In 1776, no one knew how the states should go about setting up republican institutions. Nor did Patriot leaders know if there should be a permanent central authority along the lines of the Continental Congress. It would take experiments that stretched over an entire generation to find out. It would take even longer to assimilate a new institution—the political party—into the workings of government. However, by 1820, difficult years of political conflict, compromise, and constitutional revision had resulted in republican national and state governments that commanded the allegiance of their citizens.

Diplomacy: Contending with Foreign Entanglements To create and preserve their new republic, Americans of European descent fought two wars against Great Britain, an undeclared war against France, and many battles with Indian peoples. The extension of American sovereignty and settlements into the trans-Appalachian west was a cultural disaster for Indian peoples, who were brutally displaced from their lands. The wars against Britain divided the new nation's white citizens into bitter factions—Patriots against Loyalists in the War of Independence, and pro-war Republicans versus antiwar Federalists in the War of 1812—and expended much blood and treasure. Despite these wars, by 1820, the United States had emerged as a strong independent state with internationally accepted boundaries. Freed from a half-century of entanglement in European wars and diplomacy, its people began to exploit the riches of the continent.

Economy: Expanding Commerce and Manufacturing By the 1760s, the expansion of farming and commerce had established the foundation for a vigorous national economy. Beginning in the 1780s, northern merchants financed a banking system and organized a rural system of manufacturing. Simultaneously, state governments used charters and other privileges to assist businesses and to improve roads, bridges, and waterways. Meanwhile, southern planters continued to use enslaved African Americans and exported a new staple crop—cotton—to markets in the North and in Europe. Many yeomen farm families migrated westward to grow grain; while those in the East turned out raw materials such as leather and wool for burgeoning manufacturing enterprises, and they made shoes, textiles, tinware, and other handicrafts for market sale. By 1820, the young American republic was on the verge of achieving economic as well as political independence.

Society: Defining Liberty and Equality As Americans confronted the challenges of creating a republican society, they became increasingly conscious of long-standing (but previously little-examined) divisions of gender, race, religion, and class. They disagreed over fundamental issues such as legal equality for women, the status of slavery, the meaning of free speech and religious liberty, and the extent of public responsibility for social inequality. As we shall see, political leaders managed to resolve some of these disputes. Legislatures abolished slavery in the North, broadened religious liberty by allowing freedom of conscience, and, except in New England, ended the system of legally established churches. However, Americans continued to argue over social equality, in part because their republican creed placed family authority in the hands of men and political power in the hands of propertied individuals. This arrangement denied power and status not only to slaves but also to free blacks, women, and middling and poor white men.

Culture: Forging Pluralism and National Identity The British colonies in North America contained a diversity of peoples and ways of life. This complexity inhibited the effort to define an American culture and identity. Native Americans still lived in their own clans and nations; and black Americans, one-fifth of the enumerated population, were developing a distinct African American culture. White Americans were enmeshed in vigorous regional cultures—New England, Middle Atlantic, and Southern—and in strong ethnic communities: English, Scottish, Scots-Irish, German, and Dutch. However, over time, the political institutions began to unite Americans of diverse backgrounds, as did their increasing participation in the market economy and in evangelical Protestant churches. By 1820, to be an American meant, for many members of the dominant white population, to be a republican, a Protestant, and an enterprising individual in a capitalist-run market system.

Essential Questions Review Exercises

Using the guidelines, maps, and graphic organizers that follow, gather evidence that helps you review concepts and themes from the period 1763–1820. Consult *America's History,* Seventh Edition, as well as any relevant materials your teacher has provided to review the information.

1. **Why did the British North American colonies revolt against Great Britain?**

   When considering why wars occur, it is often helpful to distinguish among long-term causes, short-term causes, and triggers—those catalysts that cause a tipping point to occur and change the course of history. Use the following table to record the causes of the American Revolution.

CAUSES FOR THE AMERICAN REVOLT AGAINST GREAT BRITAIN		
Long-Term Causes (Consider the long-term differences between Great Britain and the American colonies discussed in Part 1.)	**Short-Term Causes** (Consider the series of events from 1763–1775.)	**Triggers** (What caused Americans to unify and declare independence in 1776?)

2. **How did the United States defeat Great Britain during the American Revolution?**

   This is a great question with many parallels to more recent insurgent-style wars, such as the American war in Vietnam in the 1960s and 1970s. Use the map below for the following:

   - Using Maps 6.2, 6.3, and 6.4 in the textbook, mark key battle locations and dates, noting the Revolutionary War's geographic course from North to South, as well as events on the western frontier.
   - Draw a box on the map and label it "British Advantages," and then list those advantages.
   - Draw another box and label it "American Disadvantages," and list them.
   - Consider this in the space below the map: What did the British have to do to win? What did the Patriots have to do to win? Comparing strategies helps to understand why, despite their many advantages, the British decided to surrender in 1781.

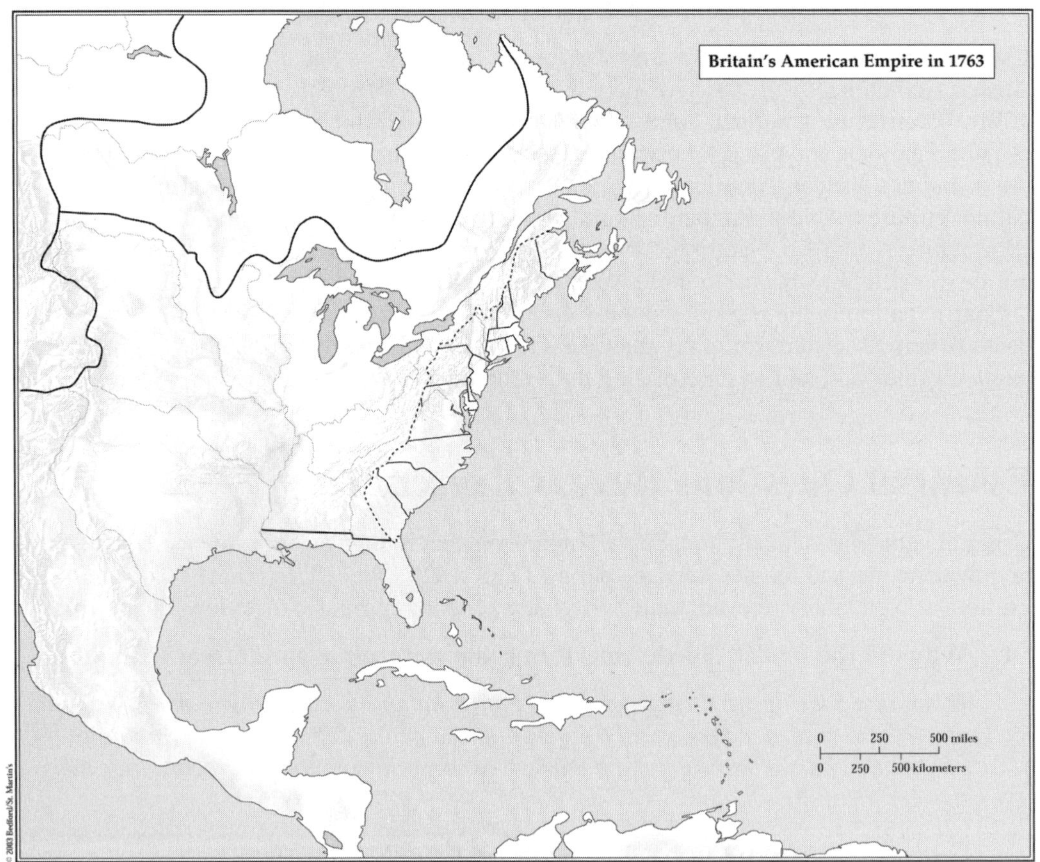

Britain's American Empire in 1763

3. **How and why did Americans craft a new government founded on republican ideals and institutions? To what extent were those ideals achieved for all Americans in this period?**

   There were two experiments in republican governance during this period: first, under the Articles of Confederation, and second, under the Constitution written in 1787. Using the table on the next page, record revolutionary and republican ideals and then ways that these two systems of government sought to further those ideals. Examples have been filled in to help you begin. Refer to Chapter 6 for help.

REPUBLICAN IDEALS	ARTICLES OF CONFEDERATION	CONSTITUTION AND BILL OF RIGHTS
No taxation without representation	Congress did not have the right to tax; only states could	
Freedom of speech		First Amendment

4. **How did European political events of the 1790s and early 1800s influence the political development of the United States?**

   The 1790s were a tumultuous time in Europe, especially in France, where the Revolution began in 1789 and caused many years of instability and war throughout Europe. Use the space below to fill out a timeline of corresponding events and their impact on the first three presidencies of the United States—Washington's, Adams's, and Jefferson's. Refer to Chapter 7 for help.

EVENTS IN EUROPE	POLITICAL DEVELOPMENTS IN THE U.S.
1789: French Revolution begins on July 15	1789: Washington elected 1796: John Adams elected 1800: Thomas Jefferson elected

5. **Why did the War of 1812 take place, and what was its impact in the Americas and Europe?**

   In the space below, write a substantive paragraph that responds to this question, reviewing the section called "The War of 1812 and the Transformation of Politics" in Chapter 7.

6. **How did the contest for power between the Federalist and Republican parties affect the newly constituted federal government?**

   Emerging directly out of the ratification debates that began in 1787 after the new Constitution was proposed, the Federalists and Republicans differed over a number of pressing political and economic issues. Using the table below (and referring to Chapter 7 for help), record the points of contention between the two parties, and consider what types of Americans were most likely to become either Republicans or Federalists.

	REPUBLICANS	FEDERALISTS
Economic Issues		
Political Issues		
Likely Party Members		

7. **In what ways did Americans seek to build a Democratic Republican society and culture?**

   Chapter 8 discusses four aspects of early national life and the impact these trends had on the emerging republican culture of the United States. Using the graphic below, note significant events and trends in each of the four areas of American life.

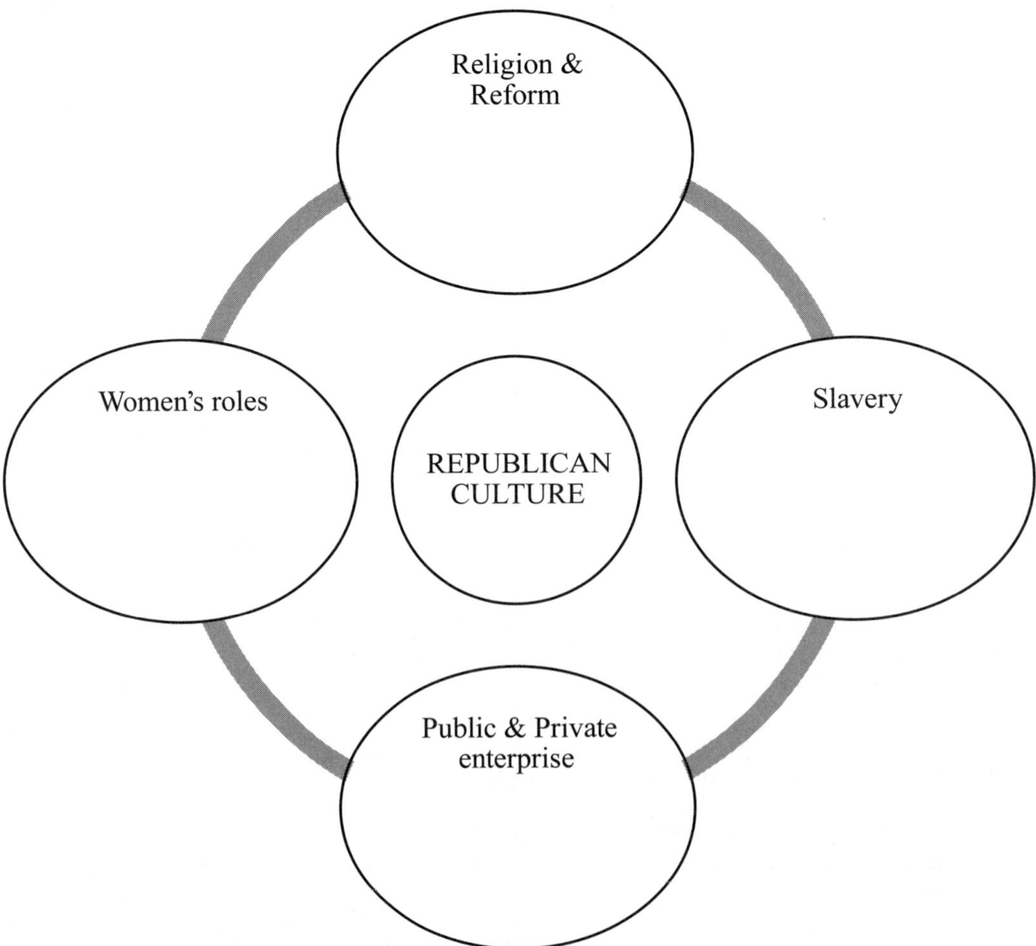

Practice Questions

The following sections allow you to test your knowledge of Part 2. The Directions are verbatim instructions from the College Board's AP Exam; the Hints offer strategies for tackling each type of AP question. Answers to all of the Part 2 practice questions follow.

Multiple-Choice Questions

Directions: Each of the questions or incomplete statements below is followed by five suggested answers or completions. Select the one that is best in each case.

Hints:

- Read each question carefully, looking out for negative words such as EXCEPT, NOT, and FALSE.
- Read all possible answers and cross out those you feel are incorrect; narrowing down your choices gives you the chance to make an educated guess.
- Be cautious of words indicating absolutes, like *most, least, all,* and *none.*
- Connect the specific information of the question to broader trends and themes.
- In questions that provide you with evidence, assess the information carefully and eliminate answers that go beyond the bounds of the evidence given.

1. Which of the following quotes best embodies the viewpoint presented in Thomas Paine's *Common Sense*?
   (A) "A government of our own is our natural right . . . TIS TIME TO PART."
   (B) "It was the best of times. It was the worst of times."
   (C) "The right to levy internal taxes was never supposed to be in Parliament as we are not represented there."
   (D) "The exercise of [Parliamentary] authority is not perfectly constitutional in respect to the colonies."
   (E) "We hold these truths to be self-evident, that all men are created equal."

2. The ideology that refutes rule by a king and embraces a representative system of government is
   (A) federalism
   (B) republicanism
   (C) democracy
   (D) diplomacy
   (E) mercantilism

3. Why was America's international ally during the Revolutionary War an unlikely partner?
   (A) The ally was a devoutly Quaker nation.
   (B) The ally was a weak nation of loosely-joined republics.
   (C) The ally was normally neutral in international affairs.
   (D) The ally was a Roman Catholic monarchy.
   (E) The ally's African colonies could have been jeopardized by joining the American cause.

4. The Philadelphia Convention's creation of the most democratic government in the world at the time was ironic because most of the delegates to the convention were
   (A) artisans
   (B) yeoman farmers
   (C) slaveholders
   (D) tenants
   (E) wealthy men

5. A political result of the American Revolution was
   (A) national equal rights for women
   (B) universal male suffrage
   (C) the end of public tax support for established churches
   (D) an increase in the number of ordinary citizens elected to state legislatures
   (E) that primogeniture and entail were eliminated

6 A result of the Loyalists' exodus during and after the Revolution was that
   (A) the leadership class had to be totally replaced
   (B) a group of entrepreneurial-minded merchants were replaced by a tradition-oriented group who invested its money in property
   (C) their land was confiscated and divided among the landless
   (D) Patriot merchants replaced Tories at the top of the economic ladder
   (E) the number of slaves declined dramatically as the Loyalists took their slaves with them

7. Which of the following was true under the Articles of Confederation?
   (A) Most of the power was vested in the central government.
   (B) Congress enforced its will through its power of taxation.
   (C) Amendments could be passed with a majority of states approving.
   (D) The real power was vested in the states.
   (E) There were three branches of government.

8. Both Shays's Rebellion and the Whiskey Rebellions were
   (A) slave revolts
   (B) insurrections over the Alien and Sedition Acts
   (C) spontaneous uprisings regarding United States foreign policy
   (D) tax revolts
   (E) Embargo Act protests

9. Of the following, who would most likely become a Federalist?
   (A) A yeoman farmer in Kentucky
   (B) A tenant in Ohio Territory
   (C) A Shaysite in western Massachusetts
   (D) A Tennessee squatter
   (E) A Pennsylvania merchant

10. An outcome of the capitalist-run market economy was
   (A) families and communities became more self-sufficient
   (B) rural families worked shorter hours with increased production
   (C) production actually decreased
   (D) families and communities lost some of their economic independence
   (E) fewer yeoman farmers than in the past needed to supplement their income by working for wages

11. In the first quarter of the nineteenth century
   (A) there was a shift in public policy that encouraged business
   (B) western farmers became wealthy
   (C) property rights of farmers were protected from encroaching business ventures
   (D) government stayed out of the daily lives of Americans
   (E) the concept of eminent domain was not yet in existence

12. An economic problem for northwestern farmers in early nineteenth century was aided by
   (A) crop rotation
   (B) irrigation
   (C) the Western Confederacy
   (D) the cotton gin
   (E) turnpikes and canals

13. Which aspect of Alexander Hamilton's financial program, as it was implemented, was most disliked by the inhabitants of western Pennsylvania?
   (A) The protective tariff
   (B) The excise tax
   (C) Bank of the United States
   (D) The revenue tariff
   (E) His insistence that there should be a national debt

14. Thomas Grimké's statement, "Give me a host of educated pious mothers and sisters and I will revolutionize a country, in moral and religious taste," was
   (A) an argument about the problems created by primogeniture
   (B) refuting public disdain for the increase in college education for women
   (C) an endorsement of the southern view of women's role
   (D) referring to the concept of republican motherhood
   (E) indicating the role both married and single women played in the Second Great Awakening

15. The slavery discussion at the time of the Missouri Compromise involved
   (A) Northern justification for the widespread acceptance of abolitionism
   (B) preserving the existing balance of power between North and South in the Senate
   (C) sectional disagreements but no real talk of abolition
   (D) a basic difference of opinion regarding slavery as a moral evil
   (E) only constitutional arguments for the continuation of slavery

Document-Based Question

Directions: The following question requires you to construct a coherent essay that integrates your interpretation of Documents A–G and your knowledge of the period referred to in the question. High scores are earned only by essays that cite key pieces of evidence from the documents *and* draw on outside knowledge of the period.

To what extent did the Constitution represent the goals of the American Revolution?

Use the documents and your knowledge of the years 1787–1820 to construct your response.

Background Reading: *America's History,* Seventh Edition, Chapter 7

Hints:

- With document-based questions, remember to move beyond the specific facts in the documents to seek their more interpretive or analytical aspects. As you read through the documents, underline key passages, jot notes in the margins, and record outside examples and facts that come to mind as you read.
- This is a "to what extent" question, meaning you are determining how well the Constitution met the goals of the Revolutionary War. Visual aids can help with questions like these. Determine where on the continuum below you would place your own interpretation:

  VERY SUCCESSFUL ←——————————→ UNSUCCESSFUL
- After reading through the documents, categorize them into groups to generate a paragraph structure for your response. Creating groups based on authors, time periods, geographical regions, and document types can often be effective.
- Keep in mind the volume of essays the exam readers must plow through. Clarity and organization are key.
- Be sure to include as many pertinent details as possible in support of your DBQ thesis.

Document A

Source: Articles of Confederation (agreed to by Congress November 15, 1777; ratified and in force March 1, 1781).

Article II. Each state retains its sovereignty, freedom, and independence, and every Power, Jurisdiction, and right, which is not by this confederation expressly delegated to the United States, in Congress assembled.

Article V. . . . No State shall be represented in Congress by less than two, nor by more than seven Members; and no person shall be capable of being a delegate for more than three years in any term of six years; nor shall any person, being a delegate, be capable of holding any office under the United States, for which he, or another for his benefit receives any salary, fees or emolument of any kind. . . .

Article VIII. All charges of war, and all other expenses that shall be incurred for the common defence or general welfare, and allowed by the United States in Congress assembled, shall be defrayed out of a common treasury, which shall be supplied by the several states, in proportion to the value of all land within each state, granted to or surveyed for any Person, as such land and the buildings and improvements thereon shall be estimated according to such mode as the United States in Congress assembled, shall from time to time direct and appoint. The taxes for paying that proportion shall be laid and levied by the authority and direction of the legislatures of the several states within the time agreed upon by the United States in Congress assembled.

Document B

Source: William Finlay, *On Democracy, Banks, and Paper Money* (1786).

Mr. Finlay: All governments being instituted for the good of the society to which they belong, the supreme legislative power of every community necessarily possesses a power of repealing every law inimical to the public safety. But the government of Pennsylvania being a democracy, the bank is inconsistent with the bill of rights thereof, which says, that government is not instituted for the emolument of any man, family, or set of men. Therefore, this institution being a monopoly, and having a natural tendency, by affording the means, to promote the spirit of monopolizing, is inconsistent with not only the frame but the spirit of our government. . . .

We are one great family: and the laws are our common inheritance. They are general rules, and common in their nature. No man has a greater claim of special privilege for his £100,000 than I have for my £5. No. The laws are a common property. The legislature are entrusted with the distribution of them. This house will not—this house has no right, no constitutional power to give monopolies of legal privilege—to bestow unequal portions of our common inheritance on favorites.

Document C

Source: Benjamin Rush, "Address to the People of the United States" (1787).

Most of the present difficulties of this country arise from the weakness and other defects of our governments.

My business at present shall be only to suggest the defects of the confederation. These consist first, in the deficiency of coercive power; second, in a defect of exclusive power to issue paper money and regulate commerce; third, in vesting the sovereign power in a single legislature; and fourth, in the too frequent rotation of its members. . . .

The people of America have mistaken the meaning of the word sovereignty; hence each state pretends to be sovereign. In Europe, it is applied only to those states which possess the power of making war and peace, of forming treaties and the like. As this power belongs only to Congress, they are the only sovereign power in the United States.

We commit a similar mistake in our ideas of the word independent. No individual state, as such, has any claim to independence. She is independent only in a union with her sister states in congress....

Patriots of 1774, 1775, 1776—heroes of 1778, 1779, 1780! Come forward! . . . Lovers of peace and order who declined to take part in the late war, come forward! Your country forgives your timidity and demands your influence and advice! Hear her proclaiming, in sighs and groans, in her governments, in her finances, in her trade, in her manufactures, in her morals, and in her manners, "The Revolution is not over!"

Document D

Source: Elbridge Gerry, A Warning to the Delegates about Leveling (1787).

Mr. Gerry: The evils we experience flow from the excess of democracy. The people do not want virtue; but are the dupes of pretended patriots. In Massachusetts it has been fully confirmed by experience that they are daily misled into the most baneful measures and opinions by the false reports circulated by designing men, and which no one on the spot can refute. One principle evil arises from the want of due provision for those employed in the administration of government. It would seem to be a maxim of democracy to starve the public servants. He mentioned the popular clamor in Massachusetts for the reduction of salaries and the attack made on that of the Governor though secured by the spirit of the Constitution itself. He had he said been too republican heretofore: he was still however republican, but had been taught by experience the danger of the leveling spirit.

Document E

Source: James Madison, *The Federalist*, No. 51 (1787).

Justice is the end of government. It is the end of civil society. It ever has been and ever will be pursued until it be obtained, or until liberty be lost in the pursuit. In a society under the forms of which the stronger faction can readily unite and oppress the weaker, anarchy may as truly be said to reign as in a state of nature, where the weaker individual is not secured against the violence of the stronger; and as, in the latter state, even the stronger individuals are prompted, by the uncertainty of their condition, to submit to a government which may protect the weak as well as themselves; so, in the former state, will the more powerful factions or parties be gradually induced, by a like motive, to wish for a government which will protect all parties, the weaker as well as the more powerful. . . In the extended republic of the United States, and among the great variety of interests, parties, and sects which it embraces, a coalition of a majority of the whole society could seldom take place on any other principles than those of justice and the general good; whilst there being thus less danger to a minor from the will of a major party, there must be less pretext, also, to provide for the security of the former, by introducing into the government a will not dependent on the latter, or, in other words, a will independent of the society itself. It is no less certain than it is important, notwithstanding the contrary opinions which have been entertained, that the larger the society, provided it lie within a practical sphere, the more duly capable it will be of self-government. And happily for the *republican cause*, the practicable sphere may be carried to a very great extent, by a judicious modification and mixture of the *federal principle.*

Document F

Source: Patrick Henry, *Virginia Ratifying Debates* (1788).

The Confederation, this despised government, merits, in my opinion, the highest encomium—it carried us through a long and dangerous war; it rendered us victorious in that bloody conflict with a powerful nation; it has secured us a territory greater than any European monarch possesses—and shall a government which has been thus strong and vigorous, be accused of imbecility, and abandoned for want of energy? Consider what you are about to do before you part with the government. Take longer time in reckoning things; revolutions like this have happened in almost every country in Europe; similar examples are to be found in ancient Greece and ancient Rome—instances of the people losing their liberty by their own carelessness and the ambition of a few. We are cautioned . . . against faction and turbulence. I acknowledge that licentiousness is dangerous, and that it ought to be provided against. I acknowledge, also, the new form of government may effectually prevent it. Yet there is another thing it will as effectually do—it will oppress and ruin the people.

Document G

Source: Henretta et al., *America's History,* Seventh Edition, Map 6.8.

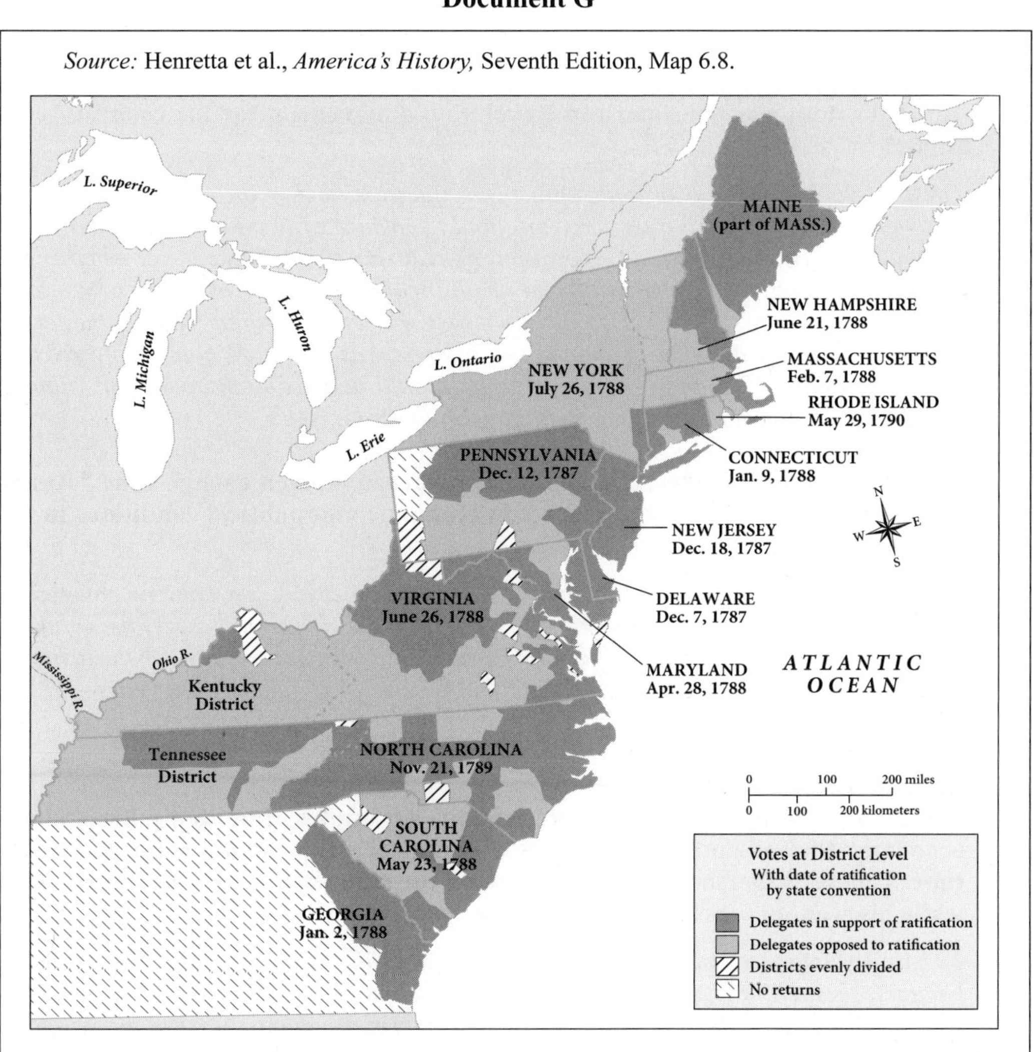

Free-Response Questions

Directions: For the following questions, you are advised to spend five minutes planning and thirty minutes writing your answer. Cite relevant historical evidence in support of your generalizations and present your arguments clearly and logically.

Hints:

- Sketch out a brief outline, recording facts and examples that you remember and organizing them in a sensible way. Each section of the outline should generate a supporting paragraph for your essay.
- Develop a thesis that takes a clear stand on the question posed. Be sure to state it in your introductory paragraph.
- Begin each supporting paragraph with a clear topic sentence.
- Consider transitions between paragraphs.
- Conclude by restating your thesis in a fresh way, perhaps by making a connection to another moment in American history.
- Keep in mind the volume of essays the exam readers must plow through. Clarity and organization are key.
- Question-specific hints follow the three sample questions.

1. **To what extent was the American Revolution a movement for the colonists' civil rights?**

   Thesis development and organization: This question draws on content covered in Chapter 5. To answer this question, you should consider what other reasons may have motivated the revolutionaries. Generations of historians have argued over whether the Patriots acted out of economic interest or political principles. Take your own stand: what evidence shows that the Patriots went to war over civil rights? What countering evidence demonstrates that economic self-interest was the more compelling reason, especially taxation? Supporting paragraphs should address both civil rights abuses and economic injustices by Great Britain upon the colonists.

2. **"The Articles of Confederation could have worked if given enough time." Assess the validity of this quote with respect to economic and political conditions in the 1780s.**

   Thesis development and organization: This question draws on content covered in Chapter 6. The strategy for responding to a question asking you to "assess the validity" is fairly easy: you either support it or disagree with it. Be sure to consider the achievements of the young United States during the Articles of Confederation years—1776–1787—as well as the limitations of that government that were addressed in the 1787 Constitutional Convention.

3. **Assess the validity of this characterization: Alexander Hamilton's ideas about economics thrived and endured while his political views did not stand the test of time. Thomas Jefferson's political views, on the other hand, thrived and endured while his economic ideas were short-lived.**

   Thesis development and organization: This question draws on content covered in Chapters 7 and 8; it is a question of legacy. The contrast between Hamilton's and Jefferson's ideals and views is another classic historical debate. "Assess the validity" means that you should take an argumentative stand on the statement. Consider how successful Hamilton's economic policies passed during his term as Treasury Secretary under President Washington were in establishing a market economy for the United States. But also consider how his Federalist mistrust for "the mob" was short-lived, given the increasing democratization that occurred in the Jacksonian era. Similarly, contrast Jefferson's opposition to such proposals—and his romantic economic views of a nation of citizen farmers—with his greater trust in democratic processes. In organizing your response, be sure to consider the four issues raised by the question: Hamilton's economic ideas and Hamilton's political views, and Jefferson's economic ideas and Jefferson's political views.

Answer Key to Part 2 Practice Questions

Multiple-Choice Questions

1. **Answer (A) "A government of our own is our natural right . . .** TIS TIME TO PART." Answer B is the only quote that does not come from a revolutionary-era document: it is the opening line from Charles Dickens' *A Tale of Two Cities*. Response E should be recognizable as language from the Declaration of Independence. Clues in answer A that point to Paine's *Common Sense* are the appeal to natural rights and the urgency of the message to separate from Great Britain. Paine's pamphlet helped to galvanize colonial sentiment for revolution in the winter of 1775–1776, leading to the writing and signing of the Declaration in July 1776. (*America's History,* Seventh Edition, Chapter 5, pp. 164–166)

2. **Answer (B) republicanism.** During the Revolution, statesmen wrote new constitutions to replace their colonial charters, essentially becoming laboratories of republican governance. The idea of representative government shaped the development of the Constitution, which relied on checks and balances to ensure that no one branch of government overpowered another. As the United States republic developed, it became more democratic, with broader voter participation and more directly elected positions. (*America's History,* Seventh Edition, Chapter 6, pp. 183–185)

3. **Answer (D) The ally was a Roman Catholic monarchy.** The ally referenced is France, which was a Catholic monarchy. The United Sates, in contrast, was a largely Protestant federation of republics. But the French were anxious to exact revenge on their longtime enemies, the British. (*America's History,* Seventh Edition, Chapter 6, p. 178)

4. **Answer (E) wealthy men.** The fifty-five delegates were mostly merchants, lawyers, and slaveholding planters. Yet all were Patriots who recognized the weaknesses of the Articles of Confederation and sought to strengthen the young nation's government. (*America's History,* Seventh Edition, Chapter 6, p. 193)

5. **Answer (D) an increase in the number of ordinary citizens elected to state legislatures.** The states' new constitutions varied in the degree to which they gave average male citizens participation in government—Pennsylvania and Vermont had the most democratic systems. But in general, average citizens did have more political power and influence. (*America's History,* Seventh Edition, Chapter 6, p. 184)

6. **Answer (D) Patriot merchants replaced Tories at the top of the economic ladder.** This was especially true in cities like Boston and Philadelphia. As supporters of the monarchy, Loyalists (also known as Tories) were conservatively minded. (*America's History,* Seventh Edition, Chapter 6, pp. 187–189)

7. **Answer (D) The real power was vested in the states.** The central government—the Congress—really only had the power to print money and declare war. Under the Articles, the United States did win the Revolutionary War and established a peaceful system for settling the West, but it was ill-equipped to deal with other challenges of the postwar period, such as addressing the problem of the war debt. (*America's History,* Seventh Edition, Chapter 6, pp. 189–191)

8. **Answer (D) tax revolts.** Shays's Rebellion in western Massachusetts was launched by farmers (many of them Revolutionary War veterans) who felt that the Boston State House did not represent their interests in the years following the war. The Whiskey Rebellion occurred during Washington's presidency in reaction against Hamilton's taxation policies. (*America's History,* Seventh Edition, Chapters 6 and 7, pp. 191–193, 207–208)

9. **Answer (E) A Pennsylvania merchant.** Federalists supported a strong central government and the economic policies of Alexander Hamilton, the first Secretary of the Treasury. Farmers and artisans were more likely to support Jefferson's party, the Republicans (other textbooks and sources sometimes refer to them as Democratic-Republicans). (*America's History,* Seventh Edition, Chapter 7, pp. 210–211)

10. **Answer (D) families and communities lost some of their economic independence.** The national economy became more interdependent, creating more opportunities but, perhaps, more vulnerability for farmers and workers. (*America's History,* Seventh Edition, Chapter 8, pp. 238–242)

11. **Answer (A) there was a shift in public policy that encouraged business.** This was called the commonwealth system or state mercantilism. (*America's History,* Seventh Edition, Chapter 8, pp. 238–242)

12. **Answer (E) turnpikes and canals.** The problem farmers had was getting their harvested crops to markets. The federal and state governments began to build a transportation infrastructure in the early decades of the Republic by public investment and by granting charters to private companies. (*America's History,* Seventh Edition, Chapter 8, p. 241)

13. **Answer (D) The revenue tariff.** Some were so angry about this tariff that they led a violent uprising: the Whiskey Rebellion. Washington sent troops to suppress it, sending a message that violent rebellion would not be countenanced—in a republic, citizens should seek change through the courts or political system. (*America's History,* Seventh Edition, Chapter 7, p. 208)

14. **Answer (D) referring to the concept of republican motherhood.** Proponents of republican motherhood did not seek a public role of citizenship for women, arguing instead that in a republic, wifely and motherly duties were ever more important for the well-being of husbands, sons, and the republic as a whole. (*America's History,* Seventh Edition, Chapter 8, p. 246)

15. **Answer (B) preserving the existing balance of power between North and South in the Senate.** The Missouri Compromise thus set a precedent for how to handle the slavery question upon admission of new states for twenty-five years to follow. (*America's History,* Seventh Edition, Chapter 8, pp. 256–258)

Document-Based Question

To what extent did the Constitution represent the goals of the American Revolution?

This question asks you to address two themes associated with the drafting and ratification of the Constitution: the extent to which the Constitution represents a continuation of the ideas that impelled colonists to revolution, and the extent to which the Constitution represented a revolution or a counter-revolution. These are among the most enduring and controversial issues in American history.

Document A is intended to invoke Americans' concern for the dangers of power in the hands of a central government represented by British imperial policies, while Document C illustrates concern that the Articles of Confederation had been too effective in limiting power. Documents B and D suggest the connections between underlying social conditions and specific governmental policies or provisions, while Documents E and F represent the different sides of the debate over ratification. Document G shows which regions ratified the constitution and which did not; note the distinction between more urban areas and the rural frontier.

Outside information that should be incorporated into your response should include the causes of the American Revolution, the challenges the United States faced after the war, and the procedures and outcome of the 1787 Constitutional Convention in Philadelphia, including its compromises and the Constitution itself as originally ratified. Remember that the original Constitution did not include a Bill of Rights; in the form of ten ratified amendments, it was added afterwards by the Congress and states (in part to respond to the objections of Antifederalists like Patrick Henry).

Free-Response Questions

1. **To what extent was the American Revolution a movement for the colonists' civil rights?**

   You may say the revolution was chiefly a movement for civil rights or you may say it was not, in which case, you will most likely say the causes of revolution were primarily economic. The most sophisticated answers will most likely refer to a combination of both types of issues, but the key is to analyze the extent to which civil rights was a factor. Below are some of the civil rights issues and economic issues that prompted the American Revolution. As you can see, some of the issues had implications for both the economy and colonists' civil rights.

   Civil Rights Issues:

   - Writs of Assistance
   - Rights of Englishmen
   - Free speech
   - Free press (Zenger Trial)
   - Trial by jury
   - Stamp Act violators being tried in vice-admiralty courts
   - Innocent until proven guilty
   - Proclamation of 1763 (restricting movement and settlement)
   - Quartering Act (right to privacy)
   - Massachusetts Government Act
   - Quebec Act (allowed the practice of Catholicism)
   - legal acknowledgment of Catholicism, which threatened Protestants
   - Pontiac's Rebellion
   - Declaratory Act
   - Boston Tea Party (right to representation and independent trade)
   - Administration of Justice Act

   Economic Issues:

   - Proclamation of 1763 (cannot make a living as farmers west of the Appalachians)
   - Taxes: Sugar, Stamp, Townshend, Tea, etc.
   - Quartering Act (must pay for housing and food)
   - Declaratory Act (Parliament can pass any tax they please)
   - Boston Tea Party (dispute over taxes)

- Boston Port Bill (cannot trade)
- Quebec Act (limits expansion by giving additional lands to Quebec)

2. "The Articles of Confederation could have worked if given enough time." Assess the validity of this quote with respect to the economic and political conditions in the 1780s.

Most students will attempt to prove the statement wrong, arguing that the Constitution "saved the country from ruin" and that because of the unanimous vote needed for amendments, the Articles could never have been incorporated. If you choose to agree with the statement, you should emphasize the successes of the government under the Articles, especially the defeat of the British in the Revolutionary War and the effective and principled resolution of the land ordinances.

Weaknesses of the Articles:

- National government couldn't tax, though it could borrow money
- No national army
- Weak central government—no executive or judicial branches
- No uniform currency
- Unanimous vote needed for amendments
- 9/13 vote needed for important laws

Problems for the Confederation:

- Ruled during a depression without power to alleviate it
- European countries "dumping" their products on the United States
- Loss of trading partners

Strengths of the Articles:

- Signed the Treaty of Paris, ending the Revolution
- The Land Ordinance of 1785 and the Northwest Ordinance
- Successfully led the nation through the Revolution

3. Assess the validity of this characterization: Alexander Hamilton's ideas on economics thrived and endured while his political views did not stand the test of time. Thomas Jefferson's political views, on the other hand, thrived and endured while his economic ideas were short-lived.

Your answer should make references to Hamilton's economic policies and his political ideas, noting whether or not the statement above is true, then repeat the process for Jefferson. Below are some key policies and ideas to keep in mind as you decide whether the statement is true. (Note: The better essays will see a conflict between Jefferson's ideals prior to his presidency and his actions as president.)

Hamilton's Economic Policies:

- National bank, which lasted until 1836
- Protective tariff, which eventually passed 1816
- Government help to industry, which eventually occurred
- Railroad subsidies

- Pro-business legislation
- Government debt to keep people and industry supporting the nation

Hamilton's Political Views:

- Elitism
- Government consisting of the upper classes
- Distrust of the peoples' abilities to participate in a democracy

Jefferson's Economic Policies:

- State banks, but no federal bank
- Against government subsidies of industry
- Agriculture as the basis for American economy
- No government debt

Jefferson's Political Views:

- Republicanism
- Government by the educated masses
- Small government, states' rights

PART 3
Overlapping Revolutions, 1820–1860

This part covers the following chapters in Henretta et al., *America's History,* Seventh Edition:

Chapter 9 Economic Transformation, 1820–1860

Chapter 10 A Democratic Revolution, 1820–1844

Chapter 11 Religion and Reform, 1820–1860

Chapter 12 The South Expands: Slavery and Society, 1800–1860

Essential Questions

After studying the chapters in Part 3, you should know how to answer the following questions:

1. How did the Industrial Revolution affect the regions of the United States—North, South, and West—differently?
2. What effects did the factory have on American social structure?
3. How and why did reform movements arise in response to social and economic change, and what impact did they have?
4. What impact did democratization have on the American party system?
5. Compare and contrast southern antebellum society with that of the North.

Resources for Review

In the following pages, you'll find the Thematic Timeline and Essay for Part 3 from *America's History,* as well as other guidance for reinforcing your knowledge of the period. In addition, you'll find AP-style questions that address the time period covered: 15 practice multiple-choice questions, 1 document-based question, and 2 free-response questions. Answers with page references to *America's History* can be found at the end of this Part 3 review.

Thematic Timeline and Part Essay

Overlapping Revolutions, 1820–1860

	ECONOMY	SOCIETY	GOVERNMENT	CULTURE	SECTIONALISM
1820	Waltham textile factory opens (1814) Erie Canal completed (1825) Market economy expands nationwide Cotton belt emerges in South	Business class develops Rural women and girls recruited as factory workers Mechanics form craft unions Waged-work increases	Spread of universal white male suffrage Rise of Andrew Jackson and Democratic Party Anti-Masonic Party rises and declines	American Colonization Society (1817) Benevolent reform movements Revivalist Charles G. Finney Emerson and transcendentalism	Missouri crisis and compromise (1819–1821) David Walker's *Appeal . . . to the Colored Citizens of the World* (1829) Domestic slave trade moves African Americans west
1830	Protective tariffs (1828, 1832) trigger nullification crisis Boom in cotton output Panic of 1837 U.S. textiles compete with British Canal systems link eastern United States	Charles G. Finney leads revivals Depression (1837–1843) shatters labor movement New urban popular culture appears	Indian Removal Act (1830) Whig Party forms (1834) Second Party System emerges Jackson destroys Second Bank and expands executive power	Joseph Smith founds Mormonism Temperance crusade expands Middle-class culture spreads Female Moral Reform Society (1834)	Ordinance of Nullification (1832) and Force Bill (1833) W. L. Garrison forms American Anti-Slavery Society (1833) Texas independence

	ECONOMY	SOCIETY	GOVERNMENT	CULTURE	SECTIONALISM
1840	Irish immigrants join labor force *Commonwealth v. Hunt* (1842) assists unions; but workers remain "servants" Machine Tool Industry expands	Working-class districts emerge in cities Irish and German inflow sparks nativist movement	Log cabin campaign (1840) mobilizes voters Tyler's policies disrupt Whig agenda	Fourierist and other communal settlements founded Mormons resettle in Utah Seneca Falls women's convention (1848)	Slavery defended as a "positive good" Antislavery Liberty Party (1840) Abolitionist movement splinters

"The procession was nearly a mile long . . . [and] the democrats marched in good order to the glare of torches," a French visitor remarked in amazement during the election of 1832. "These scenes belong to history . . . the wondrous epic of the coming of democracy." As we will see in Part 3, history was being made in many ways between 1820 and 1860. A series of overlapping revolutions were transforming American society. One was political: the creation of a genuinely democratic polity. The second was economic: in 1820, the United States was predominately an agricultural nation; by 1850, the northern states boasted one of the world's foremost industrial economies. Third, there was far-reaching social and cultural change, including the Second Great Awakening, great movements of social reform, and the advent of a complex intellectual culture. These transformations affected every aspect of life in the North and Midwest and brought important changes in the South as well. Here, in brief, is an outline of that story.

Economy: Making an Economic Revolution Impressive advances in industrial production, transportation, and trade transformed the nation's economy. Factory owners used high-speed machines and a new system of labor discipline to boost the output of goods dramatically. Manufacturers produced 5 percent of the country's wealth in 1820 and nearly 20 percent by 1850. And thanks to enterprising merchants and entrepreneurs, who developed a network of canals and an integrated system of markets, they now sold their products throughout an expanding nation.

Society: Forging a New Class Structure The new economy created a class-based society in the North and Midwest. A wealthy elite of merchants, manufacturers, bankers, and entrepreneurs rose to the top of the social order. To maintain social stability, they adopted a paternalistic program of benevolent reform. But an expanding urban middle class created a distinct material and religious culture, and it lent support to movements for radical social reform. A mass of propertyless workers, including impoverished immigrants from Germany and Ireland, joined enslaved African Americans at the bottom of the social order. The growth of large cities, primarily in the North, fostered the emergence of new urban and popular cultures. Meanwhile, slavery expanded in numbers and scope as planters created new plantations as far south and west as Texas.

Government: Creating a Democratic Polity The rapid growth of white male suffrage and political parties sparked the creation of a competitive and responsive democratic polity.

Interest groups created various short-lived organizations, notably the Anti-Masonic, Workingmen's, and Liberty parties. Farmers, workers, and entrepreneurs persuaded governments to improve transportation, shorten workdays, and award valuable corporate charters. Catholic immigrants from Ireland and Germany entered local and state politics to protect their cultures from restrictive legislation advocated by Protestant nativists and reformers.

With Andrew Jackson at its head, the Democratic Party led a political and constitutional revolution that cut government aid to financiers, merchants, and corporations. To contend with the Democrats, the Whig Party devised a competing program that stressed economic development, moral reform, and individual social mobility. This party competition engaged the energies of the electorate and helped to unify a fragmented social order.

Culture: Reforming People and Institutions Between 1820 and 1850, a series of reform movements, many with religious roots and goals, swept across America. Ministers and pious church members embarked upon a program of Benevolent Reform, preaching the gospel of temperance, Sunday observance, prison reform, and many other causes. A few Americans pursued their social dreams in utopian communities, but most reformers worked within the existing society. Then, abolitionists and women's rights activists demanded radical social changes: the immediate end of slavery and the overthrow of the patriarchal legal order. However, southern planters increasingly defended slavery as a "positive good" and restated their commitment to a society based on white supremacy and forced labor.

Sectionalism: Compromising Over Slavery The economic revolution and social reform sharpened sectional divisions: the North developed into an urban industrial society based on free labor, whereas the South remained a rural agricultural society dependent on slavery. Beginning in the 1820s, the two sections fought over economic policy. Northern manufacturers, workers, and farmers won protective tariffs, which southern planters bitterly opposed. Eventually, there was a sectional compromise, as the North accepted tariff reductions. The sections clashed again over the expansion of slavery into Missouri and once again political leaders devised a compromise solution. But slavery—and the social and economic differences it symbolized—increasingly divided the nation.

The economic and cultural transformation of the North and, to a lesser extent, of the Midwest made those regions increasingly different from the South. And the democratic political revolution that affected all sections injected greater volatility and potential for conflict into the political system.

Essential Questions Review Exercises

Using the guidelines and graphic organizers that follow, gather evidence that helps you review concepts and themes from the period 1820 to 1860. Consult *America's History,* Seventh Edition, as well as any relevant materials your teacher has provided to review the information.

1. **How did the Industrial Revolution affect the regions of the United States—North, South, and West—differently?**

   Each region of the United States made unique contributions to the emerging market economy. Using the map on the next page, list ways that the Industrial Revolution affected the three regions of the antebellum (pre–Civil War) United States. Consult Chapters 9 and 12.

2. What effects did the factory have on American social structure?

To review this idea, think about what is meant by "social structure." Families? Communities? Social classes? Use the flow chart below to review what American society was like before early industrial development and how society was affected after it. See Chapter 9.

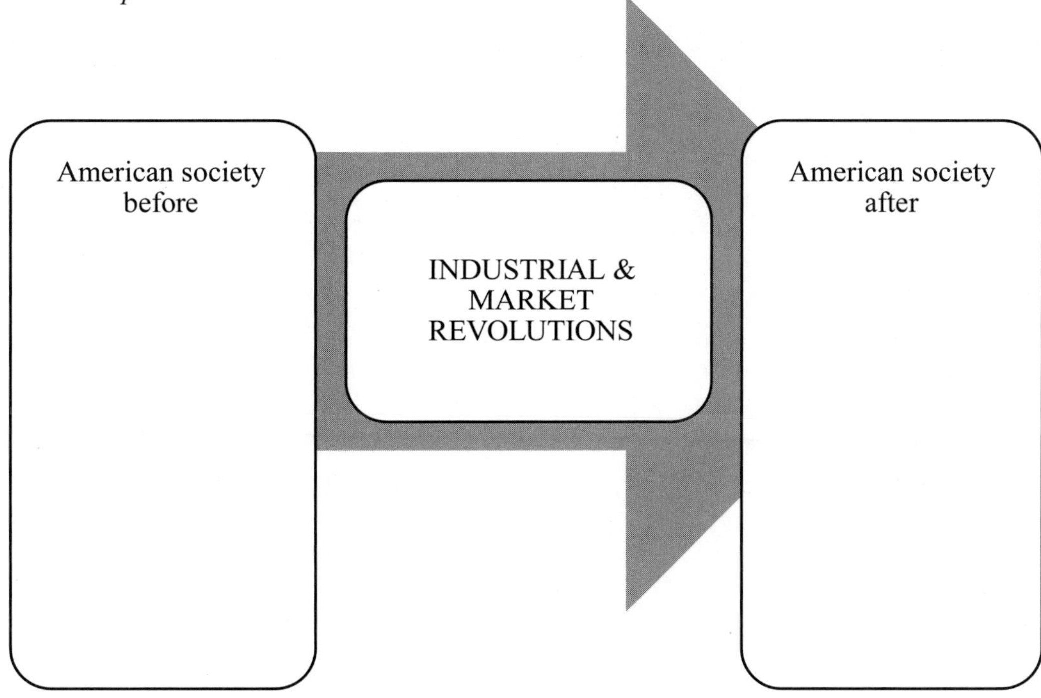

3. How and why did reform movements arise in response to social and economic change, and what impact did they have?

Consider the economic changes explained in Chapter 9 as you review the various religious, reform, and cultural currents described in Chapter 11. This is another process or change over time question, and flow charts like the one below are very helpful to review such processes.

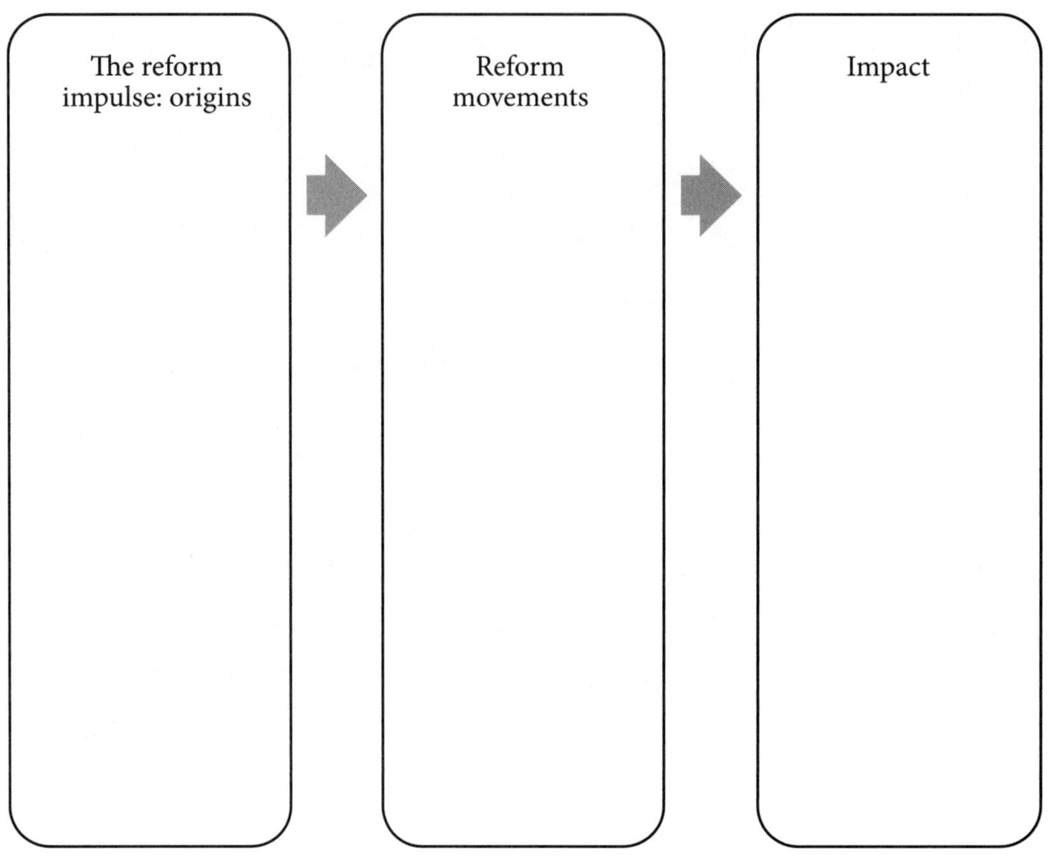

4. What impact did democratization have on the American party system?

The period from 1820–1838, covered in Chapter 10, is often called the era of the common man, and the presidency of Andrew Jackson as well as the rise of the second party system (Democrats and Whigs) are its two most significant events. Use the table below to help you brainstorm about the second party system.

THE SECOND PARTY SYSTEM	
Democrats	**Whigs**
Typical Supporters	
Views on the Duties and Limits of Government	

5. Compare and contrast southern antebellum society with that of the North.

You may draw on content from all four chapters in this Part to find similarities and differences between the two regions. It is useful to examine each society from economic, political, cultural, and social perspectives. After filling in the chart below with some of the characteristics of each region, compare similarities and contrast differences.

	NORTH	SOUTH
Economic Characteristics		
Political Characteristics		
Cultural Characteristics		
Social Characteristics		

Practice Questions

The following sections allow you to test your knowledge of Part 3. The Directions are verbatim instructions from the College Board's AP Exam; the Hints offer strategies for tackling each type of AP question. Answers to all of the Part 3 practice questions follow.

Multiple-Choice Questions

Directions: Each of the questions or incomplete statements below is followed by five suggested answers or completions. Select the one that is best in each case.

Hints:

- ✦ Read each question carefully, looking out for negative words such as EXCEPT, NOT, and FALSE.
- ✦ Read all possible answers and cross out those you feel are incorrect; narrowing down your choices gives you the chance to make an educated guess.
- ✦ Be cautious of words indicating absolutes, like *most, least, all,* and *none.*
- ✦ Connect the specific information of the question to broader trends and themes.
- ✦ In questions that provide you with evidence, assess the information carefully and eliminate answers that go beyond the bounds of the evidence given.

1. Which of the following was most responsible for encouraging the growth of domestic markets in the first half of the nineteenth century?
   (A) An increase in the number of large factories
   (B) Better transportation networks
   (C) The national bank's loan policy
   (D) The national government's economic subsidies
   (E) Increased farm production

2. Jacksonian democracy and Jeffersonian republicanism were most similar in their
   (A) dealings with native peoples
   (B) support for average Americans
   (C) treatment of the national bank
   (D) views on patronage
   (E) efforts to consolidate executive power

3. Of the following, which two presidents had the most strained relationship with the Supreme Court of the United States?
   (A) Washington and Quincy Adams
   (B) Van Buren and Adams
   (C) Madison and Tyler
   (D) Jefferson and Jackson
   (E) Washington and William Henry Harrison

4. The antebellum reform movement was, in large part, precipitated by
   (A) national government initiatives
   (B) a religious revival movement
   (C) state government initiatives
   (D) an economic recession
   (E) nativist pressures

5 Which of the following is a true statement about the Indian Removal Act?
   (A) Some Cherokee Indians promoted it.
   (B) It eliminated the Seminole Indians from Florida.
   (C) It was precipitated by Black Hawk's War.
   (D) Congress passed it despite much public outcry.
   (E) John Marshall upheld the act in *Worcester v. Georgia*.

6. Which of the following religious movements originated in the United States?
   (A) Mormonism
   (B) Puritanism
   (C) Presbyterianism
   (D) Unitarianism
   (E) Catholicism

7. The American Republican Party, which later became the Know-Nothing Party, was created in opposition to
   (A) women's rights advocates
   (B) nativists
   (C) Irish and German immigrants
   (D) abolitionists
   (E) supporters of the Mexican War

8. President Jackson's main argument for destroying the bank was that the
   (A) bank had not been successful at stabilizing the currency
   (B) bank was not able to influence credit in a satisfactory manner
   (C) government was forced to play too large a role in managing the bank
   (D) bank was a monopoly that benefited only a few owners, some of whom were foreigners
   (E) bank was powerless to keep inflationary policies of wildcat banks in check

9. The Whigs supported all of the following EXCEPT
   (A) the American System
   (B) tariffs
   (C) Indian removal
   (D) the national bank
   (E) internal improvements

10. "I will be as harsh as truth, and as uncompromising as justice. On this subject I do not wish to think, or speak, or write, with moderation. No! No! Tell a man whose house is on fire, to give a moderate alarm; tell him to moderately rescue his wife from the hands of a ravisher; tell the mother to gradually extricate her babe from the fire into which it has fallen;—but urge me not to use moderation in a cause like the present. I am in earnest—I will not equivocate—I will not excuse—I will not retreat a single inch—AND I WILL BE HEARD."

    The above quote from William Lloyd Garrison exemplifies what inspiration for antebellum reform?

    (A) Opposition to Andrew Jackson's policies
    (B) Transcendental intellectualism
    (C) Anti-British sentiment following the War of 1812
    (D) Republican motherhood
    (E) Religious fervor of the Second Great Awakening

11. The biggest deterrent to industrialization in the south was

    (A) its increased immigration
    (B) its dependence on slavery
    (C) absence of an entrepreneurial class
    (D) lack of raw materials
    (E) its need for labor

12. Which of the following is true of free blacks in the south?

    (A) They became the backbone of the south's urban artisan workforce.
    (B) Their numbers decreased between 1800 and 1860.
    (C) Most free African Americans distanced themselves from the masses of impoverished slaves.
    (D) They were expelled as a threat to slavery.
    (E) They were kept isolated from plantation slaves.

13. The notion of slavery as a "necessary evil" and a "positive good" was supported by which idea?

    (A) In a slave country, every free man is an aristocrat.
    (B) Slavery gave whites the psychological satisfaction of knowing they ranked above blacks.
    (C) Slavery allowed a civilized lifestyle for whites and provided tutelage for genetically inferior blacks.
    (D) Whites educated and Christianized slaves in return for their labor and loyalty.
    (E) Slavery was an economic necessity that promoted greater economic opportunity for all white people.

14. In the first half of the nineteenth century, American manufacturers' main advantage over the British mills was that they

    (A) had cheaper shipping
    (B) had lower interest rates
    (C) had more natural resources
    (D) had a ready supply of cheap labor
    (E) were more established

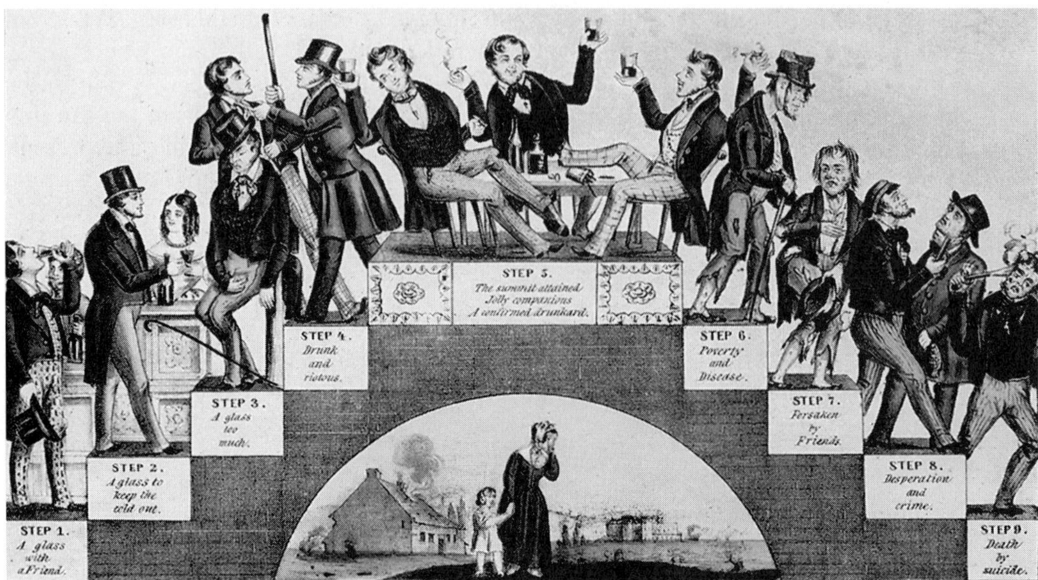

Library of Congress.

15. Which of the following is most directly a result of the situation depicted in the lithograph above?
    (A) The Christian Evangelist
    (B) The Cold Water Army
    (C) The Sunday School Movement
    (D) More funding for public education
    (E) The Benevolent Empire

Document-Based Question

Directions: The following question requires you to construct a coherent essay that integrates your interpretation of Documents A–E and your knowledge of the period referred to in the question. High scores are earned only by essays that cite key pieces of evidence from the documents and draw on outside knowledge of the period.

In what ways did women's roles reflect changes in antebellum life in the United States? Use the documents and your knowledge of the period to construct your response.

Background reading: *America's History,* Seventh Edition, Chapters 9 and 11

Hints:

- With document-based questions, remember to move beyond the specific facts in the documents to seek their more interpretive or analytical aspects. As you read through the documents, underline key passages, jot notes in the margins, and record outside examples and facts that come to mind as you read.
- This "in what ways" question challenges you to identify, select, and explain some ways that women's changing lives reflected the larger social changes of American politics, culture, and economy in the antebellum period. To answer the question well, consider the concept of Republican motherhood from the early national period as well as the leadership women took in Second Great Awakening–inspired reform movements. You should also include ways that women contributed to the emerging market economy.

- After reading through the documents, categorize them into groups to generate a paragraph structure for your response.
- Keep in mind the volume of essays the exam readers must plow through. Clarity and organization are key.

Document A

Source: Judith Sargent Murray, "On the Equality of the Sexes," 1790.

[W]hile we are pursuing the needle, or the superintendency of the family, I repeat, that our minds are at full liberty for reflection; that imagination may exert itself in full vigor; and that if a just foundation is early laid, our ideas will then be worthy of rational beings. If we were industrious we might easily find time to arrange them upon paper, or should avocations press too hard for such an indulgence, the hours allotted for conversation would at least become more refined and rational. Should it still be vociferated, "Your domestick employments are sufficient"—I would calmly ask, is it reasonable, that a candidate for immortality, for the joys of heaven, an intelligent being, who is to spend an eternity in contemplating the works of the Deity, should at present be so degraded, as to be allowed no other ideas, than those which are suggested by the mechanism of a pudding, or the sewing the seams of a garment? Pity that all such censurers of female improvement do not go one step further, and deny their future existence; to be consistent they surely ought.

Yes, ye lordly, ye haughty sex, our souls are by nature *equal* to yours; the same breath of God animates, enlivens, and invigorates us; and that we are not fallen lower than yourselves . . .

I know there are those who assert, that as the animal powers of the one sex are superiour, of course their mental faculties must also be stronger; thus attributing strength of mind to the transient organization of this earth born tenement. But if this reasoning is just, man must be content to yield the palm to many of the brute creation.

Document B

Source: Catherine Beecher, "The Profession of a Woman," 1829.

What is the *profession of a Woman?* Is it not to form immortal minds, and to watch, to nurse, and to rear the bodily system, so fearfully and wonderfully made, and upon the order and regulation of which, the health and well-being of the mind so greatly depends?

But let most of our sex, upon whom these arduous duties devolve, be asked; have you ever devoted any time and study, in the course of your education, to any preparation for these duties? . . . [W]e have attended to almost every thing more than to this; we have been taught more concerning the structure of the earth; the laws of the heavenly bodies; the habits and formation of plants; the philosophy of languages; more of *almost any thing,* than the structure of the human frame and the laws of health and reason . . .

. . . [W]e have acquired wisdom from the observation and experience of others, on almost *all other* subjects, but the philosophy of the direction and control of the human mind has not been an object of thought or study. And thus it appears that though it is woman's *express business* to rear the body, and form the mind, there is scarcely anything to which her attention has been less directed . . .

If all females were not only well educated themselves, but were prepared to communicate in an easy manner their stores of knowledge to others; if they not only knew how to regulate their own minds, tempers and habits, but how to effect improvements in those around them, the face of society would speedily be changed. The time may come when the world will look back with wonder to behold how much time and effort have been given to the mere cultivation of the memory, and how little mankind have been aware of what every teacher, parent, and friend could accomplish in forming the social, intellectual and moral character of those by whom they are surrounded.

Document C

Source: Sarah Grimké, "On the Condition of Women in the United States," 1838.

During the early part of my life, my lot was cast among the butterflies of the *fashionable* world; and of this class of women, I am constrained to say, both from experience and observation, that their education is miserably deficient; that they are taught to regard marriage as the one thing needful, the only avenue to distinction; hence to attract the notice and win the attentions of men, by their external charms, is the chief business of fashionable girls. . . . Fashionable women regard themselves, and are regarded by men, as pretty toys or as mere instruments of pleasure; and the vacuity of mind, the heartlessness, the frivolity which is the necessary result of this false and debasing estimate of women, can only be fully understood by those who have mingled in the folly and wickedness of fashionable life; and who have been called from such pursuits by the voice of the Lord Jesus, inviting their weary and heavy laden souls to come unto Him and learn of Him, that they may find something worthy of their immortal spirit, and their intellectual powers; that they may learn the high and holy purposes of their creation . . .

There is another way in which the general opinion, that women are inferior to men, is manifested, that bears with tremendous effect on the laboring class, and indeed on almost all who are obliged to earn a subsistence, whether it be by mental or physical exertion—I allude to the disproportionate value set on the time and labor of men and of women. A man who is engaged in teaching, can always, I believe, command a higher price for tuition than a woman—even when he teaches the same branches, and is not in any respect superior to the woman. This I know is the case in boarding and other schools with which I have been acquainted, and it is so in every occupation in which the sexes engage indiscriminately. As for example, in tailoring, a man has twice, or three times as much for making a waistcoat or pantaloons as a woman, although the work done by each may be equally good . . .

There is another class of women in this country, to whom I cannot refer, without feelings of the deepest shame and sorrow. I allude to our female slaves. Our southern cities are whelmed beneath a tide of pollution; the virtue of female slaves is wholly at the mercy of irresponsible tyrants, and women are bought and sold in our slave markets, to gratify the brutal lust of those who bear the name of Christians. In our slave States, if amid all her degradation, and ignorance, a woman desires to preserve her virtue unsullied, she is either bribed or whipped into compliance…

Nor does the colored woman suffer alone: the moral purity of the white woman is deeply contaminated. In the daily habit of seeing the virtue of her enslaved sister sacrificed without hesitancy or remorse, she looks upon the crimes of seduction and illicit intercourse without horror, and although not personally involved in the guilt, she loses that value for innocence in her own, as well as the other sex, which is one of the strongest safeguards to virtue. She lives in habitual intercourse with men, whom she knows to be polluted by licentiousness, and often is she compelled to witness in her own domestic circle, those disgusting and heart-sickening jealousies and strifes which disgraced and distracted the family of Abraham.

Document D

Source: Alexis de Tocqueville, "Education of Young Women in The United States," 1840.

Among almost all Protestant nations young women are far more the mistresses of their own actions than they are in Catholic countries. This independence is still greater in Protestant countries like England, which have retained or acquired the right of self-government; freedom is then infused into the domestic circle by political habits and by religious opinions. In the United States the doctrines of Protestantism are combined with great political liberty and a most democratic state of society, and nowhere are young women surrendered so early or so completely to their own guidance.

Long before an American girl arrives at the marriageable age, her emancipation from maternal control begins; she has scarcely ceased to be a child when she already thinks for herself, speaks with freedom, and acts on her own impulse . . .

Although the Americans are a very religious people, they do not rely on religion alone to defend the virtue of women; they seek to arm her reason also. In this respect they have followed the same method as in several others: they first make vigorous efforts to cause individual independence to control itself, and they do not call in the aid of religion until they have reached the utmost limits of human strength.

I am aware that an education of this kind is not without danger; I am sensible that it tends to invigorate the judgment at the expense of the imagination and to make cold and virtuous women instead of affectionate wives and agreeable companions to man. Society may be more tranquil and better regulated, but domestic life has often fewer charms. These, however, are secondary evils, which may be braved for the sake of higher interests. At the stage at which we are now arrived, the choice is no longer left to us; a democratic education is indispensable to protect women from the dangers with which democratic institutions and manners surround them.

Document E

Source: Two Weavers, c. 1860.

American Textile History Museum, Lowell, MA.

Free-Response Questions

Directions: For the following questions, you are advised to spend five minutes planning and thirty minutes writing your answer. Cite relevant historical evidence in support of your generalizations and present your arguments clearly and logically.

Hints:

- Sketch out a brief outline, recording facts and examples that you remember and organizing them in a sensible way. Each section of the outline should generate a supporting paragraph for your essay.
- Develop a thesis that takes a clear stand on the question posed. Be sure to state it in your introductory paragraph.
- Begin each supporting paragraph with a clear topic sentence.
- Consider transitions between paragraphs.
- Conclude by restating your thesis in a fresh way, perhaps by making a connection to another moment in American history.
- Keep in mind the volume of essays the exam readers must plow through. Clarity and organization are key.
- Question-specific hints follow the three sample questions.

1. **To what extent was the American political process democratized in the decades after 1820?**

   Thesis development and organization: There is a spectrum of possible interpretations here. You may emphasize the ways that American politics became more inclusive and representative in the Jacksonian era, particularly in regards to white men. Or you may emphasize the limits of the "era of the common man" by pointing to the continued exclusion and further repression of nonwhite men (Native Americans and enslaved African Americans in particular) and women. A convincing and thorough answer will account for both trends.

2. **By 1820 African Americans had created a distinct and relatively unified rural culture. Discuss the nature of this culture and its impact on the United States.**

   Thesis development and organization: Note the question's active verb: had created. This is a question of historical agency, emphasizing the choices African Americans made despite being subjugated by the slave system. Your thesis should address the very real lack of autonomy, freedom, and rights American slaves endured while pointing to the cultural agency of such trends as Evangelical Black Protestantism, enduring West African customs, and the unique agency and limitations of free African American Americans. There are many possible ways to organize your evidence; for example, a thematically structured response might have paragraphs organized by religious, social, and economic practices among enslaved and free African Americans.

Answer Key to Part 3 Practice Questions

Multiple-Choice Questions

1. **Answer (B) Better transportation networks.** These innovations helped to transform the United States to an industrial state because products were better able to get to market and be sold. (*America's History,* Seventh Edition, Chapter 9, pp. 283–288)

2. **Answer (B) support for average Americans.** As a man of his era, Jefferson would have likely recoiled from some of the rougher aspects of democracy in the Jacksonian era. But both Jefferson and Jackson supported smaller, less intrusive government as well as a faith in the common man. Despite his status as a general and plantation aristocrat, Jackson successfully fashioned himself a man of the people. (*America's History,* Seventh Edition, Chapter 10, pp. 319–321)

3. **Answer (D) Jefferson and Jackson.** Jefferson had to reckon with the Federalist Chief Justice John Marshall's support for federal power; Jackson had to respond to Marshall's invalidation of the Removal Act (which Jackson simply ignored). (*America's History,* Seventh Edition, Chapters 7 and 10, pp. 217–218, 318–319)

4. **Answer (B) a religious revival movement.** The Second Great Awakening generated a sentiment of moral activism among many Americans, which they applied to movements combating alcoholism, slavery, prostitution, and other social ills between 1820 and 1850. (*America's History,* Seventh Edition, Chapter 11, pp. 335–352)

5. **Answer (A) Some Cherokee Indians promoted it.** Like any community of people, public sentiment is rarely unanimous, so it stands to reason that a few Cherokees did support the idea. And the historical record backs up this supposition. The other responses are all false: Marshall's Supreme Court in fact ruled that the Removal Act was unconstitutional, but Jackson famously ignored that ruling. (*America's History,* Seventh Edition, Chapter 10, pp. 315–319)

6. **Answer (A) Mormonism.** All of the other listed Christian sects have European origins. Joseph Smith founded the Church of Latter Day Saints in upstate New York during the Second Great Awakening; after a westward odyssey the Mormons eventually settled in present-day Utah. (*America's History,* Seventh Edition, Chapter 11, pp. 339–341)

7. **Answer (C) Irish and German immigrants.** Officially known as the American Republican Party, their xenophobic platform of anti-immigration sentiment was kept secret. The party's founders were opposed to the large wave of new immigrants coming from Germany and Ireland from the 1830s–1850s. (*America's History,* Seventh Edition, Chapter 11, p. 344)

8. **Answer (D) bank was a monopoly that benefited only a few owners, some of whom were foreigners.** A master politician, Jackson destroyed the legacy of national banking established by Alexander Hamilton by calling attention to the elitism of the bank's supporters and shareholders, many of whom were British. (*America's History,* Seventh Edition, Chapter 10, p. 314)

9. **Answer (C) Indian removal.** The Whig Party opposed Democratic President Andrew Jackson on most issues. Whigs included merchants, businessmen, and reformers inspired by the Second Great Awakening. Many reformers were opposed to the Removal Act on moral grounds. (*America's History,* Seventh Edition, Chapter 10, pp. 318–323)

10. **Answer (E) religious fervor of the Second Great Awakening. Garrison was among the fieriest of abolitionist activists.** He launched his abolitionist publication *The Liberator* in 1831 and bravely faced scorn, ridicule, and violence for his positions—as did countless other men and women, white and African American, from 1830 to the Civil War. (*America's History,* Seventh Edition, Chapter 11, pp. 349–350)

11. **Answer (B) its dependence on slavery.** The domestic slave trade created a lot of wealth in the South, but southerners pinned their fortunes on slavery rather than investing in industrialization and a mixed economy that would have provided more long-term production, infrastructure, and wealth. (*America's History,* Seventh Edition, Chapter 12, p. 368)

12. **Answer (A) "They became the backbone of the south's urban artisan workforce."** This was due in part to the fact that white skilled workers choose to immigrate to non-slaveholding states. The overall populationof free blacks in the South increased from 94,000 in 1810 to 225,000 in 1860; and while some free blacks did take pains to keep their lives spearate from enslaved blacks, most did maintain ties to the slave community. (*America's History,* Seventh Edition, Chapter 12, p. 388–389)

13. **Answer (C) "Slavery allowed a civilized lifestyle for whites and provided tutelage for genetically inferior blacks."** The two quoted phrases in the question actually reflect the development of slavery's defense from an institution that couldn't be avoided—"necessary evil"—to the more proactive "positive good," an idea heard more frequently from slaveholders starting in the 1830s—right around the time when abolitionists began their campaign to expose slavery for the brutal system it was. (*America's History,* Seventh Edition, Chapter 12, pp. 371–373)

14. **Answer (C) had more natural resources.** While Great Britain was the first country in the world to industrialize, the United States quickly gained on its former mother country due to its access to natural resources including rivers for water power, and cotton from the South. (*America's History,* Seventh Edition, Chapter 9, p. 277)

15. **Answer (B) The Cold Water Army.** This was a temperance organization founded by preacher Thomas Poage Hunt. The title of the lithograph is "The Drunkard's Progress: From the First Glass to the Grave." (*America's History,* Seventh Edition, Chapter 9, p. 297)

Document-Based Question

In what ways did women's roles reflect changes in antebellum life in the United States? Use the documents and your knowledge of the period to construct your response.

In this exercise, the new roles women played in public life serve as a window into the changes that marked antebellum reforms. Note the themes of individualism, education, the common good, and participation in economic change. While the document-based question you encounter on the AP Exam will likely include shorter but more numerous excerpts, the focus and content of these sources sharpen the same skills of reading, analysis, and writing.

Documents A, B, and C reflect women's own criticisms of their status. Document D presents de Tocqueville's attempt to reconcile American democratic institutions with the status of women in American society. Document E, echoing earlier coverage of the Lowell Mills, refers to women in the factory system, prompting you to think again about the impact of industrialization on American society and on the status of women in particular.

Outside information that should be included is the concept of Republican motherhood; the Second Great Awakening and how it inspired women to take a larger role in their churches, and then in reform movements; public education; intellectual currents; and economic changes in the antebellum period.

Free-Response Questions

1. **To what extent was the American political process democratized in the decades after 1820?**

Successful answers will include the following information:

- Most significant was the gradual elimination of property requirements for voting, thus broadening the franchise.
- Yeoman farmers and others in an emerging middle class challenged established hierarchies, seeking lower taxes and reforms in property and debt laws.
- Martin Van Buren of the Democrats orchestrated a new system of party government that included state and local party machines, patronage to reward election supporters, and caucuses that democratized the selection of candidates.
- The second party system emerged, with Democrats appealing to the masses and the Whigs representing the merchant and (to a lesser extent) planter classes who supported economic nationalism. The Whig party also welcomed social reforms such as temperance.
- Andrew Jackson's presidency (1828-1836) epitomized the "era of the common man" in politics.
- However, citizenship privileges were extended for white men only. Even the Cherokees in the southeast, who had Americanized willingly in earlier decades, found themselves unable to prevent a forced relocation to Oklahoma Territory in the 1830s.
- The spoils system was one example of the corrupt and contentious elements of antebellum politics.
- Women and African Americans remained out of the public sphere of politics, although some did find a public voice in the reform movements that developed in the 1830s, including abolitionism and temperance.

PART 4
Creating and Preserving a Continental Nation, 1844–1877

This part covers the following chapters in Henretta et al., *America's History,* Seventh Edition:

Chapter 13 Expansion, War, and Sectional Crisis, 1844–1860

Chapter 14 Two Societies at War, 1861–1865

Chapter 15 Reconstruction, 1865–1877

Chapter 16 Conquering a Continent, 1861–1877

Essential Questions

After studying the chapters in Part 4, you should know how to answer the following questions:

1. Why did sectional discord between the North and the South culminate in war?
2. How did the Civil War transform the South? The North?
3. What were the successes and failures of Reconstruction?
4. How was westward expansion tied to accelerating American industrialization in the nineteenth century?

Resources for Review

In the following pages, you'll find the Thematic Timeline and Essay for Part 4 from *America's History,* exercises to review your knowledge of the period, and AP-style questions that address the time period covered: 15 practice multiple-choice questions, 1 document-based question, and 2 free-response questions. Answers with page references to *America's History* can be found at the end.

Thematic Timeline and Part Essay

Creating and Preserving a Continental Nation, 1844–1877

	CONTINENTAL EMPIRE	SECTIONALISM	GOVERNMENT	ECONOMY	SOCIETY
1840	Texas annexation (1845), acquisition of Oregon (1846), and Mexican War (1846–1848), extend U.S. boundaries to Pacific Wars against Seminoles in Florida (1835–1842, 1855–1858)	Mexican War and Wilmot Proviso (1846) increase sectional conflict Gold Rush makes California eligible for statehood—free or slave?	Free-Soil Party (1848) Seneca Falls convention seeks votes for women (1848)	Recession causes some states to default on bonds issued to build canals Walker Tariff (1846) lowers rates, increases trade	Whites migrate to Oregon and California Hispanics incorporated as citizens in Southwest
1850	President Pierce opens Japan to trade; seeks expansion of American territory and slavery in Caribbean Comanche and Sioux dominate Great Plains trade in horses and buffalo hides	Compromise of 1850 Harriet Beecher Stowe's *Uncle Tom's Cabin* (1852) Kansas-Nebraska Act (1854) and "Bleeding Kansas"	Whig Party disintegrates; Know-Nothing Party emerges Republican Party founded (1854) Rise of southern secessionists	Surge of cotton output in South Expansion of farm society into trans-Mississippi west Railroads and manufacturing intensify in North and Midwest	Indians resettled throughout West Arrival of millions of German and Irish immigrants *Dred Scott* decision (1857) implies slavery throughout United States

	CONTINENTAL EMPIRE	SECTIONALISM	GOVERNMENT	ECONOMY	SOCIETY
1860	Union triumphs in Civil War, preserving a continental nation Secretary of State Seward buys Alaska from Russia (1867) Homesteaders, cattlemen, and miners settle Plains and West	South Carolina leads secession movement (1860) Confederate States of America (1861–1865) Radical Republicans seek to reconstruct postwar South	Freedman's Bureau assists ex-slaves Fourteenth Amendment (1868) extends legal and political rights	Republicans enact Whigs' policy agenda: Homestead Act (1862), railroad aid, high tariffs, and national banking	Emancipation Proclamation (1863) and Thirteenth Amendment (1865) end slavery Blacks in the South struggle for freedom, land, and education
1870	Wars against Plains Indians: Cheyennes, Sioux, Apaches, and Nez Pierce	Ku Klux Klan and white vigilantes attack Reconstruction governments Compromise of 1877 ends Reconstruction	Fifteenth Amendment (1870) extends vote to black men Rollback of Republican control of Congress (1874)	Rise of sharecropping in the South Depression of 1873 halts railway expansion	White elites challenge ideal of universal suffrage Dawes Act (1887) seeks Indian assimilation

Between 1844 and 1877, the United States became a continental nation by fighting—and winning—three wars and creating a stronger central government. In the 1840s, it took over much of western North America through diplomatic negotiations with Great Britain and a war of conquest with Mexico. Geographic expansion sharpened political conflicts between the free and slave states and led to the South's secession in 1861. The Union government consolidated national authority by defeating the secessionists in a long Civil War, freeing millions of slaves, and reconstructing the Union under the ideals of the Republican Party.

Reconstruction included far more than reincorporating the South. After the war, the national government opened up newly acquired western lands for Euro-Americans by conquering Indian peoples and confining them to reservations. These events created new conflicts and systems of race relations. Native Americans found themselves negotiating between policies of "race uplift" and potential citizenship, and their desire to retain their traditional cultural and tribal ties. Meanwhile, Reconstruction offered hope for millions of workers of African ancestry, who fought for a fairer labor system and equal citizenship rights as African Americans. The story of these transforming events falls into five interconnected parts.

Continental Empire: Diplomatic and Military Expansion The romantic spirit of Manifest Destiny pervaded American culture during the 1840s, prompting southerners to push for the annexation of Texas and Midwesterners to demand control over Oregon. Railroad entrepreneurs championed expansionism, as did northeastern merchants, who were eager to expand trade across the Pacific. The quest for western lands sparked wars against Mexico and the Cheyennes, Sioux, and Comanches, among other Indian peoples. The purchase of Russian claims to Alaska, and efforts to acquire overseas coaling stations, marked policymakers' rising interest in foreign markets. On the continent, Anglo-American settlement of California and the Southwest overturned Spanish and Mexican customs and land claims. It rapidly opened up the region to white miners, farmers, and ranchers.

Sectionalism: Secession and Reunion The Mexican War prompted a decadelong debate over the constitutional status of newly acquired lands. This increasingly bitter political struggle led to the Compromise of 1850, a multifaceted legislative agreement that won little support either in the North or the South. The Kansas-Nebraska Act of 1854 and the 1857 *Dred Scott* decision began a downward spiral of conflict that ended in the Civil War. Though sectional conflict would continue, the Union emerged stronger from the Civil War, as Republican policies bound the nation together. Never again would a region seek to leave the nation and establish its independence.

Government: Democracy Challenged Continental expansion and sectional conflict triggered the disintegration of the Second Party system. As Southern Whigs became Democrats and Northern Whigs turned into Republicans, party allegiances split along sectional lines and created political divisions that persisted well into the twentieth century. Political developments brought about by the Civil War greatly enhanced the military power and the constitutional authority of the national government. Three wartime constitutional amendments changed the nature of federalism by altering the nature of American citizenship — prohibiting slavery, mandating suffrage for black men, and forbidding state action that denied people equal protection under the law. After the war, the U.S. army remained a significant force, enforcing Reconstruction in the South, suppressing Indian peoples, and upholding legal authorities in the West.

Economy: Public Support for Private Enterprise The Civil War created a powerful American state. To fight the war, the Union government mobilized millions of men and billions of dollars. In the process, it created a modern fiscal system, an elaborate network of national banks, and — for the first time in American history — a significant national bureaucracy. Inspired by Whig ideology, Republican-run Congresses enacted aggressive policies to promote economic development. They granted huge subsidies to railroad companies, protected industries and workers through high protective tariffs, promoted education and economic research, and gave western land to farmers and cattlemen. They mapped and distributed western resources, including timber and mineral rights. A great postwar boom in railway construction, land speculation, and agricultural production collapsed in 1873, as a worldwide decline in prices led to a lengthy depression.

Society: New Peoples, New Statuses The ethnic composition and racial distinctions of the United States changed dramatically during the decades before, during, and just after the Civil War. Millions of Irish, German, and British immigrants prompted a sharp nativist reaction. Increasingly, the elite classes of the North doubted the wisdom of universal male suffrage. The freedom granted to 4 million African Americans raised a similar issue for southern whites, who maintained their privileged racial status by denying full political and civil rights for freedmen. In the trans-Mississippi West, whites jostled uneasily with conquered Hispanic residents, subject Indian peoples, and despised Chinese emigrants. These decades, which began with the romantic quest for continental empire, ended on the bitter notes of racial struggles and half-won freedoms.

Nonetheless, many European Americans looked back on the era as one of unprecedented progress. The United States had claimed a vast, resource-rich empire in the West. Railroads and industrial cities were growing, from Chicago to San Francisco, and merchants and traders looked eagerly across the Pacific. The nation had fought a great war that preserved the Union and vanquished slavery. And America's dynamic postwar economy began to draw immigrants from many continents. These achievements, by no means predictable in 1840, had set the nation on a course toward global power.

Essential Questions Review Exercises

Using the guidelines, grids, maps, and schematics that follow, gather evidence that helps you to review concepts and themes from the period 1844 to 1877. Consult *America's History,* Seventh Edition, as well as any relevant materials your teacher has provided to review the information.

1. **Why did sectional discord between the North and the South culminate in war?**

   When considering why wars occur, it is often helpful to distinguish among long-term causes (causes existing for decades or longer), short-term causes (causes arising in the decade or so prior), and triggers—those catalysts that immediately cause a tipping point to occur and change the course of history. A table like the one below is often a useful organizational tool when reviewing these different levels of causation. Consulting Chapter 13 and using the following table, review the causes of the Civil War.

CAUSES OF THE CIVIL WAR		
Long-Term Causes *(Consider the ways northern and southern states differed since colonial times—economically, politically, and socially.)*	**Short-Term Causes** *(Consider the ways westward expansion emphasized those fundamental differences in the 1840s and 1850s.)*	**Triggers** *(What events in the years 1858–1861 escalated the conflict to a point of no return?)*

2. How did the Civil War transform the South? The North?

Chapter 14 highlights the key battles, strategies, advantages, and disadvantages of both sides of the U.S. Civil War. And while many experiences were shared—both the United States and the Confederacy resorted to a draft (conscription), and both armies endured extraordinary casualties—some aspects of wartime experiences were regionally distinct. Use the chart below to consider how the northern and southern states were different before the war (and you should draw on your review of earlier chapters for that), how their wartime experiences differed, and how both regions were irrevocably changed by the conflict (you may draw on Chapter 15 for the latter).

THE SOUTH (The Confederate States of America)	THE NORTH (The United States of America)
Key Characteristics Before (1800–1860)	
Wartime Experiences (1861–1865)	
Postwar Conditions (1865–1900)	

3. What were the successes and failures of Reconstruction?

When answering a question like this about Reconstruction, it is important to remember that the two main challenges the United States faced following the Civil War were these:

- How should the rebel states be readmitted into the Union?
- How should the former slaves be treated?

Chapter 15 reviews what some historians have referred to as a "crooked path" to resolving these two challenges. In the space on the next page, write one paragraph each that summarizes the answers the Reconstruction presidents and congressional leaders devised in response to those two challenges. Later, you may want to consider the extent to which either of these issues was resolved successfully; for now, simply recall and review the decisions that were made between the years 1865 and 1877.

On the readmission of rebel states:

On how to treat former slaves:

4. **How was westward expansion tied to accelerating American industrialization in the nineteenth century?**

The settlement of the West is a story of scarcity and abundance. The varied landscape offered both resources (such as mined metals and farmed crops) and markets (railroad expansion and other building) to American businesses. On the map below, first record important environmental characteristics of the trans-Mississippi West from the textbook's Map 16.4 ("The Natural Environment of the West, 1860s"). Then review the coverage of the West in Chapter 16 and note key resources, events such as the Indian Wars (and dates), the intercontinental railroad line, types of settlement that occurred, and what industries were important.

Practice Questions

The following sections allow you to test your knowledge of Part 4. The Directions are verbatim instructions from the College Board's AP Exam; the Hints offer strategies for tackling each type of AP question. Answers to all of the Part 4 practice questions follow.

Multiple-Choice Questions

Directions: Each of the questions or incomplete statements below is followed by five suggested answers or completions. Select the one that is best in each case.

Hints:

- Read each question carefully, looking out for negative words such as EXCEPT, NOT, and FALSE.
- Read all possible answers and cross out those you feel are incorrect; narrowing down your choices gives you the chance to make an educated guess.
- Be cautious of words indicating absolutes, like *most, least, all,* and *none.*
- Connect the specific information of the question to broader trends and themes.
- In questions that provide you with evidence, assess the information carefully and eliminate answers that go beyond the bounds of the evidence given.

1. Prior to the Civil War, the Republican Party's stand on slavery corresponded most closely with the principles of the
   (A) Free Soil Party
   (B) Liberty Party
   (C) American Party
   (D) Whig Party
   (E) Constitutional Union Party

2. American annexation of Texas and subsequent statehood
   (A) spurred Lincoln's victory
   (B) sparked the Mexican War
   (C) had originally been proposed by President Van Buren
   (D) was opposed by residents of the Lone Star Republic
   (E) weakened "Oregon Fever"

3. Popular sovereignty temporarily solved which issue?
   (A) The dispute over states' versus federal control over voter qualifications
   (B) Whether States had the right to secede from the Union
   (C) Whether Congress had the authority to legislate slavery in the territories
   (D) Whether states had to abide by federal laws that conflict with state laws
   (E) States' rights versus the Supremacy Clause of the U.S. Constitution

4. The Wilmot Proviso
   (A) was included in the Treaty of Guadalupe Hidalgo
   (B) proposed the prohibition of slavery in any new territories acquired from Mexico
   (C) was promoted by John C. Calhoun
   (D) caused the most trouble in California
   (E) called for a gradual end to slavery in Texas

5. Which of the following was the greatest problem for President Lincoln during the Civil War?
   (A) Congressional oversight
   (B) Loyalty within his cabinet
   (C) Secretary Cameron's problems
   (D) Finding a capable general
   (E) His indecisiveness

6. President Lincoln's most significant foreign policy achievement during the Civil War was
   (A) purchasing Alaska
   (B) getting Russian support for the Union cause
   (C) meeting Mexico's challenge to the Monroe Doctrine
   (D) keeping European powers from aiding the Confederacy militarily
   (E) securing extradition of copperhead traitors from the Canadian government

7. The Civil War is said to be the first total war in modern times. A "total war" is best defined as
   (A) one fought by people of the same country; no other nations are involved
   (B) a world war
   (C) one where all resources, including civilians, are mobilized for war
   (D) when every available man has to fight
   (E) when the war is not over without total victory by one side

8. Which is true of the role played by African Americans in the Civil War?
   (A) Blacks were not allowed to fight in either Union Army.
   (B) Blacks served in segregated regiments and showed great valor.
   (C) Some slaves gladly fought for the Confederacy.
   (D) Black men refused to fight in the "white man's war."
   (E) Military service assured an end of racial discrimination for blacks.

9. Southerners responded to the end of slavery with
   (A) Black Codes
   (B) the Freedman's Bureau
   (C) an Ordinance of Nullification
   (D) resignation
   (E) the Civil Rights Act of 1866

10. The technical reason for which Congress impeached Andrew Johnson was
    (A) his violation of the Tenure of Office Act
    (B) his attempt to undermine radical Reconstruction
    (C) his implication in the Whiskey Ring scandal
    (D) that he refused to support the Civil War amendments
    (E) that he encouraged miscegenation (mixing) between the races

11. One tangible success story of the Reconstruction era in the South was
    (A) the establishment of schools and colleges for African Americans
    (B) achievement of full civil rights for African Americans
    (C) the advancement of women's rights
    (D) enduring African American leadership
    (E) that the "solid south" voted Republican for nearly 100 years

12. Which statement is most true of sharecropping?
    (A) It created an equal partnership between tenant farmer and owner.
    (B) Sharecropper wives were partners with their husbands, laboring side by side with them on the farm.
    (C) Sharecroppers were little better off than slaves.
    (D) Through sharecropping, freed slaves were able to advance very well economically.
    (E) Some sharecroppers were so successful they bought out their former masters and took control of their plantations.

13. Which of the following made surviving on the plains easier?
    (A) The amount of rainfall and sunshine
    (B) The abundance of water and wind
    (C) The moderate climate and new fencing
    (D) Steel plows and new strains of wheat
    (E) The closeness of neighbors

14. The last great Indian "battle" was a massacre of Sioux Indians
    (A) known as the Great Northern War
    (B) in Mesa Verde
    (C) in Oklahoma
    (D) at Wounded Knee
    (E) at Little Big Horn

15. The Exodusters were
    (A) Scandinavian settlers in Minnesota
    (B) blacks who migrated to Kansas
    (C) Mexicans who immigrated to the United States
    (D) Chinese who were forced to leave California
    (E) women homesteaders

Document-Based Question

Directions: The following question requires you to construct a coherent essay that integrates your interpretation of Documents A–F and your knowledge of the period referred to in the question. High scores will be earned only by essays that add both key pieces of evidence from the documents *and* draw on outside knowledge of the period.

To what extent did the policies of Reconstruction transform the lives of African Americans?

Use the documents and your knowledge of the period to construct your response.

Background Reading: *America's History,* Seventh Edition, Chapter 15

Hints:

- With document-based questions, remember to move beyond focusing on the specific facts in the documents and seek their more interpretive or analytical aspects. As you read through the documents, underline key passages, jot notes in the margins, and record outside examples that come to mind as you read.

- After reading through the documents, categorize them into sub-sections to generate a paragraph structure for your response. Considering legal, social, and economic impacts of Reconstruction policies is one way to sort through the evidence.
- Your ultimate focus here should be an assessment of the impact of Reconstruction on the lives of African Americans. Did its policies succeed or fail the freed slaves? Use the evidence to support a credible thesis.
- Keep in mind the volume of essays the exam readers must plow through. Clarity and organization are key.

Document A

Barrow Plantation–1860

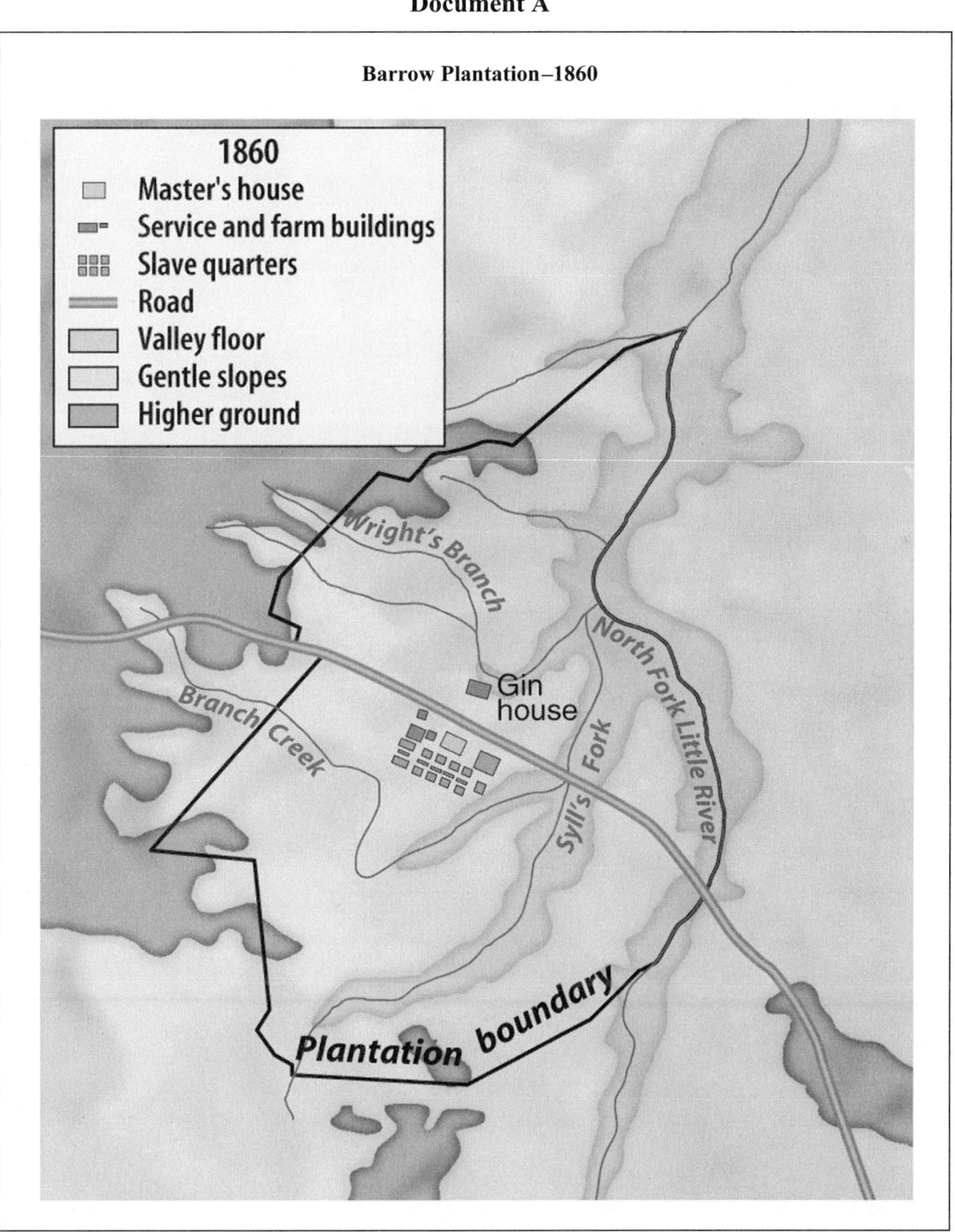

Document B

Barrow Plantation–1881

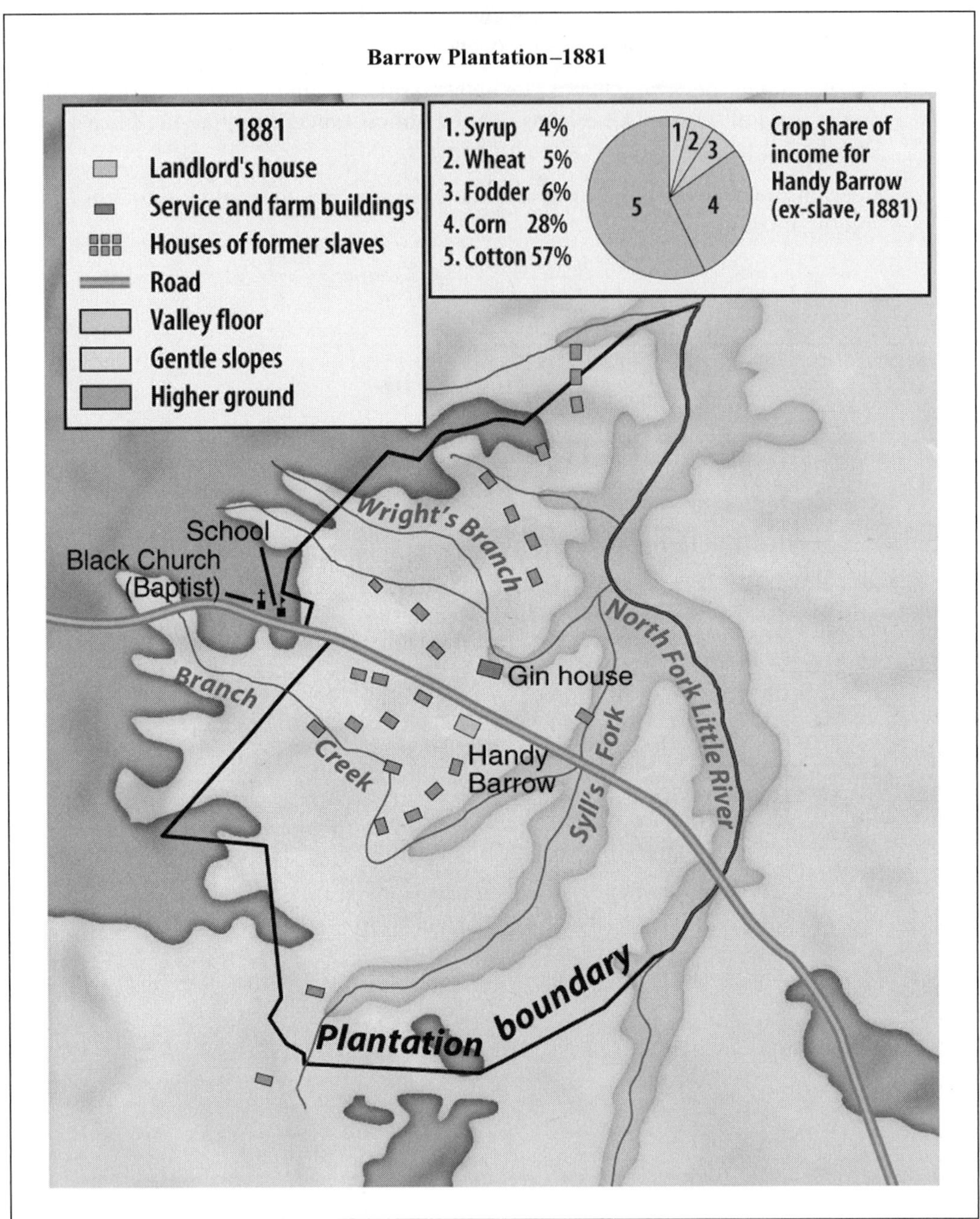

Document C

Source: Charlotte Forten, "Life on the Sea Islands," 1864.

L. and I had one day an interesting visit to a plantation about six miles from ours. The house is beautifully situated in the midst of noble pine-trees, on the banks of a large creek. The place was owned by a very wealthy Rebel family, and is one of the pleasantest and healthiest on the island. The vicinity of the pines makes it quite healthy. There were a hundred and fifty people on it, one hundred of whom had come from Edisto Island at the time of its evacuation by our troops. There were not houses enough to accommodate them, and they had to take shelter in barns, out-houses, or any other place they could find. They afterwards built rude dwellings for themselves, which did not, however, afford them much protection in bad weather. The superintendent told us that they were well-behaved and industrious. . . .

The church in which we taught school was particularly damp and cold. There was no chimney, and we could have no fire at all. Near the close of the winter a stove came for us, but it could not be made to draw; . . . We got so thoroughly chilled and benumbed within, that for several days we had school out-of-doors, where it was much warmer. Our school-room was a pleasant one, for ceiling the blue sky above, for walls the grand old oaks with their beautiful moss-drapery, but the dampness of the ground made it unsafe for us to continue the experiment. . . .

Daily the long-oppressed people of these islands are demonstrating their capacity for improvement in learning and labor. What they have accomplished in one short year exceeds our utmost expectations. . . . We cannot but feel that the day of final and entire deliverance, so long and often so hopelessly prayed for, has at length begun to dawn upon this much-enduring race. An old freedman said to me one day, "De Lord make me suffer long time, Miss. 'Peared like we nebber was gwine to git troo. But now we's free."

Document D

Source: Mississippi Black Code, November 1865.

AN ACT to confer Civil Rights on Freedmen, and for other purposes.

Be it enacted by the Legislature of the State of Mississippi. That all freedmen, free negroes and mulattoes may sue and be sued, . . . may acquire personal property . . . and may dispose of the same, in the same manner . . . that white persons may: . . .

That all freedmen, free negroes and mulattoes may intermarry with each other . . . ,who do now and have heretofore lived and cohabited together as husband and wife shall be taken and held in law as legally married, and the issue shall be taken and held as legitimate for all purposes. That it shall not be lawful for any freedman, free negro or mulatto to inter-marry with any white person; nor for any white person to inter-marry with any freedman, negro or mulatto . . .

That every freedman, free negro and mulatto, shall, on the second Monday of January, one thousand eight hundred and sixty-six, and annually thereafter, have a lawful home or employment, and shall have written evidence thereof . . .

That all contracts for labor made with freedmen, free negroes and mulattoes, for a longer period than one month shall be in writing and in duplicate, . . . and if the laborer shall quit the service of the employer, before expiration of his term of service, without good cause, he shall forfeit his wages for that year, up to the time of quitting . . . That every civil officer shall, and every person may arrest and carry back to his or her legal employer any freedman, free negro or mulatto, who shall have quit the service of his or her employer before the expiration of his or her term of service without good cause, and said officer and person, shall be entitled to receive for arresting and carrying back every deserting employee aforesaid, the sum of five dollars, and ten cents per mile from the place of arrest to the place of delivery, [to] be paid by the employer.

Document E

Source: Charles Nordhoff, *The Cotton States,* 1875.

No thoughtful man can examine the history of the last ten years in the South, as he may hear it on the spot and from both parties, without being convinced that it was absolutely necessary to the security of the blacks, and the permanent peace of the Southern communities, to give the negro, ignorant, poor, and helpless as he was, every political right and privilege which any other citizen enjoys. That he should vote and that he should be capable of holding office was necessary, I am persuaded, to make him personally secure, and, what is of more importance, to convert him from a *freedman* into a *free man.*

That he has not always conducted himself well in the exercise of his political rights is perfectly and lamentably true; but this is less his fault than that of the bad white men who introduced him to political life. But on the other hand, the vote has given him what nothing else could give—a substantive existence . . .

The negro, whose vote will be important to both parties, will find security in that fact. No politician will be so silly as to encroach upon his rights, or allow his opponents to do so; and the black man appears to me to have a sense of respectability which will prevent him, unencouraged by demagogues, from trying to force himself into positions for which he is unfit . . .

Whenever the Federal interference in all its shapes ceases, it will be found, I believe, that the negroes will not at first cast a full vote; take away petty Federal "organizers," and the negro, left face to face with the white man, hearing both sides for the first time; knowing by experience, as he will presently, that the Democrat is not a monster, and that Democratic victory does not mean his re-enslavement, will lose much of his interest in elections . . .

Of course, as soon as parties are re-arranged on a sound and natural basis, the negro vote will re-appear; for the leaders of each party, the Whig or Republican and the Democrat, will do their utmost to get his vote, and therein will be the absolute security of the black man. I believe, however, that for many years to come, until a new generation arrives at manhood perhaps, and, at any rate, until the black man becomes generally an independent farmer, he will be largely influenced in his political affiliations by the white. He will vote as his employer, or the planter from whom he rents land, or the white man whom he most trusts . . . But, at any rate, he will vote or not, as he pleases. And it is far better for him that he should act under such influences than that his vote should be massed against the property and intelligence of the white people to achieve the purposes of unscrupulous demagogues.

Document F

Source: U.S. Supreme Court, *United States v. Reynolds,* 1914.

The facts to be gathered from the indictments and pleas, upon which the court below decided the cases and determined that no offense was charged against the statutes of the United States as above set forth, are substantially these: one Ed Rivers, having been convicted in a court of Alabama of the offense of petit larceny, was fined $15, and costs, $43.75. The defendant Reynolds appeared as surety for Rivers, and a judgment by confession was entered up against him for the amount of the fine and costs, which Reynolds afterwards paid to the state. On May 4, 1910, Rivers, the convict, entered into a written contract with Reynolds to work for him as a farmhand for the term of nine months and twenty-four days, at the rate of $6 per month, to pay the amount of fine and costs. The indictment charges that he entered into the service of Reynolds, and under threats of arrest and imprisonment if he ceased to perform such work and labor, he worked until the 6th day of June, when he refused to labor. Thereupon he was arrested upon a warrant issued at the instance of Reynolds from the county court of Alabama, on the charge of violating the contract of service. He was convicted and fined the sum of 1 cent for violating this contract, and additional costs in the amount of $87.05, for which he again confessed judgment with G.W. Broughton as surety, and entered into a similar contract with Broughton to work for him as a farm hand at the same rate, for a term of fourteen months and fifteen days.

This labor is performed under the constant coercion and threat of another possible arrest and prosecution in case he violates the labor contract which he has made with the surety, and this form of coercion is as potent as it would have been had the law provided for the seizure and compulsory service of the convict. Compulsion of such service by the constant fear of imprisonment under the criminal laws renders the work compulsory, as much so as authority to arrest and hold his person would be if the law authorized that to be done.

There can be no doubt that the State has authority to impose involuntary servitude as a punishment for crime. This fact is recognized in the Thirteenth Amendment, and such punishment expressly excepted from its terms. Of course, the State may impose fines and penalties which must be worked out for the benefit of the State, and in such manner as the State may legitimately prescribe . . . But here the State has taken the obligation of another for the fine and costs, imposed upon one convicted for the violation of the laws of the State . . . The convict must work it out to satisfy the surety for whom he has contracted to work [and] must be kept, under pain of re-arrest, and another similar proceeding for its violation, and perhaps another and another. Thus, under pain of recurring prosecutions, the convict may be kept at labor, to satisfy the demands of his employer.

In our opinion, this system is in violation of rights intended to be secured by the Thirteenth Amendment, as well as in violation of the statutes to which we have referred, which the Congress has enacted for the purpose of making that amendment effective.

Free-Response Questions

Directions: For the following questions, you are advised to spend five minutes planning and thirty minutes writing your answer. Cite relevant historical evidence in support of your generalizations and present your arguments clearly and logically.

Hints:

- Sketch out a brief outline, recording facts and examples that you remember and organizing them in a sensible way. Each section of the outline should generate a supporting paragraph for your essay.
- Develop a thesis that takes a clear stand on the question posed. Be sure to state it in your introductory paragraph.
- Begin each supporting paragraph with a clear topic sentence.
- Consider transitions between paragraphs.
- Conclude by restating your thesis in a fresh way, perhaps by making a connection to another moment in American history.
- Keep in mind the volume of essays the exam readers must plow through. Clarity and organization are key.
- Question-specific hints follow the questions.

1. **"The Civil War was an irrepressible conflict." Assess the validity of this statement.**

   Thesis development and organization: the statement says that the Civil War was inevitable. What evidence might you point to in order to support it? How far back might you go: the writing of the Constitution, the Revolutionary War, colonial divergences of development (slave-based vs. free labor-based economies)? If you would like to refute (disagree with) this statement, you will probably want to emphasize the series of disastrous political events of the 1850s.

2. **"Nineteenth-century Manifest Destiny was just another name for imperialism." Assess the validity of this statement with regard to the United States' relationships with Native Americans and Mexico.**

   Thesis development and organization: this question is actually a global one. It demands that you understand what imperialism is and what European imperialists were up to around the world in the nineteenth century. Make sure that you have a clear definition for imperialism in your mind; if you do not have a background in nineteenth-century European imperialism, consider the imperial trends during the colonial era (1500s–1700s) that you've learned in this course. Be sure to identify what Manifest Destiny means to Americans and then consider the War with Mexico and conflicts with Indians. How were the motives different from or similar to the motives of the British, Spanish, Dutch, and French colonists in the earlier period? What was different about American expansion from other forms of imperialism? To what extent was westward expansion a way for the United States to become a more powerful nation?

Answer Key to Part 4 Practice Questions

Multiple-Choice Questions

1. **Answer (A) Free Soil Party.** The Republican Party encompassed both abolitionists who opposed slavery for moral reasons and business-oriented northerners who opposed slavery for economic reasons. The Republican platforms in 1856 and 1860 endorsed a restriction on any further expansion of slavery in the West, but not its abolition in the South. (*America's History,* Seventh Edition, Chapter 13, pp. 419–420, 424)

2. **Answer (B) sparked the Mexican War.** Texas is the only state that has ever been its own country: after its American residents successfully fought Mexican rule, it was known as the Lone Star State. When it was annexed by the United States, the Mexican government responded bitterly. In the name of expansion, a border skirmish was inflated by President Polk to justify war. (*America's History,* Seventh Edition, Chapter 13, pp. 405–408)

3. **Answer (C) Whether Congress had the authority to legislate slavery in the territories.** Since 1820, Congress had kept a balance of free and slave states represented in Congress as they managed the admission of new states into the Union. By the 1850s, the balance became harder to achieve—thus Senator Stephen Douglas's invention of "popular sovereignty," which gave people living in a given territory the right to choose whether or not they would allow slavery. It was a neat way for Congressmen to sidestep these contentious political decisions, but a disastrous policy that ultimately led to the events known as Bleeding Kansas. (*America's History,* Seventh Edition, Chapter 13, pp. 415–418)

4. **Answer (B) proposed the prohibition of slavery in any new territories acquired from Mexico.** Northerners like David Wilmot of Pennsylvania worried that the new territories won in the War with Mexico would expand the slave South's power in Congress; in 1846 at the start of the war, Wilmot proposed a plan to prevent the expansion of slavery into those territories. The proviso was voted down, but foreshadowed the growing conflict between slave and free states. (*America's History,* Seventh Edition, Chapter 13, p. 408)

5. **Answer (D) finding a capable general.** Lincoln's conflict with General George B. McClellan was so nasty that McClellan ran against Lincoln for president in the 1864 election. It wasn't until 1863, after his success on the western frontier at Vicksburg, that Lincoln found a general willing to do what was necessary to win such a bloody conflict: Ulysses S. Grant. The Confederacy's Robert E. Lee was one of the South's great assets throughout the war. (*America's History,* Seventh Edition, Chapter 14, pp. 436–439, 451)

6. **Answer (D) keeping European powers from supporting the Confederacy Military.** If the Confederacy had been able to win recognition and support from either France or Great Britain, they might have shared the same advantages Americans enjoyed during the Revolutionary War when the alliance with France was forged (in 1777). The other answers offer some half-truths, but note what the question is asking: the only foreign policy issue relevant to the Civil War is D. (*America's History,* Seventh Edition, Chapter 14, p. 435)

7. **Answer (C) one where all the resources, including civilians, are mobilized for war.** The general who best epitomized the concept was General William Tecumseh Sherman: his brutally effective "March to the Sea" from Atlanta helped to win the war but embittered southerners. (*America's History,* Seventh Edition, Chapter 14, p. 453)

8. **Answer (B) Blacks served in segregated regiments and showed great valor.** While many northerners opposed the idea of African American soldiers, these men endured segregation, humiliating conflicts over pay, and many other indignities in their effort to support the Union's cause. (*America's History,* Seventh Edition, Chapter 14, pp. 449–451)

9. **Answer (A) Black Codes.** These were laws passed in the immediate aftermath of the war that attempted to severely restrict the activities of African Americans. Answer C is irrelevant to this question; answers B and E were measures passed by Radical Republicans in Congress and were not widely supported among white southerners. And while some may have felt resigned to slavery's end, we can only speculate whether that is true. (*America's History,* Seventh Edition, Chapter 15, p. 464)

10. **Answer (A) his violation of the Tenure of Office Act.** This was the legal basis for launching impeachment proceedings, but the real reason why the Radical Republicans were so angry with Johnson was his failure to support their plans for Reconstruction. The Whiskey Ring scandal refers to the corruption in President Ulysses S. Grant's administration, which came a bit later. (*America's History,* Seventh Edition, Chapter 15, p. 468)

11. **Answer (A) the establishment of schools and colleges for African Americans.** While many of the achievements of Reconstruction such as citizenship and voting rights for African Americans were short-lived, the schools established during the period had true and lasting impact on the lives of generations of students. (*America's History,* Seventh Edition, Chapter 15, p. 482)

12. **Answer (C) Sharecroppers were little better off than slaves.** While the eradication of slavery was profoundly meaningful, economically sharecropping was similar because sharecroppers were usually in debt to the landowners for life and couldn't easily escape their situation. There was nothing equal about the relationship between tenant farmer and owner. (*America's History,* Seventh Edition, Chapter 15, pp. 476–477)

13. **Answer (D) Steel plows and new strains of wheat.** These technological innovations, along with others including barbed wire and of course railroads, helped Americans to survive and often thrive on the Great Plains. The climate was variable and not always conducive, and neighbors were few and far between. (*America's History,* Seventh Edition, Chapter 16, p. 504)

14. **Answer (D) at Wounded Knee.** Two important events to remember from the Indian wars are the defeat of Custer at Little Big Horn and the civilian massacre at Wounded Knee, which burned in the memories of plains Indians for generations. (*America's History,* Seventh Edition, Chapter 16, p. 518–520)

15. **Answer (B) blacks who migrated to Kansas.** While a majority of former slaves became mired in sharecropping arrangements in the South (most not far from where they had served as slaves), some moved west seeking better opportunities. The Exodusters are important to remember; they predated the massive northern migration of African Americans to jobs in cities in the first half of the twentieth century. (*America's History,* Seventh Edition, Chapter 16, pp. 504–505)

Document-Based Question

To what extent did the policies of Reconstruction transform the lives of African Americans?

This exercise requires a multidimensional view of Reconstruction. The best answer will examine the effects of Reconstruction on several areas of African American life. My sample answer references the legal, social, and economic impacts of Reconstruction. The benefit of this type of question is that you can note varying degrees of progress in the different areas you choose to examine. Remember to clearly state and define the areas you will address; given the evidence offered and outside information from the textbook, you can thoroughly consider the legal, social, and economic impacts of reconstruction policies.

Your response should make note of the attempt to reconstruct a labor system in the Reconstructed South in the maps of the Barrow Plantation (Document A), the Black Codes (Document D), and *United States v. Reynolds* (Document F). Similarly, the table of home and land ownership (Document B) and Charlotte Forten's essay (Document C) illustrate a sense of the enormous potential for upward economic mobility in the immediate aftermath of the war. Lastly, Nordhoff's *The Cotton States* (Document E) reasserts the structures of bound labor, as does Document F. You should have also drawn on your knowledge of the Reconstruction Amendments (thirteenth, fourteenth, and fifteenth), the Reconstruction Act of 1867, Jim Crow laws, and the mechanisms of tenant farming and sharecropping to substantiate your response. Review Chapter 15 for further insights.

Free-Response Questions

1. **"The Civil War was an irrepressible conflict." Assess the validity of this statement.**

   Was the Civil War avoidable or not? Whichever argument you made, you should have incorporated references to some or all of the following events, ideas, and trends:

   - Compact versus contract theory of government
   - Social/cultural differences between the North and South
   - Vital interests—tariff, slavery, free land, internal improvements, reform
   - Economic differences between the North and the South
   - Compromises: Missouri (1820), 1850, Kansas-Nebraska (1854)
   - Dred Scott decision; Bleeding Kansas

2. **"Nineteenth-century Manifest Destiny was just another name for imperialism." Assess the validity of this statement with regard to the United States' relationships with Native Americans and Mexico.**

   On the issue of the treatment of Native Americans, the topics that ought to have been considered in your response from Chapters 10, 13, and 16 include:

   - Indian Removal Act
   - Trail of Tears
   - Reservations
   - Broken treaties
   - Indian Wars
   - Assimilation policies

On the issue of the treatment of Mexico, the topics from Chapter 13 that ought to have been considered in your response include:

- Annexation of Texas
- Mexican War
- Gadsden Purchase

Your answer should include discussions of how these issues were resolved, and whether the issues were similar to earlier imperial policies and ideals.

PART 5
Bold Experiments in an Era of Industrialization, 1877–1929

This part covers the following chapters in Henretta et al., *America's History,* Seventh Edition:

Essential Questions

After studying the chapters in Part 5, you should know how to answer the following questions:

1. Why and how did American society industrialize during the late nineteenth century?
2. What were the causes and consequences of urbanization?
3. How did political change and progressive reform gain momentum after 1900?
4. How did the United States emerge as a world power by 1918?
5. What tensions between the old and new existed in the 1920s?

The 1920 Census revealed that a majority of Americans (51 percent) lived in urban areas for the first time. Part 5 covers the accelerating trends that led up to this important shift in American life from the agrarian to the urban. As you review these chapters, in addition to the questions above, notice what stayed constant in American life despite astonishing economic growth, political upheaval, the rise of a mass culture, and the United States' new role on the world stage. Various conflicts between tradition and innovation would consume Americans from the 1880s to the 1920s.

Resources for Review

In the following pages, you'll find the Thematic Timeline and Essay for Part 5 from *America's History,* exercises to review your knowledge of the period, and AP-style questions that address the time period covered: 15 practice multiple-choice questions, 1 document-based question, and 3 free-response questions. Answers with page references to *America's History* can be found at the end.

Thematic Timeline and Part Essay

Bold Experiments in an Era of Industrialization, 1877–1929

	ECONOMY	POLITICS AND LAW	REFORM	CULTURE	FOREIGN RELATIONS
1870	Economic depression of 1870s	Reconstruction ends (1877)	Great Railroad Strike of 1877	National League launches professional baseball (1876)	Treaty brings Hawaii within U.S. orbit
1880	First vertically integrated firms Rockefeller establishes Standard Oil Trust Emergence of white-collar managerial work Women enter paid labor as office workers	Era of close party competition, 1876–1894 Chinese exclusion (1882–1943) Pendleton Act (1883) Interstate Commerce Act (1887)	Woman's Christian Temperance Union (WCTU) becomes largest women's reform movement Knights of Labor at peak (mid 1880s) Hull House (1889)	William Dean Howells calls for realism in literature (1881)	
1890	Economic depression (1893–1897)	Sherman Antitrust Act (1890) Republican victories (1894–1896) Rise of Democratic "Solid South" Supreme Court upholds segregation in *Plessy v. Ferguson* (1896)	People's Party (1890) Sierra Club (1892) Coxey's Army (1894) Consumers League (1899)	William Randolph Hearst pioneers "yellow journalism" Disfranchisement and Jim Crow in the South Rise of Social Gospel	War of 1898 Hawaii annexed (1898) Philippine-American War (1899–1902)

	ECONOMY	POLITICS AND LAW	REFORM	CULTURE	FOREIGN RELATIONS
1900	U.S. Steel becomes first corporation with billion-dollar valuation (1901)	William McKinley assassinated; Theodore Roosevelt becomes president (1901) Hepburn Act regulates railroads (1906)	Growth of American Federation of Labor (AFL) American Socialist Party (1901) NAACP (1909)	Popularity of ragtime music First World Series in baseball (1903)	Platt Amendment sets limits on Cuban autonomy (1902) Roosevelt corollary to Monroe Doctrine (1904) Panama Canal begun (1904)
1910	Triangle Shirtwaist Fire (1911) U.S. becomes a creditor nation Great Migration of African Americans to factory work in the North	Woodrow Wilson elected president (1913) Eighteenth Amendment: Federal income tax (1913)	Women's suffrage movement grows	Armory Show (1913) Anti-German nativism during WWI "Red Scare" (1919)	Wilson intervenes in Mexico (1914) U.S. enters WWI (1917) Wilson's Fourteen Points (1918)
1920	Economic prosperity (1922–1929)	Republican ascendancy (1920–1932) National women's suffrage (1921) Prohibition (1921–1933)	Heyday of second Ku Klux Klan	Rise of Hollywood Harlem Renaissance Emergence of jazz	Treaty of Versailles rejected by U.S. Senate (1920)

Visiting the United States in 1905, British visitor James Bryce remarked on its "prodigious material development." He wrote that "rural districts are being studded with villages, the villages are growing into cities, the cities are stretching out long arms of suburbs." Bryce was witnessing America's birth as a global industrial power. In 1866 the nation was overwhelmingly rural and dependent on foreign capital as it recovered from a crippling civil war. By 1929, industrialization had introduced new ways of working and living. The United States also began to assert itself on the world stage, claiming overseas territories and playing a decisive role in World War I. Industrialization required political innovation. As former president Theodore Roosevelt declared in 1910, American citizens needed to "effectively control the mighty commercial forces which they have called into being." Workers, farmers, and urban Progressives worked to clean up politics, regulate corporations, and fight poverty. In their creative responses to the problems of a new industrial age, such reformers gave their name to the Progressive Era.

Economy: Industrialization and the Rise of Corporations The post–Civil War economy grew rapidly, a trend intensified by industrial production during World War I. Millions of immigrants arrived from around the globe; though millions found places in the economy, Asians faced legal exclusion, and restrictions on overall numbers of immigrants were enacted in the 1920s. Giant corporations developed national and even global networks of production, marketing, and finance. Their complex structures opened new career opportunities for middle-class managers, salesmen, and women office workers. Traditional craftsmen, however, found themselves displaced, while factory workers and miners endured harsh conditions, low pay, and cycles of unemployment. Farmers also suffered from falling crop prices, caused by expanding world production.

Politics and Law: State Building and Economic Regulation The fierce struggles of post–Reconstruction politics centered on the scope of government power. In the 1880s, Republicans increasingly became champions of business. Though Republican Theodore Roosevelt championed key reforms during his presidency (1901–1909), much reform energy passed to other parties. The Greenback-Labor, People's (or Populist), and Progressive parties all proposed expanding government powers in response to industrialization and concentrated wealth. While none won national power, these parties shaped the course of reform. Democrats, who had long called for limited government, began in the 1880s to advocate stronger government intervention to fight poverty and restrain big business. The party had little opportunity to enact national programs during the Republican-dominated years of 1894–1910 and the prosperous, complacent decade of the 1920s. But in between, during the presidency of Democrat Woodrow Wilson (1913–1921), the party enacted an impressive slate of reforms. By 1929, when the Great Depression hit, Democrats were poised to enact the New Deal.

Reform: Labor, Reform, and Protest Movements An array of reformers, loosely known as progressives, arose in response to the problems caused by industrialization. More radical proposals tended to come from mass-based coalitions of workers and farmers; pressure from such groups combined with the efforts of middle-class urban reformers to generate new policies. Reformers sought to enhance democracy, rein in the growing power of corporations, uphold labor rights, and promote public health and safety. Progressives ran up against formidable political obstacles, especially from the Supreme Court. Nonetheless, by 1920, national, state, and local governments enacted a range of landmark laws, representing the early emergence of the modern state.

Culture: Immigration and Urbanization: The Origins of Modern Mass Culture While the nineteenth-century values of hard work, thrift, piety, and domesticity never entirely faded, they faced serious challenges in the era of industrialization. Women asserted more independent roles within the family and in public life. The secular pleasures of consumer culture encouraged Americans to spend money and have fun. Americans cheered for professional sports teams, and by the 1920s flocked to the movies and purchased millions of automobiles. As early as the 1880s, literary realism marked a break with Victorian culture as one element of the modernism that led to such innovations as jazz music and abstract art.

Foreign Relations: An Emerging World Power Policymakers of the post–Civil War era focused on overseas trade. Victorious against Spain in the War of 1898, the United States claimed overseas colonies and asserted control over the Caribbean basin. Though President Woodrow Wilson attempted to maintain neutrality at the start of World War I, trade ties helped draw America into the conflict on the Allied side. Wilson sought to influence the peace, but Allied leaders ignored his proposals and the U.S. Senate rejected the treaty altogether. At war's end, though America exerted tremendous clout in global affairs, its role on the world stage remained uncertain.

Essential Questions Review Exercises

Using the guidelines, maps, and graphic organizers that follow, gather evidence that helps you to review concepts and themes from the period 1877–1929. Consult *America's History,* Seventh Edition, as well as any relevant materials your teacher has provided to review the information.

1. **Why and how did American society industrialize during the late nineteenth century?**

   There were a variety of factors that contributed to the extraordinary process of industrialization in the United States at this time. Government policies and protections such as patent laws, open immigration, railroad regulation, and trade tariffs facilitated growth. Use the matrix below to review how the economic factors contributed in the four categories listed: workers, innovators (i.e. inventors and business leaders), resources, and markets.

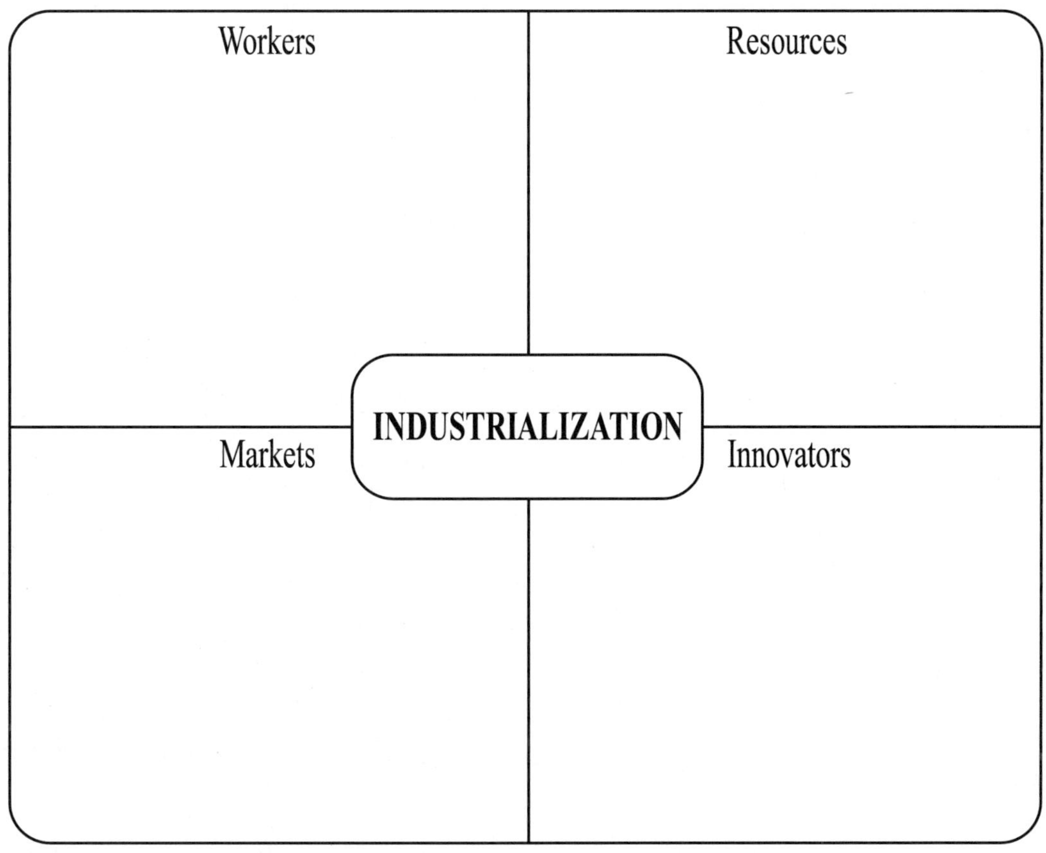

2. What were the causes and consequences of urbanization?

Using the flowchart below, note significant causes and effects of the explosive growth of cities in the late nineteenth and early twentieth centuries.

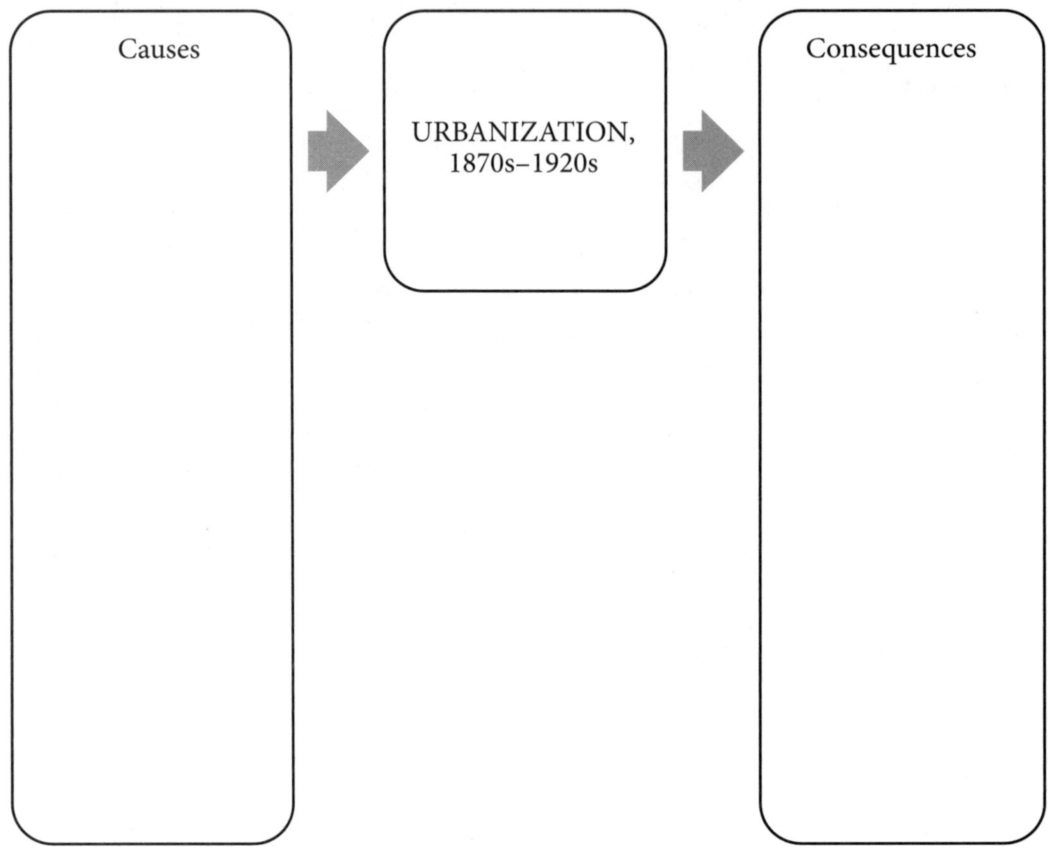

3. How did political change and progressive reform gain momentum after 1900?

While workers, reformers, and farmers sought rights and protections throughout the Gilded Age, progressive change reached national proportions in the early twentieth century. Not all Progressive reformers sought the same results, nor were they motivated by the same factors. Using the chart below, review the types of people who successfully fought for reforms in the period from 1880–1917.

SOCIAL GROUP	WHERE WERE THEY ACTIVE?	WHAT MOTIVATED THEM?	WHAT CHANGES DID THEY SEEK?	WHAT IMPACT DID THEY HAVE BY 1917?
Industrial Workers/ Union Leaders				
Populist Farmers				
Middle-Class Women				
African Americans				
State and Local Politicians				
Presidents Roosevelt and Wilson				

4. How did the United States emerge as a world power by 1918?

Using the map below, mark the regions in which the United States was active from 1877 through World War I. You may want to use a few different colors to show areas that became directly controlled by the United States, such as Cuba and the Philippines following the 1898 war with Spain; areas that saw American military intervention; and areas that were affected by American economic and cultural influences. Note dates as well. Visualizing the increase in foreign involvement on the map will help you formulate your response to this question about U.S. status as a "world power."

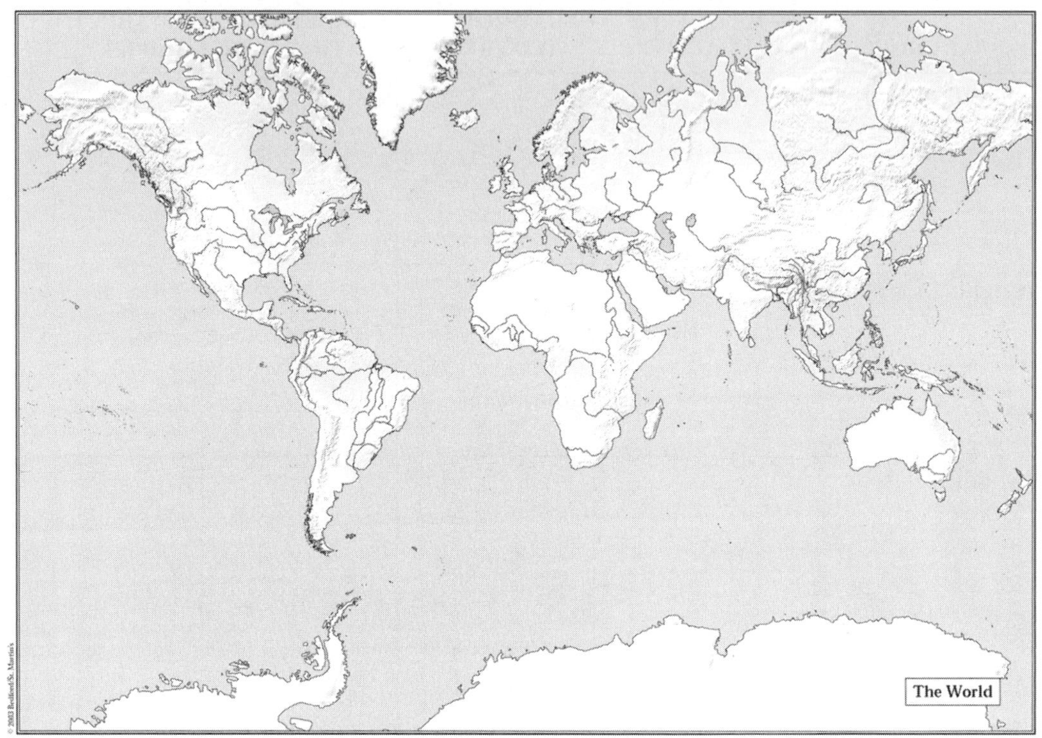

5. What tensions between the old and new existed in the 1920s?

Many historians see the 1920s as the culmination of modernizing trends that had begun to affect American life for decades: industrialization, urbanization, changing social norms, and a diversifying population, to name a few. In reaction, many Americans sought refuge in traditional ideas and attitudes. Below are listed some momentous events and trends from the 1920s. Use the chart to review the forces for tradition and modernity at play in each event and trend, and how they clashed during this decade.

EVENT/TREND	OLD/TRADITIONAL FORCES	NEW/MODERN FORCES
The Sacco/Vanzetti Trial		
The Scopes Trial		
Lindbergh's Flight		
Women's Roles		
Cars, Radios, and Other Technology		
Immigration Restriction Laws		
Harlem Renaissance		
Corporate Welfare		
Prohibition		

Practice Questions

The following sections allow you to test your knowledge of Part 5. The Directions are verbatim instructions from the College Board's AP Exam; the Hints offer strategies for tackling each type of AP question. Answers to all of the Part 5 practice questions follow.

Multiple-Choice Questions

Directions: Each of the questions or incomplete statements below is followed by five suggested answers or completions. Select the one that is best in each case.

Hints:

- Read each question carefully, looking out for negative words such as EXCEPT, NOT, and FALSE.
- Read all possible answers and cross out those you feel are incorrect; narrowing down your choices gives you the chance to make an educated guess.
- Be cautious of words indicating absolutes, like *most, least, all,* and *none.*
- Connect the specific information of the question to broader trends and themes.
- In questions that provide you with evidence, assess the information carefully and eliminate answers that go beyond the bounds of the evidence given.

1. Both Andrew Carnegie and Gustavus Swift made use of vertical integration, which is
   (A) the deliberate laying off of permanent employees to cut costs and raise profits
   (B) when a national company is capable of handling all the functions of an industry within its own structure
   (C) when a national company pushes out its competition and controls nearly the entire industry
   (D) a type of business organization where stockholders won the company
   (E) an agreement between business and government in which industries are guaranteed a profit

2. As Northern European immigration to the United States declined at the end of the nineteenth century, which immigrant group dramatically increased?
   (A) North-Central Europeans
   (B) Middle Easterners
   (C) Germans and Irish
   (D) Southern and Eastern Europeans
   (E) Southeast Asians

3. By the early 1900s, cities became a major concern for reformers who feared
   (A) William Jennings Bryan was correct in his assessment of cities in his "Cross of Gold" Speech
   (B) that city life engendered the loss of republican American ideals
   (C) increased homelessness would swell the welfare rolls
   (D) a decrease in immigration would leave the cities bereft of a working class
   (E) not enough commercial entertainment was available for the burgeoning population

4. Modern cities offered all the following amenities EXCEPT
   (A) public transportation
   (B) street lights
   (C) dance halls
   (D) comfortable, modern housing for the working classes
   (E) skyscrapers

5. Social Darwinists believed that
   (A) government should create social services to aid the poor
   (B) human competition is a law of nature and the fittest individuals rise to the top
   (C) evolution should be taught in society's public schools
   (D) private agencies should be responsible for assisting the needy
   (E) religion and politics do not mix

Picture Researh Consultants & Archives.

6. The advertisement above shows the significance of what phenomenon in the late 1800s?
   (A) The importance of proper labeling on food packages
   (B) Businesses creating demand for brand names
   (C) Government intervention to ensure pure food and drugs
   (D) The increased number of Americans who switched from bacon and eggs to cereal for breakfast
   (E) The influence of immigration on advertising

7. In *Plessy v. Ferguson* (1896),
   (A) the Supreme Court upheld the sanctity of contracts
   (B) state laws were declared inferior to national laws
   (C) discrimination and segregation were upheld
   (D) previous court decisions were overturned
   (E) the Supreme Court upheld that a civilian could not be tried in a military court if a civilian court is available

8. New York legislation dealing with safety in factories and wages-and-hour laws for women and children was enacted because of the
   (A) Anthracite Coal Strike
   (B) Danbury Hatters Boycott
   (C) Niagara Movement
   (D) Triangle Shirtwaist fire
   (E) Square Deal

9. As a result of the war with Spain in 1898, the United States gained all of the following EXCEPT
   (A) Guam
   (B) the Philippines
   (C) Puerto Rico
   (D) Hawaii
   (E) the Guantanamo Bay, Cuba, naval base

10. A unilateral declaration that the United States was the "policeman of the western hemisphere" was the
    (A) Roosevelt Corollary to the Monroe Doctrine
    (B) Platt Amendment to the declaration of war with Cuba
    (C) Open Door Policy
    (D) Pan American Policy
    (E) White Man's Burden

11. A lasting legacy of America's participation in World War I was the
    (A) emergence of the modern bureaucratic state
    (B) Sixteenth Amendment
    (C) American participation in the League of Nations
    (D) suspension of antitrust laws
    (E) promotion of further reforms

12. The "Great Migration" refers to
    (A) women moving to the cities to take the jobs vacated by men off to war
    (B) African Americans moving from the South to the North during World War I
    (C) the American Expeditionary Force traveling en masse to Europe to fight
    (D) Mexican Americans leaving farm labor for industrial jobs in southwestern cities
    (E) the massive influx of immigrants before World War I who became part of the war effort

13. The battle in the Senate over the Treaty of Versailles centered around Article X, which was
    (A) a section of the League of Nations' covenant that called for military action
    (B) a plan for reparation payments
    (C) a proposal for the creation of new nations in Europe and the Middle East
    (D) an international army
    (E) a new map of Europe

14. A major impact of advertising and mass media in the 1920s and later was the
    (A) standardization of culture and dissemination of the values of consumerism
    (B) creation of new syndromes and phobias
    (C) reinforcement of production-oriented societal values and the work ethic
    (D) growth of a more organized, more bureaucratic, and more complex economy
    (E) increase of regional differences

15. The fact that a person cannot yell "fire" in a crowded theater because it would pose a "clear and present danger" is an outgrowth of
    (A) the Sedition Act of 1918
    (B) *Munn v. Illinois*
    (C) The Supreme Court's actions against the AAA
    (D) *Plessy v. Ferguson*
    (E) *Schenck v. United States*

Document-Based Question

Directions: The following question requires you to construct a coherent essay that integrates your interpretation of Documents A–G and your knowledge of the period referred to in the question. High scores will be earned only by essays that both cite key pieces of evidence from the documents *and* draw on outside knowledge of the period.

To what extent were the justifications for restricting Chinese immigration to the United States illustrative of attitudes toward the "New Immigrants"?

Background reading: *America's History,* Seventh Edition, Chapters 16–17

Hints:

- With document-based questions, remember to move beyond the specific facts in the documents and seek their more interpretive or analytical aspects. As you read through the documents, underline key passages, jot notes in the margins, and record outside examples that come to mind as you read.
- After reading through the documents, categorize them into sub-sections to generate a paragraph structure for your response. Was the perceived threat to native labor that Chinese immigrants posed explained in social, economic, or racial terms? Does the statistical evidence support such fears?
- Your ultimate focus here should be a comparison of Asian and European immigration trends to the United States to determine whether the fears that led to the Chinese Exclusion Act were justified. Use the evidence to support a credible thesis.
- Keep in mind the volume of essays the exam readers must plow through. Clarity and organization are key.

Document A

Source: Selected Census Data, 1870–1880.

STATE	TOTAL POPULATION	NUMBER OF CHINESE
1870 CENSUS		
Arkansas	484,471	98
California	560,247	49,310
Massachusetts	1,457,351	97
Nebraska	122,993	0
Nevada	42,491	3,152
Oregon	90,923	3,330
Tennessee	1,285,520	0
Texas	818,579	25
U.S. Total	38,155,505	56,186
1880 CENSUS		
Arkansas	805,525	133
California	864,894	75,218
Massachusetts	1,783,085	237
Nebraska	452,402	18
Nevada	62,266	5,419
Oregon	174,768	9,512
Tennessee	1,542,359	25
Texas	1,591,749	136
U.S. Total	49,371,340	93,923

Document B

Source: "Immigration East and West," 1881.

Document C

Source: Chinese Exclusion Act, passed by the U.S. Senate on April 28, 1882.

Whereas, In the opinion of the Government of the United States, the coming of Chinese laborers to this country endangers the good order of certain localities within the territory thereof; therefore

It is enacted, etc., That from and after the expiration of 90 days next after the passage of this act, and until the expiration of 10 years next after the passage of this act, the coming of Chinese laborers to the United States be and the same is hereby suspended; and during such suspension it shall not be lawful for any Chinese laborer to come, or having so come after the expiration of said 90 days, to remain within the United States.

Document D

Source: George D. Kellogg (owner of Choice Mountain Fruit) to P.J. Healy (District Statistician, Knights of Labor), 1886.

Dear Sir:

In reply to Your queries, in their regular order:

I have repeatedly made this proposition, to the public: "When I can have my work done as satisfactorily by white help, at double the expense, as I can get it done by china help, I will discharge every chinaman that I have got." The majority of my work can be done by white help better, and I give them the preference, every time. I have never yet been able to get a white man that could pack my fruit or pick my berries in a satisfactory manner, I expect to hire no more china help than I have now, but keep those I now have to teach new white help on the ranch how to pack and ensure my fruit being packed in a marketable manner, which is an ESSENTIAL IN THE FRUIT BUSINESS.

I pay my chinamen $1.00 per. day, and they board themselves.

I am paying for my white help, to 1, $15. and board, to another, $20. and board to others $50. and they board themselves.

Document E

Source: U.S. Supreme Court, *United States v. Wong Kim Ark,* 1898.

The question presented by the record is whether a child born in the United States, of parents of Chinese descent, who, at the time of his birth, are subjects of the Emperor of China, but have a permanent domicil and residence in the United States, and are there carrying on business, and are not employed in any diplomatic or official capacity under the Emperor of China, becomes at the time of his birth a citizen of the United States, by virtue of the first clause of the Fourteenth Amendment of the Constitution, "All persons born or naturalized in the United States, and subject to the jurisdiction thereof, are citizens of the United States and of the State wherein they reside.". . . And the right of the United States, as exercised by and under those acts, to exclude or expel from the country persons of the Chinese race, born in China, and continuing to be subjects of the Emperor of China, though having acquired a commercial domicil in the United States, has been upheld by this court.

The fact, therefore, that acts of Congress or treaties have not permitted Chinese persons born out of this country to become citizens by naturalization, cannot exclude Chinese persons born in this country from the operation of the broad and clear words of the Constitution. . . . Upon the facts agreed in this case, the American citizenship of Wong Kim Ark acquired by birth within the United States has not been lost or taken away by anything happening since his birth. No doubt he might himself, after coming of age, renounce this citizenship, and become a citizen of the country of his parents, or of any other country; for by our law, as solemnly declared by Congress, "the right of expatriation is a natural and inherent right of all people,". . . "said Wong Kim Ark has not, either by himself or his parents acting for him, ever renounced his allegiance to the United States, and that he has never done or committed any act or thing to exclude him therefrom."

[These facts] were to present for determination the single question . . . whether a child born in the United States, of parents of Chinese descent . . . becomes at the time of his birth a citizen of the United States. For the reasons stated above, this court is of the opinion that the question must be answered in the affirmative.

Document F

Source: The Immigration Act of 1924.

Section 11 (a). The annual quota of any nationality shall be 2 per centum of the number of foreign-born individuals of such nationality resident in continental United States as determined by the United States census of 1890, but the minimum quota of any nationality shall be 100.

Document G

Source: Henry Pratt Fairchild, *The Melting Pot Mistake,* 1926.

It has been repeatedly stated that the consequences of nonassimilation is the destruction of nationality. This is the central truth of the whole problem of immigration, and it cannot be overemphasized. An immigration movement that did not involve nonassimilation might be tolerated, though it might have other evil consequences which would condemn it. But an immigration movement that does involve nonassimilation—like the movement to the United States during the last fifty years at least—is a blow at the very heart of nationality. . . . Any force that tends to impair our capacity for leadership is a menace to mankind and a flagrant violation of the spirit of liberalism.

Unrestricted immigration was such a force. It was slowly, insidiously, irresistibly eating away the very heart of the United States. What was being melted in the great Melting Pot, losing all form and symmetry, all beauty and character, all nobility and usefulness, was the American nationality itself.

Document H

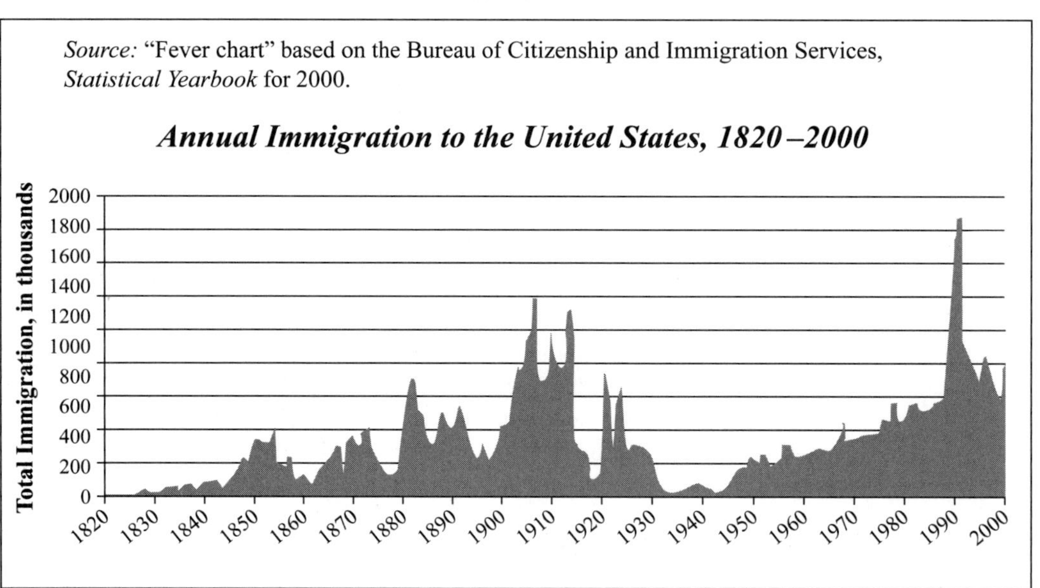

Source: "Fever chart" based on the Bureau of Citizenship and Immigration Services, *Statistical Yearbook* for 2000.

Immigration Statistics, Table 1, p.6, at uscis.gov.

Free-Response Questions

For the following questions, you are advised to spend five minutes planning and thirty minutes writing your answer. Cite relevant historical evidence in support of your generalizations and present your arguments clearly and logically.

Hints:

- ✦ Sketch out a brief outline, recording facts and examples that you remember and organizing them in a sensible way. Each section of the outline should generate a supporting paragraph for your essay.
- ✦ Develop a thesis that takes a clear stand on the question posed. Be sure to state it in your introductory paragraph.
- ✦ Begin each supporting paragraph with a clear topic sentence.
- ✦ Consider transitions between paragraphs.
- ✦ Conclude by restating your thesis in a fresh way, perhaps by making a connection to another moment in American history.
- ✦ Keep in mind the volume of essays the exam readers must plow through. Clarity and organization are key.
- ✦ Question-specific hints follow the questions.

1. **American big business, which grew nearly unhampered in the late nineteenth and early twentieth century, was eventually curbed by the same factors that contributed to its growth. Assess this statement with regard to the following:**

   court decisions
   public opinion
   government action

   Thesis development and organization: assess *means to determine whether or not the statement is plausible. The statement is based on the premise that court decisions, public opinion, and government action all initially helped, but then eventually curbed, big business Because you are given the three areas to consider—court decisions, public opinion, and government action (other than court decisions)—your supporting paragraph structure should be obvious. Be sure to show what helped and what hurt American big business in each category.*

2. **Analyze the extent to which the rise of cities challenged traditional republican ideals.**

   Thesis development and organization: analyze *means you must support a position. Did urbanization threaten Thomas Jefferson's ideal of a nation of citizen farmers? And if so, did the opportunities and changes caused by urbanization make American society more or less democratic? Essentially you should decide whether cities were a force for social good or social decay, and support your analysis with relevant examples. One possible way to organize your paragraphs is to consider political, economic, and social/cultural effects of urbanization. Whether your analysis asserts the positive or negative consequences of cities, these categories could work.*

3. **Contrast the causes and consequences of the United States' involvement in the Spanish-American War of 1898 and World War I.**

   Thesis development and organization: contrast *means that you should highlight distinctions between these two military engagements. What caused the United States to declare war on Spain in 1898, and what were the effects of the conflict? Why did the United States get involved in the European war that broke out in 1914? To what extent were these engagements wars of choice, and what legacies did they leave? After establishing your thesis in an introductory paragraph, you might consider giving each war its own supporting paragraph in which you can highlight the reasons why the United States acted. Then with one more supporting paragraph consider the overall legacy of the two conflicts in terms of the U.S. role on the world stage, and in terms of their domestic impact.*

Answer Key to Part 5 Practice Questions

Multiple-Choice Questions

1. **Answer (B) when a national company is capable of handling all the functions of an industry within its own structure.** When one corporate entity controlled a whole industry—"from raw materials to finished goods"—they could charge what they wished, endangering the mechanisms of the free market. Cattle dealer Gustavus Swift pioneered vertical integration when he developed efficient ways to slaughter and process meat, and then he took it further by developing refrigerated cars for transporting his product to markets around the country. Incorrect response C defines "horizontal integration," another form of market control or monopoly that crowded out competition. John D. Rockefeller is credited with this strategy, absorbing competing firms into what became known as Standard Oil. (*America's History,* Seventh Edition, Chapter 17, pp. 531–533)

2. **Answer (D) southern and Eastern Europeans.** After the 1850s, rural Europeans faced difficulties caused by commercialized agriculture and population growth. While the Irish and Germans caused an earlier, pre–Civil War immigration wave, they were overwhelmingly joined after the 1870s by Italian, Greek, Polish, Czech, Russian, and other immigrants from central and southern Europe. Southeast Asian immigration (made up largely of refugees from American wars there) would soar much later, after the 1965 immigration reform act. (*America's History,* Seventh Edition, Chapter 17, pp. 544–546)

3. **Answer (B) that city life engendered the loss of republican American ideals.** Because reformers' motivations varied, generalizations about them can be tricky. But the process of elimination shows that B is the best answer here: Bryan's speech concerned farmers and the gold standard; welfare rolls were not yet an issue; there was an overabundance of immigrant workers, not a shortage; and reformers did not generally approve of commercial entertainment. (*America's History,* Seventh Edition, Chapter 19, pp. 591–592)

4. **Answer (D) comfortable, modern housing for the working classes.** While various forms of public transportation, street lights (first gas, then electric), dance halls, and skyscrapers all were defining elements of modern cities, housing choices for the working class were grim, dangerous and severely overcrowded. (*America's History,* Seventh Edition, Chapter 19, pp. 596–600)

5. **Answer (B) human competition is a law of nature and the fittest individuals rise to the top.** British philosopher Herbert Spencer and American sociologist William Graham Sumner were proponents of the application of Charles Darwin's theory of evolution to human societies. (*America's History,* Seventh Edition, Chapter 18, p. 579)

6. **Answer (B) Businesses creating demand for brand names.** By looking at the advertisement carefully, it is easy to eliminate answers that refer to ideas not present. What is present is the brand name of the cereal shown, Kellogg's®. (*America's History,* Seventh Edition, Chapter 17, pp. 533–535)

7. **Answer (C) discrimination and segregation were upheld.** The Supreme Court promoted the doctrine of "separate but equal" with this decision; your textbook authors observe that it "protected theoretical rights while ignoring reality." It is one of the most important Supreme Court cases to remember and remained the law of the land until 1954, when the *Brown v. Board of Education* decision outlawed segregation. (*America's History,* Seventh Edition, Chapter 20, p. 635)

8. **Answer (D) Triangle Shirtwaist fire.** It took this terrible 1911 tragedy, in which 146 (mostly young, female) employees died, to break through the barriers to reform in New York state. Machine politicians, led by Tammany Hall's Wagner and Smith, finally backed workplace reform laws. (*America's History,* Seventh Edition, Chapter 19, p. 614)

9. **Answer (D) Hawaii.** Although it also happened in 1898, the annexation of Hawaii was a separate process from the conflict with Spain, from which all of the other places listed were gained. Hawaii had been an independent nation, but American sugar planters had long influenced the island by the time annexation finally became a reality. (*America's History,* Seventh Edition, Chapter 21, p. 656)

10. **Answer (A) Roosevelt Corollary to the Monroe Doctrine.** Theodore Roosevelt was a progressive who applied the ideas of strong central government to foreign policy. The words "unilateral declaration" are a clue that the correct answer was neither a policy nor a treaty—they apply to the Roosevelt Corollary to the Monroe Doctrine, which was Roosevelt's justification for intervening in Caribbean affairs on behalf of U.S. interests. (*America's History,* Seventh Edition, Chapter 21, p. 665)

11. **Answer (A) emergence of the modern bureaucratic state.** The agencies established by President Wilson to mobilize the American people for war—such as the War Industries Board, the War Finance Corporation, and the Food Administration—set the precedent for an activist central government that would lay rather dormant during the 1920s but become renewed after 1932, when President Franklin D. Roosevelt sought strong measures to pull the United States out of its Great Depression. (*America's History,* Seventh Edition, Chapter 21, pp. 672–673)

12. **Answer (B) African Americans moving from the South to the North during World War I.** This marked one of the most significant internal migrations of Americans in history. Although African Americans faced race riots, discrimination, and violence in northern cities, the war created job opportunities that were unavailable in the South. Mexican Americans in the West also moved into cities for wartime jobs in significant numbers. (*America's History,* Seventh Edition, Chapter 21, pp. 674–676)

13. **Answer (A) a section of the League of Nations' covenant that called for military action.** Republicans in Congress objected to the idea that the United States could get dragged into external conflicts again; they invoked President Washington's warning against "entangling alliances" in their justifications for opposing the League. (*America's History,* Seventh Edition, Chapter 21, p. 681)

14. **Answer (A) standardization of culture and dissemination of the values of consumerism.** The 1920s saw the acceleration of the rise of mass American culture particularly through the promotion and availability of consumer products. Advertisements and mail-order catalogs connected Americans across the country to the goods and services that began to be seen as necessities, such as radios, cars, and household appliances. (*America's History,* Seventh Edition, Chapter 22, pp. 703–709)

15. **Answer (E) *Schenck v. the United States.*** Both *Schenck* and the following *Abrams v. United States* (also decided in 1919) upheld restrictions on the First Amendment right of freedom of speech during times of "clear and present danger." The cases reflect the first "Red Scare" that occurred after World War I and included the Palmer Raids, the Sacco and Vanzetti conviction, and the establishment of the ACLU in response to perceived governmental restrictions of constitutional rights. (*America's History,* Seventh Edition, Chapter 21, p. 674)

Document-Based Question

To what extent were the justifications for restricting Chinese immigration to the United States illustrative of attitudes toward the "New Immigrants"?

This question uses Chinese exclusion as a vehicle for understanding the course of immigration policy from about 1870 to 1952. Unlike most textbooks, *America's History,* Seventh Edition, gives equal weight to both European and Asian immigration in Chapter 17, "Immigrants East and West." By reviewing this section you will be well-prepared to write a persuasive response to the document-based question posed.

Focusing on assimilation, you should evaluate the threat Californians, and the nation as a whole, believed Chinese immigration to be through an examination of census data (Document A). Consider the extent to which the threat to native labor was believed to be social, economic, or racial (Documents B, D, and E). This information then can be correlated to overall immigration rates to America (Document H).

How does Kellogg's argument about the hiring of Chinese immigrations (Document D) speak to rationales for Chinese immigration restriction? To what extent can the two acts of Congress (Documents C and F) be seen as racial/cultural exclusion? How does the decision in the Wong Kim Ark case (Document E) reflect the continued concern about the Chinese in America? Do you see any irony in this decision?

What the documents are asking you to consider is how a specific historical phenomenon—Chinese exclusion—fits within a larger historical context (race, immigration policy, and the profound economic and social changes that occurred in the several decades following the Civil War). The more you can integrate your specific knowledge of immigration policy with your general knowledge of changes in American life—the growth and transformation of cities; the connection between westward settlement and Eastern urbanization; the arrival of the "New Immigrants," the rise of industry and government bureaucracy, and the changing role of the United States in the world—the richer your answer will be.

Free-Response Questions

1. **American big business, which grew nearly unhampered in the late nineteenth and early twentieth century, was eventually curbed by the same factors that contributed to its growth. Assess this statement with regard to the following:**

   court decisions
   public opinion
   government action

   Drawing mostly from Chapters 17, 18, and 19, the following evidence should have been considered. Stronger essays will mention positive and negative effects of each factor.

Court Decisions

Helped big business:

- The Pullman Strike—American Railway Union leaders were jailed for contempt after refusing to stop the strike.
- President of the A.R.U., Eugene V. Debs, appeals his contempt decision but fails.
- The E.C. Knight case outcome limited the control government had over monopolies.
- The Wabash Railroad case outcome limited states' rights to control interstate commerce.

Hurt big business:

- The *Munn v. Illinois* case outcome allowed states more control over businesses within the state.
- In the Standard Oil case, the Court decided that Standard Oil held an illegal monopoly on petroleum industry.
- The Court upheld the breakup of the Northern Securities Co.
- *Muller v. Oregon*—upheld Oregon law restricting women to ten-hour workdays.

Public Opinion

Helped big business:

- Much of the public in the late nineteenth century was enamored of the wealthy capitalists.
- Horatio Alger's "rags to riches" stories led people to believe that they too could acquire riches.
- Social Darwinism celebrated capitalists as winners whose success meant that they were the "fittest" in the human race.
- Ward McAllister's list of 500 included industrialists who had replaced much of the landed gentry in the American social elite.
- There was widespread anti-union sentiment among many who believed in rugged individualism.

Hurt big business:

- In the 1890s, Populists began to sway public opinion toward anger at exploitative capitalist practices.
- The Omaha Platform demanded government ownership of railroads.
- Progressives from all social classes began to call for reforms from both the consumer and worker perspectives.
- Muckrackers (Ida Tarbell, Lincoln Steffens, Frank Norris, Upton Sinclair, etc.) published widely read articles and books that exposed some of the most nefarious practices of big business.

Government Action

Helped big business:

- "Laissez-faire" policy existed in name only.
- The governor of Pennsylvania put Homestead under martial law during the steel strike; the leaders were arrested.
- President Cleveland sent in federal troops to put down the Pullman Strike.
- President Hayes sent in federal troops to stop the Railroad Strike of 1877.
- The McKinley Tariff set tariff rate for imports, hurting farmers.
- The government provided railroad subsidies.
- Police action intervened at the Haymarket bombing in Chicago.

Hurt big business:

- The Clayton Antitrust Act strengthened antitrust laws and benefited consumers.
- Teddy Roosevelt's platform of Square Deal legislation allowed government intervention in cases of corporate abuse.
- Granger Laws fixed maximum railroad rates, grain elevators, protected farmers and short-haul shippers.
- The government busted trusts.
- The ICC (Interstate Commerce Commission) regulated railroads.

2. **Analyze the extent to which the rise of cities challenged traditional republican ideals.**

   Successful answers could include some or all of the following examples. For additional review of cities from the 1870s through the 1920s, see Chapters 18 and 21; for more on Progressive reforms in cities, see Chapter 20.

Factors showing cities as the antithesis of Jeffersonian ideals:

- Corruption, prostitution, crime
- Nickelodeons and vaudeville as destroyers of traditional American values
- Negative impact of "new immigrants"
- Poor living conditions
- Loss of individual autonomy

- Billy Sunday
- Stephen Crane's *Maggie: Girl of the Streets*
- Theodore Dreiser's *Sister Carrie* and *An American Tragedy*
- The New Woman
- Political machines

Factors showing cities as strongholds of republican ideals:

- Frederick Law Olmsted's parks
- Museums
- Opera houses, theaters, symphonies
- Libraries
- Newspapers
- Gathering places for people, ideas, movements (labor strikes, Progressivism)
- Economic opportunities for business owners and workers
- Progressive triumphs in city politics, workplace and living conditions, settlement houses, consumer protections

3. **Contrast the causes and consequences of the United States' involvement in the Spanish-American War of 1898 and World War I.**

To review, see Chapter 20. Successful answers will include some or all of the following examples:

Causes of the Spanish-American War:

- Americans had long looked hungrily at Cuba's sugar plantations.
- The "yellow press" of the 1890s helped whip up war fever against Spain.
- The explosion in Havana Harbor of the *U.S.S. Maine* (later determined to be an accident) bolstered war fever.
- European imperialism led some Americans to argue for an increase of American power overseas, e.g., Mahan's 1890 *The Influence of Sea Power upon History.*

Consequences of the Spanish-American War:

- The United States took control of the Philippines in addition to Cuba and inherited an insurgent revolution against Filipino nationalists that cost thousands of American and Filipino lives.
- A heated debate about the appropriateness of an American empire divided Americans.
- The United States bore new responsibilities as an emerging global power.
- President McKinley enjoyed a surge of popularity as Americans perceived their victory in a "splendid little war."
- Theodore Roosevelt, under-secretary to the Navy before the war, rose to national prominence during the conflict.

Causes of U.S. involvement in World War I:

- Most Americans did not want their country to get involved in a European conflict.
- German affronts to American neutrality, such as the sinking of the *Lusitania,* began to shift public opinion, as did the Zimmerman telegram incident.
- President Woodrow Wilson, who campaigned for reelection in 1916 on the message that "He Kept Us Out of War," finally asked for a declaration of war in 1917.
- In eighteen months the United States was able to mobilize its military and economy to help the British and French defeat the Germans and Ottomans.

Consequences of U.S. involvement in World War I:

- Although their victory was swift, most Americans retreated to an isolationist stance in the years following the war.
- Wilson's Fourteen Points advocated a new world order that followed democratic ideals.
- American rejection of the Treaty of Versailles (1918) meant that Wilson's vision would be deferred.
- The massive mobilization effort, which included the Committee on Public Information to shape public opinion, led to a suppression of dissent and free expression.

PART 6
The Modern State and the Age of Liberalism, 1929–1973

This part covers the following chapters in Henretta et al., *America's History,* Seventh Edition:

Chapter 23	The Great Depression and the New Deal, 1929–1939
Chapter 24	The World at War, 1937–1945
Chapter 25	Cold War America, 1945–1963
Chapter 26	Triumph of the Middle Class, 1945–1963
Chapter 27	Walking into Freedom Land: The Civil Rights Movement, 1941–1973
Chapter 28	Uncivil Wars: Liberal Crisis and Conservative Rebirth, 1964–1972

Essential Questions

After studying the chapters in Part 6, you should know how to answer the following questions:

1. What were the dramatic changes and upheavals experienced by the American economy in the 1930s, and how did the federal government respond?
2. How and why did America transform from an isolationist state to a leader of the Allied coalition in World War II?
3. What caused the Cold War to develop between the United States and Soviet Union, and how did it impact the United States domestically? How did it impact the world?
4. What were some significant characteristics of American life and culture during the early years of the Cold War?
5. How did the civil rights movement come into existence when it did? What did it accomplish? What did it fail to accomplish?
6. Why did the United States become involved in the Vietnam conflict, and what impact did it have on the "age of liberalism" in American politics?

Resources for Review

In the following pages, you'll find the Thematic Timeline and Essay for Part 6 from *America's History*, exercises to review your knowledge of the period, and AP-style questions that address the time period covered: 15 practice multiple-choice questions, 1 document-based question, and 3 free-response questions. Answers with page references to *America's History* can be found at the end.

Thematic Timeline and Part Essay

The Modern State and the Age of Liberalism, 1929–1973

	ECONOMY	DIPLOMACY	POLITICS	SOCIETY	CULTURE
1932	Great Depression, 1929–1941 WPA aids development Rise of CIO and organized labor	Rise of European fascist powers Spanish Civil War (1936–1939) Japan invades China (1937) Atlantic Charter (1941) U.S. enters World War II	Franklin Roosevelt elected president (1932) First New Deal (1933) Second New Deal (1935) Social welfare liberalism	Bonus Army (1932) Social Security created (1935) Rural electrification Federal Housing Authority (1937)	Documentary impulse in arts WPA assists artists
1945	War spending ends depression Married women enter workforce Bretton Woods system established: World Bank, IMF	Atomic bombing of Japan (1945) Marshall Plan (1947) Containment strategy emerges	Truman's Fair Deal Loyalty-Security Program Taft-Hartley Act (1947) Truman reelected	Imprisonment of Japanese Americans Segregation in armed services Rural blacks and whites migrate to cities for war jobs Early civil rights organizing	Film industry aids war effort Rationing curbs consumer spending

	ECONOMY	DIPLOMACY	POLITICS	SOCIETY	CULTURE
1950	Rise of military-industrial complex Real wages increase Economy based on consumption Government stimulates growth	NATO created (1949) Permanent mobilization: NSC-68 Korean War (1950–1953) U.S. in Iran, Guatemala, Vietnam	Cold War liberalism McCarthyism and Red Scare Eisenhower's liberal Repub-licanism	Treaty of Detroit (1950) *Brown v. Board of Education* (1954) Montgomery Bus Boycott (1955)	Growth of suburbia and Sunbelt Baby boom Jazz, Bebop, the Beats Youth culture develops
1960	Economic boom Government spending on Vietnam and Great Society	Cuban missile crisis (1962) Vietnam War escalates (1965) Tet offensive (1968); peace talks begin	Kennedy's New Frontier Kennedy assassinated (1963) War on Poverty; Great Society Nixon elected (1968)	March on Washington (1963) Civil Rights legislation (1964, 1965) Student and antiwar activism Black Power	Shopping malls and fast food Baby boomers swell college enrollments Hippie counter-culture
1970	Inflation	Nixon invades Cambodia (1971)	Nixon landslide (1972)	Revival of women's movement Conservative resurgence	Consumer safety movement

"What Rome was to the ancient world," proclaimed the influential journalist Walter Lippmann in 1945, "America is for the world of tomorrow." Lippmann believed that the United States, having emerged from World War II triumphant, was poised to play a leading role in world affairs. What Lippman underestimated were the challenges, global and domestic, confronting the postwar United States. In this Part 6, covering the years 1929–1973, we track how the United States responded to the depression by creating a modern welfare state, enlarged that state to fight a war on three continents, and then entered a prolonged period of international tension and conflict known as the Cold War. These developments were intertwined with the predominance of liberalism in American politics. One might think of an "age of liberalism" in this era, encompassing the social welfare liberalism of the New Deal and the rights liberalism of the 1960s—inspired by the modern civil rights movement—both of which fell under the larger umbrella of Cold War liberalism.

Economy: Era of the Middle Class and Social Welfare In response to the Great Depression, President Franklin Roosevelt's New Deal expanded federal responsibility for the welfare of ordinary citizens, sweeping away much of the laissez-faire individualism that dominated earlier eras. Wartime measures went even further, as the government mobilized the entire economy and tens of millions of citizens to fight the Axis Powers. After the war, prodded by liberal ideas about the good that government can do, legislators from both political parties helped create the largest middle class in the nation's history, through such measures as the GI Bill, subsidies for suburban homeownership, and educational initiatives. More than ever, the American economy was driven by mass consumption and the accompanying process of suburbanization. Poverty, however, affected nearly one-third of Americans in the 1960s. The lack of economic opportunity became a driving force in the civil rights movement and in the Great Society under President Lyndon Johnson.

Diplomacy: The Cold War and Third World Revolution Faced with the rise of fascist powers in Europe and Japan and of isolationist sentiment at home, the Roosevelt administration steered a middle course. In the late 1930s, it began to send aid to its traditional ally Great Britain without committing U.S. military forces. This strategy kept the nation out of the brewing wars in Europe and the Pacific until late 1941. When the United States officially joined World War II, it entered into a "Grand Alliance" with England and the Soviet Union. That alliance proved impossible to sustain after 1945, as the United States and the Soviet Union became competitors to shape postwar Europe, Asia, and the developing world. The resulting Cold War lasted four decades, during which the United States extended an unprecedented political and military reach onto every continent.

Politics: Rise and Fall of the Liberal Consensus The New Deal set the tone for American politics throughout this period. Though Democrats and Republicans differed over key issues—such as the power of the labor movement—there was broad agreement that a modern welfare state was necessary to regulate the economy and provide a basic safety net for the nation's citizens. Anti-communism was another unifying force. Political leaders from both parties sought to contain communism abroad and isolate "subversives" at home. The result was "Cold War liberalism," a centrist politics that rejected radicalisms of both the left and the right. By the late 1960s, however, Cold War liberalism was under attack from the antiwar and civil rights movements on the left and new conservative groups on the right. The liberal coalition fractured and split, and by the 1970s a new conservative age had dawned.

Society: Social Movements and the Rights Revolution A defining characteristic of the "age of liberalism" was the growth of the American middle class. Rising wages, increasing access to higher education, and the availability of suburban home ownership raised living standards and allowed more Americans than ever to afford consumer goods. Suburbanization transformed the nation's cities, and the Sunbelt led the nation in population growth. But the new prosperity had mixed results. Cities declined, and new racial and ethnic ghettoes formed. These conditions, alongside continued southern segregation, helped to fuel the civil rights movement, a decades-long effort to ensure equal opportunity for African Americans. Adopting the civil rights model, women, Mexican Americans and other Latino groups, Native Americans, and gays and lesbians helped spawn a "rights" revolution.

Culture: Consumer Culture and Its Critics Two powerful forces shaped American culture in this era: the advent of television and the youth-centered baby boom. By the mid-1950s, nearly every household in the country had a television. Americans increasingly experienced defining events—the Cuban Missile Crisis, the assassination of President Kennedy, and the Vietnam War, for instance—through television. Through this new medium, the advertising industry attained unprecedented power to create consumer desire and shape purchasing habits. Meanwhile, baby boom children embraced new musical forms (rock 'n' roll, rhythm and blues, and the folk revival, especially), experimented with countercultural sexual values, and forged a "youth culture" that remains influential to this day.

Essential Questions Review Exercises

Using the guidelines and graphic organizers that follow, gather evidence that helps you review concepts and themes from the period 1929 to 1973. Consult *America's History*, Seventh Edition, as well as any relevant materials your teacher has provided to review the information.

1. **What were the dramatic changes and upheavals experienced by the American economy in the 1930s and how did the federal government respond?**

   The causes of the Great Depression are still being discussed, analyzed, and disagreed upon by historians and economists today. But most generally agree that the three main causes were overproduction, under-consumption, and bank failure—three interrelated trends that caused a downward spiral. While emphasizing such causes arguably overlooks signs of weakness in the economy of the 1920s—such as the plight of farmers, and growing inequality between the very rich and the rest of the country—it is a helpful way to review this material. Use the chart below to note examples of the economic crisis that began in earnest in 1929 and consumed the presidencies of Herbert Hoover and Franklin D. Roosevelt. Then note how the government addressed each cause.

CAUSES OF THE GREAT DEPRESSION		
Overproduction *(List some commodities produced in quantities too large for the demand.)*	**Under-Consumption** *(List products Americans could no longer afford to purchase.)*	**Bank Failure** *(List reasons why they failed.)*
GOVERNMENT RESPONSES		

2. How and why did America transform from an isolationist state to a leader of the Allied coalition in World War II?

As you consider the events and decisions that led up to the bombing of Pearl Harbor on December 7, 1941, and subsequent U.S. entry into World War II, use the map of the world below to record the key events and battles of the war on both the European and Pacific fronts. Use the maps in Chapter 24 for guidance. You can also use this map to record other events of the war, including Japanese internment and industrial mobilization within U.S. borders. Considering this information visually should make clear the extent of U.S. involvement on the world stage during this period.

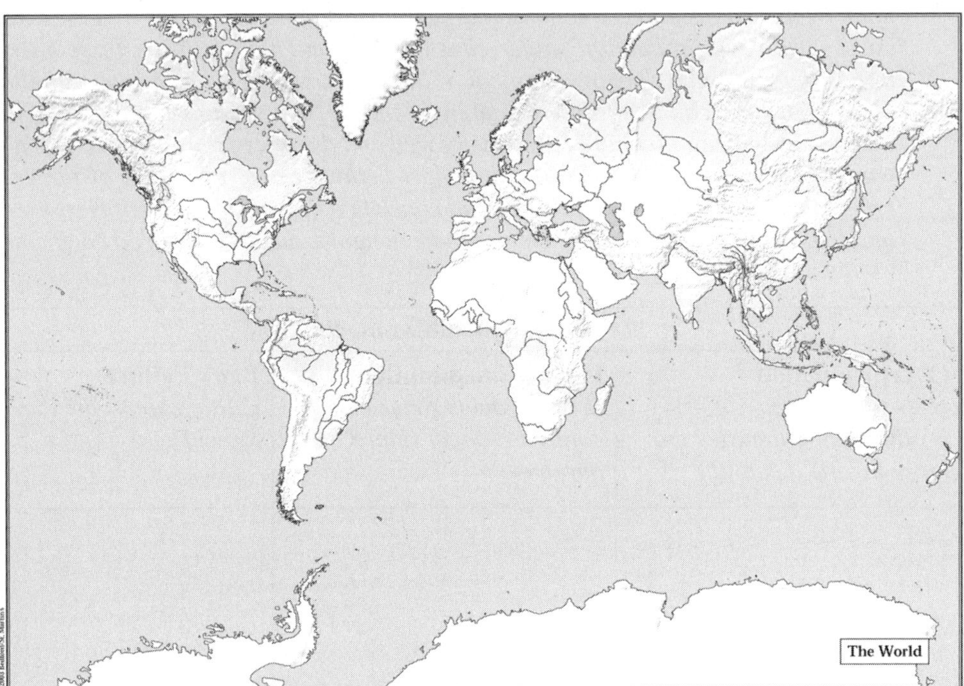

3. What caused the Cold War to develop between the United States and Soviet Union, and how did it impact the United States domestically? How did it impact the world?

Using the chart below, review the key Cold War events of each period listed, and consider the impact those events had on the United States and the world.

COLD WAR STAGE	KEY EVENTS	DOMESTIC IMPACT	GLOBAL IMPACT
1941–1945: WWII and Seeds of Discord			
1945–1954: Calculations, Nuclear Fears, Suspicion			
1955–1973: Crises and Aversions			

4. What were some significant characteristics of American life and culture during the early years of the Cold War?

Chapter 26 provides an overview of how Cold War fears helped to fuel social conservatism and conformity even as technology developed and young people rejected the old expectations (not to mention the civil rights and social movements covered in Chapter 27). Using the three categories below, record some reasons why Americans were concerned or anxious, in what ways they chose to conform in response to those anxieties, and what consumer products helped to facilitate the continued rise of mass American culture during the 1950s.

CONCERNS	CONFORMITY	CONSUMERISM

5. How did the civil rights movement come into existence when it did? What did it accomplish? What did it fail to accomplish?

The civil rights era was arguably the most significant grassroots movement in American history and was an era of tremendous change in American society. Historians like to talk about "top/down" and "bottom/up" change; for example, in the Progressive Era, change came both from the top—Presidents Teddy Roosevelt and Woodrow Wilson—and from the bottom—reformers and activists from labor union members to settlement house workers and countless others. Considering the series of events outlined in Chapter 27, consider the changes that came both from ordinary Americans from all walks of life as well as those from the highest levels of power in the years 1941 to 1973. It may be helpful to consider legal, social, and economic changes as you consider the last part of this question.

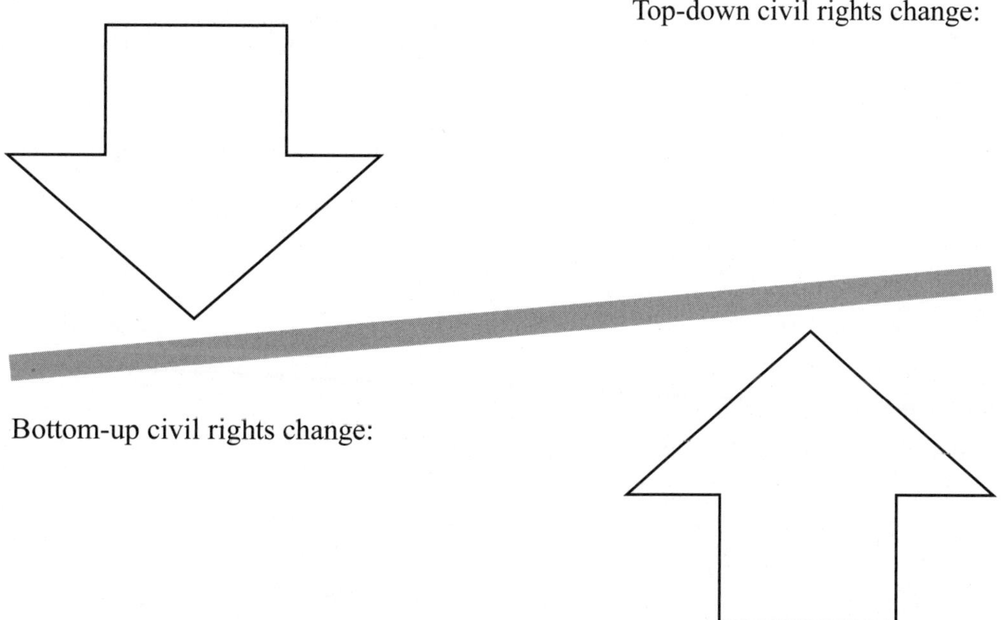

6. **Why did the United States become involved in the Vietnam conflict, and what impact did it have on the "age of liberalism" in American politics?**

   During the Cold War, American policymakers sought to counter the threat of Communist world domination by opposing Communist movements in places like Korea, Vietnam, and Latin America. American involvement in Vietnam must be understood in this Cold War context. Use the timeline below to review the causes, significant events, and effects of the long, disastrous conflict.

THE AMERICAN WAR IN VIETNAM, 1954–1975			
1954–1964 Causes	**1964–1967** Key Events Surrounding American Entry	**1968–1974** Key Events Causing the Tide to Turn	**1975** Aftermath/Effects

Practice Questions

The following sections allow you to test your knowledge of Part 6. The Directions are verbatim instructions from the College Board's AP Exam; the Hints offer strategies for tackling each type of AP question. Answers to all of the Part 6 practice questions follow.

Multiple-Choice Questions

Directions: Each of the questions or incomplete statements below is followed by five suggested answers or completions. Select the one that is best in each case.

Hints:

- Read each question carefully, looking out for negative words such as EXCEPT, NOT, and FALSE.
- Read all possible answers and cross out those you feel are incorrect; narrowing down your choices gives you the chance to make an educated guess.
- Be cautious of words indicating absolutes, like *most, least, all,* and *none.*
- Connect the specific information of the question to broader trends and themes.
- In questions that provide you with evidence, assess the information carefully and eliminate answers that go beyond the bounds of the evidence given.

1. All of the following were causes of the Great Depression EXCEPT
   (A) stock market speculation
   (B) overproduction and under-consumption
   (C) sick industries and agricultural distress
   (D) government's excessive spending
   (E) unequal distribution of wealth

2. Senator Huey Long from Louisiana was one of Roosevelt's largest threats with his
   (A) call for the government to provide more jobs
   (B) Share Our Wealth Society
   (C) insistence that Roosevelt's New Deal was communistic
   (D) huge following in the northeast
   (E) ability to motivate the masses to right

3. Roosevelt heeded economist John Maynard Keynes's advice on
   (A) balancing the budget
   (B) creating the Good Neighbor Policy
   (C) proposing the NLRB
   (D) improving the Federal Reserve
   (E) deficit spending

4. Hoover was hated during the depression, partially because of the public perception that he
   (A) was unqualified to be president
   (B) did nothing to alleviate the depression
   (C) refused to give the federal government a role in stabilizing agriculture
   (D) led the nation deeply into debt
   (E) allowed Communists to gain influence in the nation

5. The Wilsonian principles of freedom of the seas, national self-determination, and collective security were reiterated in
   (A) the Atlantic Charter
   (B) the Munich Pact
   (C) *Mein Kampf*
   (D) the Yalta Conference
   (E) the Manhattan Project

6. Roosevelt's decision to recognize the Soviet Union in 1933 was influenced by
   (A) the danger of a Russian-French alliance
   (B) the rise of militarism in Germany, Italy, and Japan
   (C) a need to buy Russian wheat
   (D) the Japanese bombing of Pearl Harbor
   (E) the fact that Americans were more comfortable with the Soviet Union after it was no longer communist

Gaslight Advertising Archives, Inc.

7. The advertisement on the preceding page represents which of the following?
   (A) WACS (Women's Army Corps)
   (B) Rosie the Riveter
   (C) Frances Perkins
   (D) WAVES (Women Accepted for Voluntary Service)
   (E) Marine Corps Women's Reserves

8. *Korematsu v. United States* legitimized the
   (A) elements of the Root-Takahira Agreement
   (B) discrimination of Japanese students in schools
   (C) forced internment of Americans of Japanese descent into relocation camps
   (D) use of Americans of Japanese descent in the armed forces
   (E) deportation of Japanese aliens

9. To forestall economic difficulties, which could foster the rise of communism throughout Europe, the United States gave nearly $13 billion to a European recovery program nicknamed the
   (A) Berlin Airlift
   (B) Marshall Plan
   (C) Truman Doctrine
   (D) NATO Alliance
   (E) Eisenhower Doctrine

10. An unexpected result of building the Eisenhower interstate highway system was that it
    (A) precipitated the decay of American cities
    (B) revealed and exaggerated regional differences
    (C) hurt the petroleum industry as Americans traveled less by air and rail
    (D) created a problem in the real estate industry
    (E) hurt the construction trade

11. What attracted many industries to the South and West after World War II?
    (A) An unorganized labor force
    (B) Low taxes
    (C) Inexpensive land
    (D) The invention of air conditioning
    (E) All of the above

12. A result of Rosa Parks's arrest was
    (A) *Plessy v. Ferguson*
    (B) the Montgomery bus boycott
    (C) *Brown v. Board* of Education
    (D) Eisenhower's intervention in Little Rock, Arkansas
    (E) the creation of the Black Panthers

13. When Eisenhower said, "We must never let the weight of this combination endanger our liberties or democratic processes," he was referring to the
    (A) Sino-Soviet alliance
    (B) military-industrial complex
    (C) Axis powers
    (D) Warsaw Pact
    (E) nonaligned nations in the United Nations

14. The Nixon White House authorized
    (A) illegal surveillance on private citizens
    (B) wiretaps on private phones without warrants
    (C) the cover-up of the Watergate break-in
    (D) the IRS to harass the administration's opponents
    (E) all of the above

15. Which of the following was NOT a legacy of the Vietnam War?
    (A) Tremendous inflation
    (B) Deep distrust of government
    (C) The British invasion
    (D) Shattering of the liberal consensus
    (E) A slowing of domestic reform efforts

Document-Based Question

Directions: The following question requires you to construct a coherent essay that integrates your interpretation of Documents A–H and your knowledge of the period referred to in the question. High scores are earned only by essays that both cite key pieces of evidence from the documents *and* draw on outside knowledge of the period.

How effective were Franklin D. Roosevelt and the New Deal in addressing the problems of the Great Depression?

Use the documents and your knowledge of the era to construct your response.

Background Reading: *America's History*, Seventh Edition, Chapter 23.

Hints:

- With document-based questions, remember to move beyond focusing on the specific facts in the documents and seek their more interpretive or analytical aspects. As you read through the documents, underline key passages, jot notes in the margins, and record outside examples that come to mind as you read.
- After reading through the documents, categorize them into sub-sections to generate a paragraph structure for your response. Considering the economic successes, economic failures, opposition to the New Deal, and the New Deal's impact on the government is one way to sort through the provided evidence.
- Your ultimate focus here should be an assessment of the impact of the New Deal. In what ways did its policies succeed, and in what ways did it fail? Use the evidence to support a credible thesis.
- Keep in mind the volume of essays the exam readers must plow through. Clarity and organization are key.

Document A

Source: Rexford G. Tugwell, "Design for Government," 1933.

The success of the new spirit demanded a restoration of power to the Executive. The executive branch of the Government is not a piece of mechanism, it is a body of men. If the new program is to succeed, those men must be wise, able, ingenious and honest. The shift to a new design for government would be a total failure if they were otherwise.

President Roosevelt is establishing, at this most critical period, an enduring pattern of administrative conduct. A lesser man, a self-aggrandizing, humorless one, a person less gifted with administrative talent and less eagerly hungry for wisdom, a dogmatizer without the experimental attitude, would merely have aroused false hopes which his accomplishments would have destroyed.

Document B

Source: Lorena Hickok, Report on Arizona to Harry L. Hopkins, 1934.

Phoenix, Arizona, May 4, 1934

Dear Mr. Hopkins:

In the office of the [Federal Emergency Relief] administrator, I sat talking for an hour with half a dozen white collar clients. . . . We went over their budgets, to see if they could possibly get along on that $21 maximum.

The former businessman, who told me that, when the depression hit, he was worth $60,000—and other people told me he was telling the truth—had only three in his family, his wife, himself, and a son, who had to leave college, but who has been unable to get steady work of any kind. He is paying $15 a month rent, having recently moved out of a $25 apartment. That leaves $6 a month for food for the three of them.

Document C

Source: Mary Ross, *Why Social Security?* 1936.

The Social Security Act establishes a system of federal old-age benefits which will provide monthly payments, in 1942 and after, to many workers when they reach the age of sixty-five. The amount of a man's benefit depends on the wages he has received in his working years, after 1936, as defined in the act. . . .

In general, the Social Security Act helps to assure some income to people who cannot earn and to steady the income of millions of wage earners during their working years and their old age.

Document D

Source: Norman Thomas, "What Was the New Deal?" 1936.

To one who faces the American economic and political scene realistically, despite the program's serious theoretical and practical shortcomings, it was as much of an achievement along its own line and within capitalist limits as we could reasonably expect in a country where labor unions and other forces desiring change were so weak. It stands in sharp contrast to the Hoover record. That it is fundamentally a failure, is not primarily its fault as a New Deal of the old capitalist deck; it is the fault of the whole game.

Document E

Source: Odette Keun, "TVA in Foreign Eyes," 1937.

[The Tennessee Valley Authority] elaborated its agricultural program, invented its fertilizer, created its Agricultural Industries Division, founded its educational and training courses. It is for them, plus the small-towner, that it is waging the fight for power against the Utilities. Its goal is to secure for them a more intelligent, dignified, and assured existence, participating in the facilities our contemporary world affords but conserving the happy balance between the Jeffersonian Dream of the self-sufficing agricultural community and mechanical advantages of the Power Age.

Document F

Source: Alfred Hayes/Earl Robinson, "Joe Hill," 1938.

I dreamed I saw Joe Hill last night
Alive as you and me.
Says I, "But Joe you're ten years dead."
"I never died," says he,
"I never died," says he.
"Joe Hill ain't dead," he says to me,
"Joe Hill ain't never died.
Where working men are out on strike
Joe Hill is at their side,
Joe Hill is at their side."

"From San Diego up to Maine
in every mine and mill,
Where workers strike and organize,"
Says he, "You'll find Joe Hill,"
Says he, "You'll find Joe Hill."

Document G

Source: Dorothea Lange, *Tractored Out, Childress County, Texas,* 1938.

Library of Congress, Prints & Photographs Division, FSA/OWI Collection.

Document H

Source: Robert A. Taft, "New Problems of Government," Speech to the Institute of Public Affairs, University of Virginia, 1939.

The New Deal Program has created a vast number of new problems of government. Every activity creates a new problem, and usually an interesting one. Some are well administered; some are hopelessly inefficient; all are experimental and subject to continual change of policy. Little public attention is paid to them. Few men even in Congress have a comprehensive idea of the countless activities of government. A good many more problems have been created than solved.

Free-Response Questions

Directions: For the following questions, you are advised to spend five minutes planning and thirty minutes writing your answer. Cite relevant historical evidence in support of your generalizations and present your arguments clearly and logically.

Hints:

- Sketch out a brief outline, recording facts and examples that you remember and organizing them in a sensible way. Each section of the outline should generate a supporting paragraph for your essay.
- Develop a thesis that takes a clear stand on the question posed. Be sure to state it in your introductory paragraph.
- Begin each supporting paragraph with a clear topic sentence.
- Consider transitions between paragraphs.
- Conclude by restating your thesis in a fresh way, perhaps by making a connection to another moment in American history.
- Keep in mind the volume of essays the exam readers must plow through. Clarity and organization are key.
- Question-specific hints follow the questions.

1. **Analyze the ways in which the Cold War both constrained and assisted the emerging civil rights movement.**

   Thesis development and organization: Unlike the following two "extent" questions, this is an "analyze" question. Your answer must show both sides of the Cold War's impact on the civil rights movement. It is not necessary to choose one over the other and argue your decision; your response should be balanced and explanatory.

2. **To what extent were the 1950s a decade of conformity?**

   Thesis development and organization: By now you have probably noticed that the AP Exam writers love the question "to what extent." They use it so frequently because it provides you with a spectrum of possibilities, like this:

   CONFORMITY ⟵――――――――――――⟶ **DISSENT**

   Somewhere along this arrow is your position. Think about the many influences in American mass culture that generated conformity (television shows, for example); jot them down before you write your response. Then jot down the voices of dissent (the Beat poets, for example). When you look at your two lists, do you have more examples to emphasize conformity in your response, or dissent? Or will you choose to answer by giving both ends of the spectrum equal weight? This tells you how to frame your thesis and response.

3. **Analyze the extent to which the Watergate scandal affected American politics and culture.**

   Thesis development and organization: The Watergate scandal certainly had negative ramifications, and your answer should explain what those ramifications were. But sophisticated answers will also consider the extent to which the American system worked in the face of such a crisis. Nixon's misdeeds, after all, did not bring down the government. Consider how the political system endured despite the crisis as you examine the negative effects Watergate has had on the political process ever since.

Answer Key to Part 6 Practice Questions

Multiple-Choice Questions

1. **Answer (D) government's excessive spending.** This was not a cause of the Great Depression; if anything, the Republican presidents of the 1920s reduced spending. Franklin Roosevelt's adoption of Keynesian economics—which held that governments should go into deficit spending during a downturn—is credited with restarting the economy and restoring confidence. (*America's History*, Seventh Edition, Chapter 23, pp. 720–723; refer to Chapter 22 for a discussion of the causes of the Great Depression.)

2. **Answer (B) Share Our Wealth Society.** FDR faced opponents on both the extreme right and the extreme left; Huey Long was the governor of Louisiana, a populist who wanted to severely tax the wealthy to redistribute property to ordinary Americans. It was an extreme position on the left that threatened FDR's more centrist tendencies, but an assassin's bullet ended Long's rise in 1935. (*America's History*, Seventh Edition, Chapter 23, pp. 730–731)

3. **Answer (E) deficit spending.** As noted above for question 1, Keynesian economic theory argued that extreme economic downturns justified government intervention: to borrow money in order to "prime the pump" and get the economy on stronger footing. This went against fiscal conservatives who insisted that the government ought to balance each budget. (*America's History*, Seventh Edition, Chapter 23, pp. 732–735)

4. **Answer (B) did nothing to alleviate the depression.** Note that the question does not assert that Hoover literally did nothing; he actually took unprecedented, proactive measures to stimulate economic activity. But it was the public's *perception* that he was not doing enough. Hoover has gotten more sympathy from historians in recent years, but as your textbook authors point out, his programs did not meet the unprecedented needs that Americans faced. (*America's History*, Seventh Edition, Chapter 23, pp. 720–721)

5. **Answer (A) the Atlantic Charter.** In August 1941—a few months before the attack at Pearl Harbor would cause U.S. entry into World War II—President Roosevelt met with the British Prime Minister Winston Churchill and came to agreement on many principles for global cooperation. Their joint statement following the meeting became known as the Atlantic Charter, and it provided both ideological weight for the Allied cause and a roadmap for peace in the postwar world. (*America's History*, Seventh Edition, Chapter 24, p. 756)

6. **Answer (B) the rise of militarism in Germany, Italy, and Japan.** This decision is not directly reported in *America's History*, but you can infer the correct answer by eliminating other options. The real threat of the 1930s was the fascist regimes of Hitler and Mussolini. The Red Scare of the post–World War I era had long since subsided, and many Americans joined Communists against the Fascist Franco in Spain (the Spanish Civil War lasted from 1936–1939) in the Popular Front. These conditions made it possible for Roosevelt to formally recognize the Communist Soviet Union in 1933. Relations between the United States and the Soviet Union would deteriorate after World War II was over. (*America's History*, Seventh Edition, Chapter 24, pp. 752–756)

7. **Answer (B) Rosie the Riveter.** The woman's overalls, kerchief, and work gloves show that she is a factory worker: "Rosie the Riveter" is the popular name given to the vast numbers of American women who took jobs to help the war effort. If she had been in a military uniform, perhaps answers A, D, and E would have been plausible; be sure to look for visual clues in this type of question. (*America's History*, Seventh Edition, Chapter 24, pp. 761–762)

8. **Answer (C) forced internment of Americans of Japanese descent into relocation camps.** Japanese American internment during World War II is now viewed as a grave violation of civil liberties, but during the war, the Supreme Court deemed it acceptable "on the basis of 'military necessity' " as your textbook authors point out. The two relevant cases are *Hirabayashi v. United States* (1943) and *Korematsu v. United States* (1944). (*America's History*, Seventh Edition, Chapter 24, pp. 771–773)

9. **Answer (B) Marshall Plan.** While the Berlin Airlift (answer A) was also a relief measure for Europeans, the Marshall Plan was a much larger economic program that facilitated the recovery of western Europe's wrecked nations. Secretary of State George C. Marshall was the proponent of the plan, which was launched in 1947. Answers C and E refer to those presidents' diplomatic approaches during the Cold War, and D is not a recovery program but a formal peacetime alliance among western European nations and the United States. (*America's History*, Seventh Edition, Chapter 25, pp. 790–791)

10. **Answer (A) precipitated the decay of American cities.** Eisenhower's National Interstate and Defense Highways Act was the nation's largest public works effort ever. Its wide, fast lanes slashed through some city neighborhoods, but more importantly, the highways made it easier for American drivers to move out of the cities and commute to work. Answer B is wrong because the highway network connected various regions by car; the petroleum industry boomed as a result of the growing dependence on cars; and the real estate and construction trades enjoyed a boom as suburban sprawl spread. (*America's History*, Seventh Edition, Chapter 26, pp. 829–831)

11. **Answer (E) All of the above.** As your textbook authors note, the Sunbelt became particularly tied to the defense and energy industries of the military-industrial complex. Abundant land for sprawling subdivisions, the ability to air condition large factories, and low taxes made this region attractive. When you have an "all of the above" option and can determine that at least two of the answers are correct, even if you are unsure of the other two, the right answer is likely to be E. (*America's History*, Seventh Edition, Chapter 26, pp. 833–834)

12. **Answer (B) the Montgomery bus boycott.** You should remember that *Plessy v. Ferguson* was decided in 1896 and permitted "separate but equal" facilities; the *Brown* case was decided in 1954 and predated Rosa Park's act of civil disobedience on December 1955. Her calculated act launched the Montgomery, Alabama, bus boycott. The Black Panthers were a radical civil rights group that were formed later, in the 1960s. (*America's History*, Seventh Edition, Chapter 27, pp. 861–862)

13 **Answer (B) military-industrial complex.** Many now see it as ironic that one of America's greatest generals became the president who warned against the Cold War creation of a military-industrial complex that threatened American democracy. Eisenhower used the term in his farewell address in 1961, just as President John F. Kennedy took office. It later became a popular term among protesters of the Vietnam War and others on the left. (*America's History*, Seventh Edition, Chapter 26, pp. 820–822)

14. **Answer (E) all of the above.** Remember that if you can reasonably establish that at least two of the possible answers are true, the answer is "all of the above." The question addresses the Watergate scandal that caused the downfall of Richard Nixon's presidency. Along with the Vietnam War, Watergate is credited with eroding American trust in the government. (*America's History*, Seventh Edition, Chapter 28, pp. 910–911)

15. **Answer (C) The British invasion.** This should be a fairly easy negative question to answer, once you read the possible answers: the British invasion is a cheeky reference to 1960s bands like the Beatles who transformed rock 'n' roll, and it had nothing to

do with the war in Vietnam. (But lead singer John Lennon did become a war protester later on—his 1969 hit with the Plastic Ono Band, "Give Peace a Chance," became an anthem of the peace movement.) All of the other responses, including tremendous inflation, deep distrust of government, the shattering of the liberal consensus, and a slowing of domestic reform efforts, were regrettable effects of American military actions in Vietnam on the United States. (*America's History*, Seventh Edition, Chapter 28, pp. 906–911)

Document-Based Question

How effective were Franklin D. Roosevelt and the New Deal in addressing the problems of the Great Depression?

This question attempts to address the mixed impact of Roosevelt's New Deal policies in alleviating the depression. It is an issue over which historians, economists, politicians, and citizens continue to disagree—particularly in recent years, as policymakers struggle to respond to today's economic challenges. By reviewing Chapter 23 and considering these sources, you will be able to identify and understand the impact of the growth of government on the social and political lives of Americans; the i7mpact of government regulation on the economy; and the impact of the New Deal in ending the depression. You may also have time to consider the growth of the powers of the presidency in the twentieth century.

The authors of *America's History* examine the legacy of the New Deal in Chapter 23. They point out that for those on the left, the New Deal did not go far enough to help ordinary Americans; and for those on the right, "the New Deal state intruded deeply into the personal and financial lives of the citizenry" (p. 746). They conclude that the New Deal's social welfare legislation provided Americans with the economic security that they lacked prior to the Great Depression's crisis; certainly there was a restoration of confidence that arguably strengthened the nation sufficiently so that Americans were prepared for the daunting challenge that faced them in the 1940s: World War II.

So how will you use the given sources to examine this controversial and enduring question? Structure your response by aggregating the sources topically. Document A illustrates the tendency to emphasize the ability of the executive branch of government to deal with problems generated by the depression. Documents C and E reflect the most noteworthy accomplishments of the New Deal—the Social Security Act and the Tennessee Valley Authority. Documents B, D, and G express concern over Roosevelt and the New Deal's shortcomings. The song "Joe Hill" (Document F) reflects two important points: (1) union organizing was not a priority for Roosevelt, and (2) workers' wages did not significantly improve as a result of the Wagner Act.

The most successful responses will discuss the ways in which fiscal reforms like the FDIC and the Social Security System repaired immediate consumption and thus short-term recovery, but they also provided long-term structural reforms in American society. As you analyze this evidence that reveals the criticism Roosevelt's policies faced from both liberals and conservatives, be sure to consider this: as governments around the world sought extreme and often totalitarian solutions to the perceived failure of capitalism that the global Great Depression caused, to what extent can Franklin Roosevelt be credited with saving American-style capitalism? To what extent can he be credited with transforming American politics?

Free-Response Questions

1. **Analyze the ways in which the Cold War both constrained and assisted the emerging civil rights movement.**

   The Cold War constrained the civil rights movement in these ways:

   - Conformity and acceptance of the status quo were stressed. It was assumed that those who challenged the status quo must be Communists.
   - Dissent was distrusted and un-American. Neo-conservatives wanted to show American consensus in the face of communism, therefore dissent was not tolerated.
   - Such a dramatic change in the social fabric would be viewed as radical, and there was a built-in fear of radicalism that went along with the Cold War mentality.
   - Communists were ousted from the NAACP and labor unions, thereby silencing other militant voices.
   - African American Paul Robeson had his passport revoked in 1950 because he was an outspoken critic of the treatment of blacks in the United States. Therefore, allowing him to travel abroad would be contrary to the best interests of the United States.

   The Cold War assisted the civil rights movement in these ways:

   - Civil rights protests and brutal treatment of African Americans at the hands of police were televised and shown throughout the world.
   - American authorities were mistreating African Americans, and that did not fit with America's image of itself, especially in the face of "godless" communism.
   - The Soviets capitalized on the issue, saying that the United States fell far short of realizing its ideals of democracy and equality.

2. **To what extent were the 1950s a decade of conformity?**

   You may argue that the decade was nearly all about conformity and point to:

   - Little tolerance for difference
   - Consumer culture, reinforced by television and the print media, showing the stereotypical middle-class family with the stay-at-home mom in the suburbs
   - Specific rules for the correct way to do everything—dress, entertain, exhibit manners, set a table, display affection, and so on
   - Popular works of literature such as *The Man in the Gray Flannel Suit, The Organization Man, The Status Seekers*

   Successful answers will point out dissent as well:

   - Youth culture
   - Rock 'n' roll as an invitation to race mixing, sexual promiscuity, and juvenile delinquency
   - Gay and lesbian subcultures (although they were considered security risks and sometimes lost their jobs)
   - Beatniks: Jack Kerouac, Allen Ginsberg

   Review Chapter 26 for further insights

3. Analyze the extent to which the Watergate scandal affected American politics and culture.

Successful answers will certainly cite the negative effects:

- Nixon became the first president to resign.
- The Nixon administration was nearly paralyzed after the scandal.
- The American public became disillusioned with government and politics, and they lost confidence in their leaders and respect for public officials.
- It sparked voter cynicism; 1974 had the lowest voter turnout in thirty years.
- It weakened the Republican Party, as Nixon's scandal was likened to Teapot Dome and Crédit Mobilier.

More advanced responses will include the notion that Watergate also demonstrated the strength of American democratic institutions:

- The free press worked; Americans saw the First Amendment in action.
- The two-party system was effective; Democrats in Congress opposed the administration.
- Checks and balances prevailed.
- The concept of government by law was reinforced. No man, not even the president, is above the law.
- Presidential powers were weakened and Congressional powers strengthened.
- Congress passed laws to curtail government abuses of power, such as the Budget Reform Act, the War Powers Act, the Ethics in Government Act, and the Freedom of Information Act.
- The public's esteem for Congress increased.
- The scandal prompted a call for election-campaign reform.

The end of Chapter 28 covers the scandal itself; the first part of Chapter 29 covers the impact of Watergate.

PART 7
Global Capitalism and the End of the American Century, 1973–2011

This part covers the following chapters in Henretta et al., *America's History,* Seventh Edition:

Chapter 29 The Search for Order in an Era of Limits, 1973–1980

Chapter 30 Conservative America Ascendant, 1973–1991

Chapter 31 National Dilemmas in a Global Society, 1989–2011

Essential Questions

After studying the chapters in Part 7, you should know how to answer the following questions:

1. In what ways did the 1970s represent an era of limits for Americans—politically, economically, and socially?
2. How has the role and expectation of the presidency and the federal government changed since 1980?
3. How has the end of the Cold War and the United States' emergence as the world's lone superpower affected American foreign policy? What are the domestic implications for American international leadership?

Resources for Review

In the following pages, you'll find the Thematic Timeline and Essay for Part 7 from *America's History,* exercises to review your knowledge of the period, and AP-style questions that address the time period covered: 15 practice multiple-choice questions, 1 document-based question, and 2 free-response questions. Answers with page references to *America's History* can be found at the end.

Thematic Timeline and Part Essay

Global Capitalism and the End of the American Century, 1973–2011

	POLITICS	DIPLOMACY	ECONOMY	SOCIETY	TECHNOLOGY AND SCIENCE
1973	Arab oil embargo (1973–1974) Inflation surges, while economy stagnates (stagflation) New York City nears bankruptcy (1975) Chrysler bankruptcy averted by federal bailout (1979)	Paris Peace Accords end Vietnam War (1973) Camp David Accords between Egypt and Israel (1978) Iranian Revolution (1979); hostage crisis (1979–1981)	Endangered Species Act (1973) Watergate scandal; Nixon resigns (1974) Jimmy Carter elected president (1976) Tax revolt in California (1978)	*Roe v. Wade* (1973) STOP ERA fights Equal Rights Amendment *Bakke v. University of California* limits affirmative action (1978) Harvey Milk assassinated (1978)	Microsoft founded by Bill Gates and Paul Allen (1975) Apple Computers founded (1976)
1980	National debt begins to rise Revival of military-industrial complex with military buildup Recession (1981–1982) followed by strong growth (1982–1987)	Reagan begins arms buildup Intermediate Nuclear Forces Treaty (1988) Berlin Wall comes down (1989)	New Right helps elect Ronald Reagan president (1980) Reagan tax cut (1981) Reagan reduces government regulation G. H. W. Bush elected president (1988)	Rise in Latino and Asian immigration AIDS epidemic begins (1981) Renewed emphasis on material success and the "rich and famous" *Webster v. Reproductive Health Services* (1989)	Cable News Network (CNN) founded (1980) Apple IIe personal computer introduced (1983) Compact discs and cell phones invented

	POLITICS	DIPLOMACY	ECONOMY	SOCIETY	TECHNOLOGY AND SCIENCE
1990	Recession (1990–1991) Debt reduction and new technology spark economic growth and productivity rise NAFTA ratified (1993)	Persian Gulf War (1990) USSR breaks apart; end of Cold War Al Qaeda bombs World Trade Center (1993) U.S. peacekeeping forces in Bosnia (1995)	Bill Clinton elected (1992) Republican resurgence (1994) Welfare reform (1996) Clinton impeached and acquitted (1998–1999)	Pat Buchanan declares "cultural war" (1992) Battles over homosexuality and abortion Defense of Marriage Act (1998)	Internet gains in popularity Popularization of e-mail Biotech revolution Telecommunications Act deregulates media Google founded (1998)
2000	Bush tax cuts China purchases increasing amounts of U.S. debt Stock market and housing bubbles Great Recession (2007–2010)	Al-Qaeda attacks World Trade Center and Pentagon (2001) U.S. and allies oust Taliban from Afghanistan (2002) U.S. invasion of Iraq (2004) North Korea tests a nuclear weapon; stalemate with Iran over nuclear program	George W. Bush narrowly elected president (2000) USA PATRIOT Act (2002) Barack Obama elected first African American president (2008) Health care reform passed (2010) Tea Party Movement (2009–2010)	More than a dozen states ban gay marriage Baby boomer retirements begin; crisis forecast in Social Security Unemployment exceeds 10 percent	Broadband and wireless access grows iPod introduced (2001) Global warming becomes a scientific consensus

For historians, the recent past can be a challenge to evaluate and assess. Insufficient time has passed for scholars to weigh the significance of events and to determine which developments will have a lasting effect and which are more fleeting. Nevertheless, the period between the early 1970s and our own day has begun to emerge in the minds of historians with some clarity. Scholars generally agree on the era's three most significant developments: the resurgence of political conservatism, the end of the Cold War, and the globalization of communications and the economy. What Henry Luce had named the "American Century"—in his call for the United States to assume global leadership in the decades after World War—came decisively to an end in the last quarter of the twentieth century and the first decade of the twenty-first.

The United States lost its role as the world's dominant economy, faced rising competition from a united Europe and a surging China, and experienced a wide-ranging and divisive internal debate over its own values and priorities. Part 7 remains necessarily a work-in-progress, because events continue to unfold, but through equal parts conflict, struggle, and ingenuity, Americans collectively created a new era in national history after the 1960s.

Politics: Conservative Ascendancy The 1970s constituted a crucial transitional period between the aggressive liberalism of Lyndon Johnson's Great Society and the forthright conservatism of the Reagan era. Under Ronald Reagan, elected president in 1980, the conservative agenda combined reducing the regulatory power of the federal government, shrinking the welfare state created by liberal Democrats during the New Deal and Great Society, and expanding the military. Evangelical Christians and conservative lawmakers challenged abortion rights, feminism, and gay rights; and they brought other social issues into the political arena, setting off controversies that sharply divided the American people and produced what many called a "culture war."

Diplomacy: Ending the Cold War and Rising Conflict in the Middle East Between 1989 and 1991, the four-decade Cold War came to a stunning halt. The Soviet Union and its satellite communist regimes in Eastern Europe collapsed. The result was, in the words of President George H. W. Bush, a "new world order." Without a credible rival, the United States emerged in the 1990s as the lone military "superpower" in the world. In the absence of a clear Cold War enemy, the United States intervened in civil wars, worked to disrupt terrorist activities, and provided humanitarian aid—but on a case-by-case basis, guided more by pragmatism than principle. The foremost region that occupied U.S. attention was the Middle East, where strategic interest in oil supplies remained paramount. Between 1991 and 2011, U.S. armed forces fought three wars in the region—two in Iraq and one in Afghanistan—and became even more deeply embedded in its politics.

Economy: Globalization and Increasing Social Inequality The long post–World War II expansion of the American economy came to an end in the early 1970s. Deindustrialization eliminated much of the nation's manufacturing base. Wages stagnated. Inflation skyrocketed. In the 1980s and 1990s, however, productivity increased, military spending boosted production, and new industries—such as computer technology—emerged. These developments led to renewed economic growth for much of the last two decades of the twentieth century. More and more, though, the economy produced *services* rather than *goods*. Americans increasingly bought products manufactured overseas—in China, Southeast Asia, and Latin America. The end of the Cold War had made possible this global expansion of capitalism, as multinational corporations moved production to low-wage countries.

Society: Increasing Diversity and Culture Wars American society grew increasingly heterogeneous in this era. Immigrants from Latin America, Asia, and Africa contributed to a new racial and national diversity—the impact of changes in immigration law made in 1965. In the wake of the civil rights and women's and gay rights movements, American workplaces and educational institutions grew more diverse. These changes did not come without controversy, however. Some Americans believed that what they considered traditional culture and the family were under assault. Even as it grew more diverse, American society became more economically unequal. Conservative tax policies, deindustrialization, the decline of unions, and globalization all contributed to a widening inequality between the wealthiest Americans and the middle class and poor.

Technology and Science: The Information and Digital Revolutions Americans experienced radical changes in their day-to-day lives because of developments in science and technology. In just over three decades, computers, cell phones, satellite and cable television, and the Internet revolutionized everyday life. These dramatic changes boosted economic productivity in the United States and around the world; they made the globalization of commerce and trade possible. With new technologies came new questions and challenges: Would the Internet facilitate the export of middle-class jobs? Would enhanced surveillance techniques allow the government to monitor the activities of ordinary people? Would cell phones and computers allow terrorist networks to organize complex operations? The new world of technology altered virtually every aspect of American life.

Essential Questions Review Exercises

Using the guidelines and graphic organizers that follow, gather evidence that helps you review concepts and themes from the period of 1973–2011. Consult *America's History,* Seventh Edition, as well as any relevant materials your teacher has provided to review the information.

1. **In what ways did the 1970s represent an era of limits for Americans—politically, economically, and socially?**

   After three decades of growth, the 1970s were a time of reckoning for the American people. Using the pie chart below, note some of the key economic, political, and social events and trends that hemmed in American optimism and opportunity. Be sure to include environmental issues that arose during this decade.

AMERICAN LIMITS in the 1970s

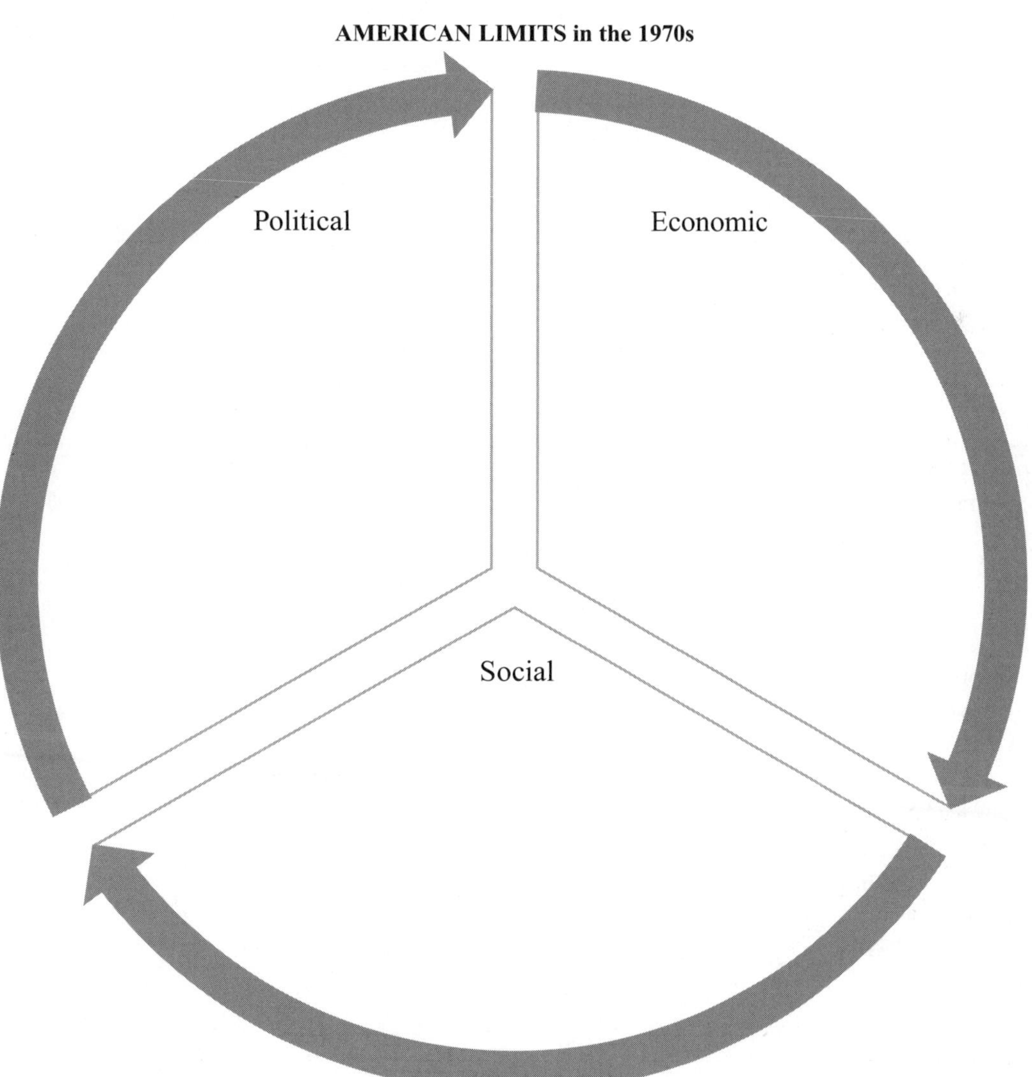

2. How has the role and expectation of the presidency and the federal government changed since 1980?

As Ronald Reagan came into office in the 1980s, he sought to counter the pessimism and angst of the 1970s. With the ignominious end of the Vietnam War, Watergate, stagflation, and profound social changes Americans experienced, by 1980 they were ready for Reagan's optimistic message that it was "morning in America" once again.

One paradox of the Reagan presidency is that his projected personality and presidential leadership became very important to Americans at the same time that he facilitated the trend toward smaller government by cutting taxes and social programs. The public, it seemed, responded positively to both trends—exhibiting both a greater dependence on the president and more profound skepticism of "big government." Democratic and Republican presidents in the decades since have had to negotiate this paradox in very dynamic and dangerous times.

Using the graphic organizer below, consider how each president's leadership style, policies, and approach to the size and scope of the federal government has differed since 1980.

	LEADERSHIP STYLE/ USE OF MEDIA	SIGNATURE POLICY CHANGES	ANALYSIS: HOW DID HIS PRESIDENCY ALTER THE SIZE AND SCOPE OF FEDERAL PROGRAMS?
Ronald Reagan, Republican (1981–1989)			
George H.W. Bush, Republican (1989–1993)			
Bill Clinton, Democrat (1993–2001)			
George W. Bush, Republican (2001–2009)			
Barack Obama, Democrat (2009–present)			

3. How has the end of the Cold War and the United States' emergence as the world's lone superpower affected American foreign policy? What are the domestic implications for American international leadership?

The pressures of the Cold War and the post–Cold War eras have meant an unprecedented increase in both American power and responsibility. Traditionally isolationist, Americans have been rather ambivalent about these powers and responsibilities over the past several decades. On the U.S. map below, indicate with arrows the pressures coming at the country from various directions overseas, as well as the pressures the United States was putting on other nations. How did these pressures affect foreign policy changes? List the domestic effects of being a superpower, from the military-industrial complex, to defense industries, to limited economic resources. The map is intended to serve as a graphical reminder of the U.S. role in the world; you do not need to label geographical locations accurately, but use the map to chart out the influences and the domestic implications that seem most important to you.

North America: Polar Projection

Practice Questions

The following sections allow you to test your knowledge of Part 7. The Directions are verbatim instructions from the College Board's AP Exam; the Hints offer strategies for tackling each type of AP question. Answers to all of the Part 7 practice questions follow.

Multiple-Choice Questions

Directions: Each of the questions or incomplete statements below is followed by five suggested answers or completions. Select the one that is best in each case.

Hints:

- Read each question carefully, looking out for negative words such as EXCEPT, NOT, and FALSE.
- Read all possible answers and cross out those you feel are incorrect; narrowing down your choices gives you the chance to make an educated guess.
- Be cautious of words indicating absolutes, like *most, least, all,* and *none.*
- Connect the specific information of the question to broader trends and themes.
- In questions that provide you with evidence, assess the information carefully and eliminate answers that go beyond the bounds of the evidence given.

1. "For the first time in the history of the world, every human being is now subjected to contact with dangerous chemicals, from the moment of conception until death. In the less than two decades of their use, the synthetic pesticides have been so thoroughly distributed throughout the animate and inanimate world that they occur virtually everywhere."

   The words above most likely come from

   (A) Betty Friedan's *The Feminist Mystique*
   (B) Rachel Carson's *Silent Spring*
   (C) James Watson's *The Double Helix*
   (D) Martin Luther King's *Why We Can't Wait*
   (E) John Kenneth Galbraith's *The Affluent Society*

2. The Equal Rights Amendment (ERA)

   (A) benefited women athletes
   (B) was opposed by Phyllis Schlafly
   (C) came about as a result of *Griswold v. Connecticut*
   (D) called for the government to buy Love Canal residents' homes
   (E) overturned state laws against the sale of contraceptives to married adults

3. President Carter's greatest foreign policy problem, which helped cost him a second term, occurred in regard to

   (A) Panama
   (B) the Soviet Union
   (C) Egypt
   (D) Israel
   (E) Iran

4. *Roe v. Wade* was decided on the basis of
   (A) misuse of federal funds
   (B) discrimination
   (C) the right to privacy
   (D) separation of church and state
   (E) community standards

5. Trends of the 1970s included all of the following EXCEPT
   (A) public cynicism about politicians and government
   (B) the rise of economic inequality
   (C) the increase in the power of the religious right
   (D) a more effective and collaborative legislative branch
   (E) more educational, political, and economic opportunities for women

6. The U.S. economy experienced "stagflation" in the 1970s when
   (A) both wages and consumer prices spiraled upward
   (B) unemployment and inflation both rose dramatically
   (C) the rate of consumer borrowing decreased suddenly
   (D) banks suddenly cut their interest rates
   (E) prices fell and unemployment dropped to historic lows

7. Which of the following is true of the Reagan presidency?
   (A) The gap between rich and poor narrowed.
   (B) The national debt tripled.
   (C) There was no homelessness.
   (D) Federal aid to poor families increased.
   (E) Taxes were raised for the wealthy.

8. Consider the following statement, made by the United States CIA director at the end of the Cold War: "We have slain a large dragon, but we live now in a jungle of poisonous snakes. And in many ways the dragon was easier to keep track of."

   To whom was the director referring when he spoke of the large dragon?
   (A) Communist China
   (B) North Vietnam
   (C) Islamic extremists
   (D) The Soviet Union
   (E) Al Qaeda

9. Sandra Day O'Connor and Ruth Bader Ginsberg were
   (A) the first women appointed to the Supreme Court
   (B) leaders of NOW during the 1980s
   (C) among the first women appointed to presidential cabinet posts
   (D) among those who spoke out publicly against the confirmation of Clarence Thomas to the Supreme Court
   (E) at the forefront of the New Right against the women's movement

10. Which is true of the labor movement in the last two decades of the twentieth century?
    (A) It was strengthened by Reagan-Bush economic policies.
    (B) Two-thirds of union membership consisted of blacks and women.
    (C) The increase in manufacturing jobs strengthened union membership.
    (D) It made great strides in organizing unskilled labor.
    (E) It was hurt by downsizing and foreign competition.

11. The new wave of immigration in the late twentieth century consisted of people from
    (A) Southern and Eastern Europe
    (B) Mexico and Canada
    (C) Latin America and Asia
    (D) Europe and Africa
    (E) Northern Europe and the former Soviet Union

12. NAFTA was created to
    (A) facilitate improved international working conditions
    (B) address Canadian workers' need for cheaper products
    (C) eliminate competition
    (D) offset the economic clout of the European Union
    (E) prevent outsourcing

13. The Bush doctrine
    (A) declared that the United States had the right to attack dangerous states even if there was no imminent threat
    (B) was stated in the USA PATRIOT Act (United and Strengthening America by Providing Appropriate Tools Required to Intercept and Obstruct Terrorism)
    (C) declared a war on government abuse of power and protected American citizenry from needless government intrusion into their private lives
    (D) upheld the treatment of detainees in custody at Guantanamo Bay as in line with international law and the Geneva Convention
    (E) confirmed the president's No Child Left Behind program for schools

14. The election of 2000 is significant historically because
    (A) it was the first time a third-party candidate swayed the results
    (B) it had the highest voter turnout since 1968
    (C) no candidate garnered a plurality of electoral votes
    (D) it was the first time the "Solid South" voted Republican
    (E) the Supreme Court intervened and decided the outcome

AP Photo/Hasan Jamali.

15. The picture above represents
    (A) entrepreneurship
    (B) globalization
    (C) outsourcing
    (D) downsizing
    (E) American multiculturalism

Document-Based Question

Directions: The following question requires you to construct a coherent essay that integrates your interpretation of Documents A–F and your knowledge of the period referred to in the question. High scores are earned only by essays that both cite key pieces of evidence from the documents *and* draw on outside knowledge of the period.

To what extent did the rise of environmental activism reflect an era of diminished expectations?

Use the documents and your knowledge of the era to construct your response.

Background Reading: *America's History,* Seventh Edition, Chapters 29 and 31

Hints:

- With document-based questions, remember to move beyond focusing on the specific facts in the documents and seek their more interpretive or analytical aspects. As you read through the documents, underline key passages, jot notes in the margins, and record outside examples that come to mind as you read.

- This is a "to what extent" question, meaning you are weighing the usefulness of the "diminished expectations" concept of the 1970s to the energy crisis specifically. To put it visually:

  Is the "diminished expectations" concept useful to explain the rise in concerns over environment and energy?

VERY USEFUL ⟵——————————⟶ **NOT USEFUL**

- After reading through the documents, categorize them into sub-sections to generate a paragraph structure for your response.
- Keep in mind the volume of essays the exam readers must plow through. Clarity and organization are key.

Document A

Source: Barry Commoner, "The First Law of Ecology: Everything is Connected to Everything Else," 1971.

In the aquatic ecosystem, each biological step also has a characteristic reaction time, which depends on the metabolic and reproductive rates of the organisms involved. The time to produce a new generation of fish may be some months; of algae, a matter of days . . . The metabolic rates of these organisms—that is the rates at which they use nutrients, consume oxygen, or produce waste—is inversely related to their size . . . If the entire cyclical system is to remain in balance, the over-all rate of turnover must be governed by the slowest step . . . Thus, the rates of the separate processes in the cycle are in a natural state of balance which is maintained only so long as there are no external intrusions on the system. When such an effect originates outside the cycle, it is not controlled by the self-governing cyclical relations and is a threat to the stability of the whole system.

Document B

Source: U.S. Department of Energy.

"At the height of the 1973 energy crisis, drivers of vehicles with odd-numbered plates were allowed to purchase gasoline on odd-numbered days of the month, while drivers with even-numbered were limited to even-numbered days."

U.S. Department of Energy.

Document C

Source: James G. Watt, Interview with *U.S. News and World Report* on Economic Development and the Environment, 1981.

Q. Why do we need more development of federal lands?

A. Because America needs more energy, more timber, more agricultural grazing. We have not had an oil-and-gas lease issued onshore Alaska since the mid-1960s. We have not had a major coal lease issued since the early 1970s. Applications have been pending for oil-and-gas leases in the overthrust belts of Wyoming, Montana and Idaho for 10 years. Our mining industry is in very bad shape. Yet we ask why there's an energy crisis.

Q. Can this country develop energy resources off its coasts without endangering fish and wildlife?

A. The marine scientists and the biologists tell us definitely we can. The history of the environmental protection from drilling on the outer continental shelf has been remarkably good. We have had only two spills of more than 1,000 barrels since 1970. Of course, a Mexican offshore well went out of control in 1979, causing damage to Padre Island, Tex., but I am advised that huge spill would not have happened under drilling procedures and environmental safeguards observed in U.S. waters.

Document D

Source: Exxon Valdiz Oil Spill Trustee Council.

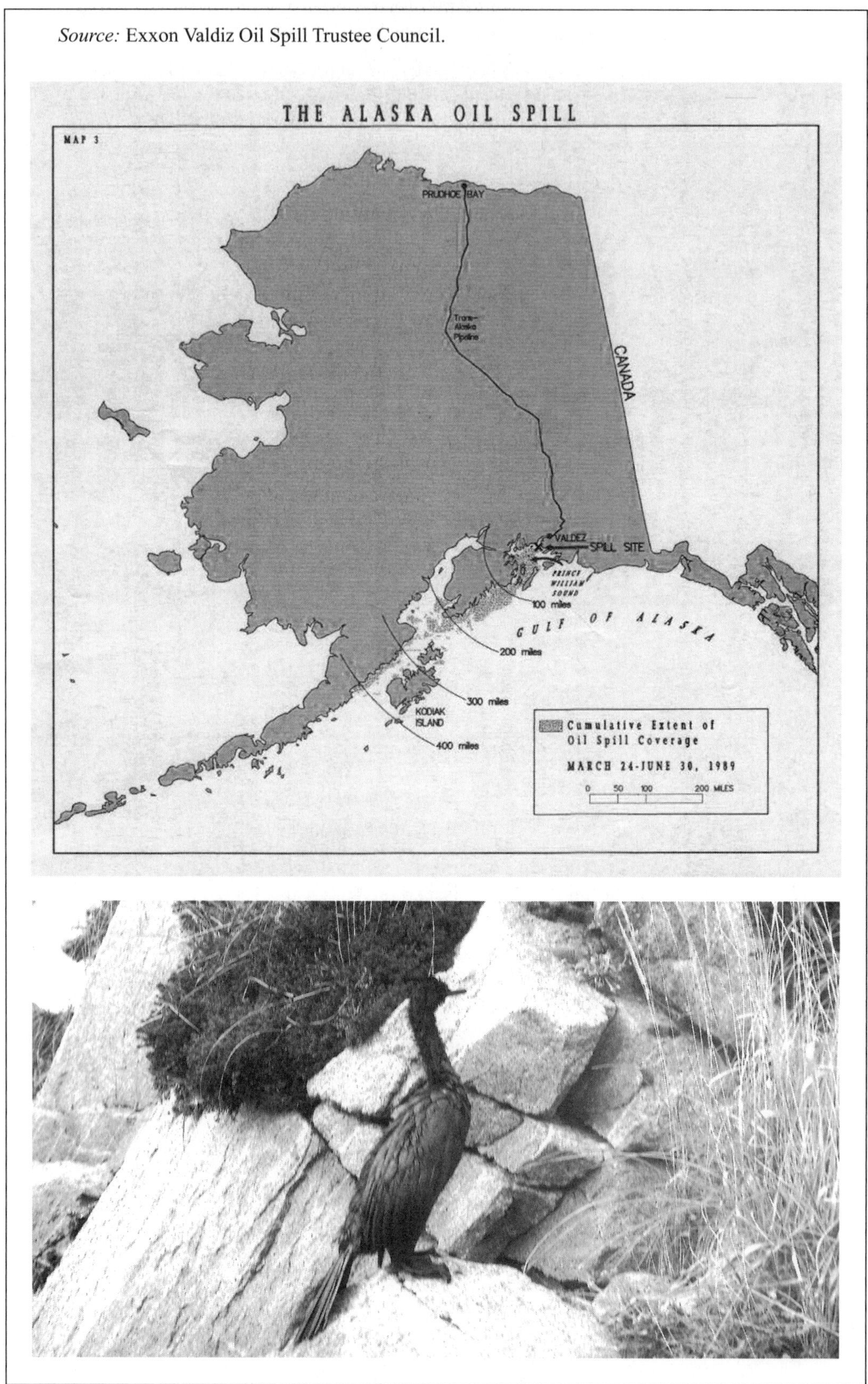

Exxon Valdez Oil Spill Trustee Council.

Document E

Source: U.S. Energy Information Administration.

U.S. Per Capita Use of Energy

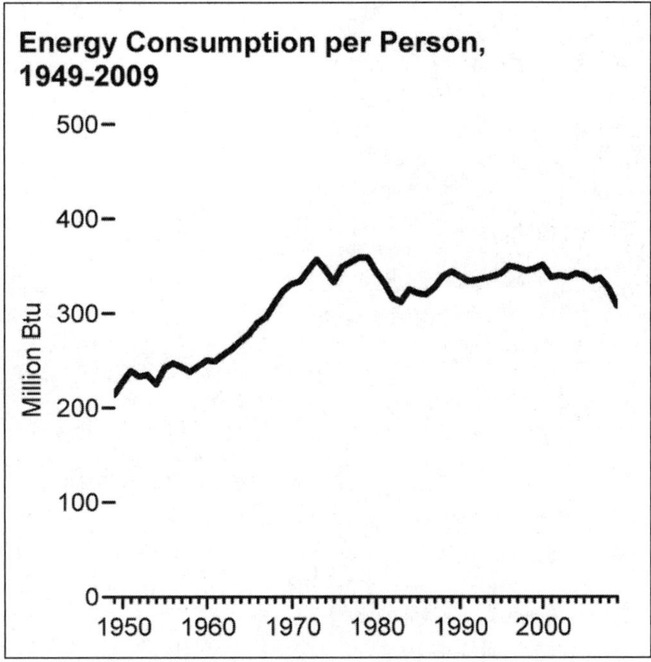

- The per capita use of energy decreased for 2 years immediately following the OPEC embargo.
- In 1978, the per capita use of energy peaked at 365 million BTU—a level not since repeated.
- Although the population rose 5.5 percent from 1978 to 1983, the energy use per person dropped 14 percent.
- The start of the decline in consumption of energy coincided with the onset and aftereffects of a second oil price increase.
- From 1983 to 1997, the energy use per person increased at a steady low rate of 0.8 percent per year.
- Energy use declined in 2001, and again after 2007, due to economic recessions.

U.S. Energy Information Administration.

Document F

Source: Mike Luckovich, *Atlanta Journal-Constitution*, June 15, 2010.

By permission of Mike Luckovich and Creators Syndicate, Inc.

Free-Response Questions

Directions: For the following questions, you are advised to spend five minutes planning and thirty minutes writing your answer. Cite relevant historical evidence in support of your generalizations and present your arguments clearly and logically.

Hints:

- Sketch out a brief outline, recording facts and examples that you remember and organizing them in a sensible way. Each section of the outline should generate a supporting paragraph for your essay.
- Develop a thesis that takes a clear stand on the question posed. Be sure to state it in your introductory paragraph.
- Begin each supporting paragraph with a clear topic sentence.
- Consider transitions between paragraphs.
- Conclude by restating your thesis in a fresh way, perhaps by making a connection to another moment in American history.
- Keep in mind the volume of essays the exam readers must plow through. Clarity and organization are key.
- Question-specific hints follow the questions.

1. **Both Presidents Franklin Roosevelt and George W. Bush faced major attacks on the United States while they were in office. Evaluate the relative effectiveness of each president in handling these attacks.**

   Thesis development and organization: this type of cross-era comparison question is most likely the way in which the AP Exam would address very recent events. You are being asked to compare and contrast President Roosevelt's and President Bush's responses to external threats, but you may also wish to touch on the nature of the two attacks. Supporting paragraphs should address events and decisions before, during, and after Pearl Harbor and the terrorist attacks of September 11, 2001.

2. **Analyze the extent to which the post-1965 immigration dispute was merely a rehash of the early twentieth-century argument on the same issue.**

   Thesis development and organization: in order to answer this question effectively, you must first be clear on what the "immigration dispute" was. At the turn of the twentieth century and in the last few decades, immigration increased dramatically, generating strong reactions from Americans. What did immigrants bring to the United States economy and society, and why did many Americans respond to new immigration with hostility? What patterns can you see in terms of the reasons for opposing immigration? If you can identify three similarities between the two periods, use those to shape supporting paragraphs.

Answer Key to Part 7 Practice Questions

Multiple-Choice Questions

1. **Answer (B) Rachel Carson's *Silent Spring*.** Even if you haven't read any words from Carson's study of the impact of pesticides on the environment, it's important to know that *Silent Spring,* published in 1962, helped to spur the environmental movement by showing in painstaking scientific detail the deleterious affects of the pesticide DDT on the food chain. The others listed are important nonfiction publications that addressed other issues. *(America's History,* Seventh Edition, Chapter 29, p. 921)

2. **Answer (B) was opposed by Phyllis Schlafly.** The ERA had first been proposed in 1923 and would have amended the Constitution to protect women's rights. Congress adopted the amendment in 1972, but progress on the amendment's ratification halted thanks to Schafly's vigorous opposition movement. Answer A refers to the Title IX provision that guaranteed equal access to athletic opportunities for female athletes. Answer C is related to answer E: the *Griswold* case is the one that addressed reproductive rights and laid the groundwork for *Roe v. Wade. (America's History,* Seventh Edition, Chapter 29, pp. 934–937)

3. **Answer (E) Iran.** Although Carter had some notable achievements in foreign policy, the hostage crisis in Iran that followed the fundamentalist revolution there in 1979 was a humiliation. In a pointed gesture, Iranian leaders released the American diplomats the morning after Carter's successor, Ronald Reagan, took office. *(America's History,* Seventh Edition, Chapter 30, pp. 949, 952)

4. **Answer (C) the right to privacy.** Following the 1965 *Griswold v. Connecticut* case, the Supreme Court continued to expand Americans' right to privacy in *Roe v. Wade.* This right is implied in the Constitution but not stated outright. The Court determined that women had the right to choose whether or not to terminate their own pregnancies, but as your textbook authors point out, the issue of abortion has been contested ever since. *(America's History,* Seventh Edition, Chapter 29, p. 935)

5. **Answer (D) a more effective and collaborative legislative branch.** Your textbook authors argue that rules changes passed in an effort to reform government after the Watergate scandal actually laid the groundwork for the partisan rancor and lobbyist influence that seems to cripple the legislative process in contemporary times. All of the other answers—public cynicism about politicians and government, the rise of economic inequality, the increase in the power of the religious right, and more educational, political, and economic opportunities for women—are key hallmarks of the 1970s and '80s. *(America's History,* Seventh Edition, Chapter 29, p. 920–935)

6. **Answer (B) unemployment and inflation both rose dramatically.** For questions like this, it's important to read the answers carefully so that you don't mix up the economic terminology. You should remember that the 1970s were a time of economic restructuring, recession, and hardship for Americans. The unique combination of rising unemployment and the rapid inflation of prices was dubbed "stagflation." *(America's History,* Seventh Edition, Chapter 29, p. 920)

7. **Answer (B) The national debt tripled.** For all of the other possible answers, the exact opposite was true of President Reagan's policies in the 1980s. He lowered taxes on the rich and cut public services to the poor. Despite a professed program of fiscal conservatism, cutting taxes did cause a huge increase in the national debt. *(America's History,* Seventh Edition, Chapter 30, p. 961)

8. **Answer (D) The Soviet Union.** On Reagan's watch, the Soviet Union—crippled by its unsuccessful war in Afghanistan and falling behind market economies for decades—began to crumble. When the Eastern bloc finally fell in the years 1989–1991, the Cold War ended, and the bipolar balance of power between the Americans and Soviets ended. Yet as the quote indicates, the post–Cold War era has had its share of dangerous "snakes." *(America's History,* Seventh Edition, Chapter 30, p. 967)

9. **Answer (A) the first women appointed to the Supreme Court.** Reagan appointed O'Connor, the first female justice, in 1981, and Clinton appointed Ginsburg in 1993. Since then, two other female justices have joined the high court: Sonia Sotomayor and Elena Kagan, both appointed by Barack Obama. *(America's History,* Seventh Edition, Chapter 30, p. 962 on O'Connor; Ginsburg is not mentioned in your textbook, but you should remember her name.)

10. **Answer (E) It was hurt by downsizing and foreign competition.** After a surge of popularity and strength from the 1930s to the 1960s, the economic trends of the 1970s to the present have not been good for America's labor unions. In particular, they lost clout in the industrial sector because many corporations began to downsize their manufacturing plants in the United States and built factories in other countries where labor was much cheaper. *(America's History,* Seventh Edition, Chapter 29, pp. 922–923, Chapter 30, p. 960)

11. **Answer (C) Latin America and Asia.** Thanks to the Immigration and Nationality Act, which your textbook calls "one of the less well-known but most influential pieces of Great Society legislation," the United States has seen a huge influx of immigrations from both Latin America and nations across the Pacific. The wars in Vietnam and Cambodia were also responsible for an influx of refugees from Southeast Asia. *(America's History,* Seventh Edition, Chapter 31, pp. 986–987)

12. **Answer (D) offset the economic clout of the European Union.** Supporters of the North American Free Trade Agreement sought a regional free-trade zone to rival the economic success of the European Union. Although a coalition of Democrats and Republicans supported the measure, its effects on working- and middle-class Americans have been hotly debated since President Clinton signed it in 1993. *(America's History,* Seventh Edition, Chapter 31, p. 981)

13. **Answer (A) declared that the United States had the right to attack dangerous states even if there was no imminent threat.** In the wake of the terrorist attacks on September 11, 2001, President Bush pursued a dramatic new direction in American foreign policy. While international law allows nations to attack other nations only under imminent threat, proponents of the Bush doctrine argued that the United States could act preemptively. *(America's History,* Seventh Edition, Chapter 31, p. 1003)

14. **Answer (E) the Supreme Court intervened and decided the outcome.** Because of faulty ballot design and a number of other electoral problems in Florida, a key swing state, election night 2000 came and went without a winner declared. It was not until December 12 of that year—over a month later—after weeks of attempted recounting of ballots in Florida that the Supreme Court intervened, put an end to the recount, and declared George W. Bush the victor over Al Gore. *(America's History,* Seventh Edition, Chapter 31, p. 1000)

15. **Answer (B) globalization.** The first four answers all address economic trends of the last few decades, some—such as outsourcing and downsizing—possible ramifications of globalization. The most important clues of the photo are the man in Arabic clothing, the words in Arabic, and the McDonald's sign: as your textbook explains, by the 1990s, "'McWorld' had become a popular shorthand term for globalization." *(America's History,* Seventh Edition, Chapter 31, pp. 981–982)

Document-Based Question

To what extent did the rise of environmental activism reflect an era of diminished expectations?

This exercise provides a core of documents that illustrates the larger thematic issue of environmental activism. The question seeks to address how the concern over the environment raised competing, complex objectives. Commoner's concern for the environment (Document A) illustrates the general sense—confirmed by incidents like the Exxon Valdez (Document D), the Santa Barbara oil spills, and Love Canal—of the need for greater conservation and the development of alternative energy sources. Yet the costs of conservation, as illustrated by the comments of Secretary Watt (Document C), and the dependence on private passenger automobiles, as exemplified so dramatically during the energy crisis of 1973 (Document B), also highlight the economic aspects of environmentalism.

However, consider these documents as an extension of the challenging economy of the 1970s. After economic growth in the 1980s and 1990s, in recent years Americans are once again facing economic and environmental limits as they did in the 1970s. Indeed, very recent events—including growing evidence of global warming, and the 2010 Gulf oil spill—have once again brought environmental concerns to the fore.

Free-Response Questions

1. **Both Presidents Franklin Roosevelt and George W. Bush faced major attacks on the United States while they were in office. Evaluate the relative effectiveness of each president in handling these attacks.**

   Things to keep in mind regarding Roosevelt's response to the attack on Pearl Harbor:

   - He had to balance the desire of many to immediately fight only Japan with the need to assist Europe in its efforts against the Nazis.
   - He was involved in decisions regarding the military strategies on both fronts of World War II. How effective were the strategies? It is important to include the ultimate decision to drop the atomic bomb—the August 1945 decision was made by Truman, but FDR was the one who authorized the Manhattan Project.
   - His response involved decisions that limited civil liberties, such as the internment of Japanese Americans.

   Things to keep in mind regarding George W. Bush's response after the terrorist attacks on September 11, 2001:

   - He was involved in the decision to order attacks on the Taliban in Afghanistan and search for Osama Bin Laden.
   - He declared the War in Iraq and the War on Terror. Have these been effective as a response to the 9/11 attacks?

   Important comparisons to make between the two:

   - Compare the Patriot Act's civil-liberties restrictions with FDR's internment of Japanese Americans.
   - Compare Bush's unilateral decision making in Iraq with FDR's negotiations with allies Great Britain and the Soviet Union.

   To review, see Chapter 24 on World War II and Chapter 31 on 9/11 and its aftermath.

2. Analyze the extent to which the post-1965 immigration dispute was merely a rehash of the early twentieth-century argument on the same issue.

Explain the influx of new immigrants from the 1880s–1920s and more recent immigration trends from 1965 to the present. Savvy students will make note of the differences in immigrant populations, while discussing the fears that Americans exhibited during both times.

Some important fears Americans had regarding immigration:

- Xenophobia, or the fear of foreigners
- Loss of jobs and economic instability
- Loss of culture, as immigrant populations tried to retain their own.
- Fear of insurgency from anarchists with southern and eastern European origins, Communists, terrorists

Some ways in which Americans reacted to immigration:

- Push for stricter immigration legislation
- Government legislated exclusion versus inclusion: Chinese Exclusion Act of 1882, Emergency Immigration Act of 1921, and Johnson-Reed Act (1924–1929), versus the Immigration Reform and Control Act (1986) and building a wall to keep out illegal immigrants
- The Immigration Act of 1965, which opened up immigration after decades of restriction following the acts of the 1920s, and changed American demographics dramatically
- The persistence of blaming outsiders when Americans are threatened by worsening economic conditions

SECTION 3
AP-Style Practice Exams

PRACTICE EXAM 1

UNITED STATES HISTORY SECTION I

Multiple-Choice Questions
(Time — 55 minutes)
Number of Questions—80

Directions: Each of the questions or incomplete statements below is followed by five suggested answers or completions. Select the one that is best in each case.

1. English, Spanish, and French colonies in North America were most alike in that they all
   (A) discouraged feudalistic landholding policies
   (B) served as asylums for people fleeing religious persecution
   (C) had elected representative assemblies
   (D) followed mercantilist policies
   (E) were created by trading companies

2. The greatest legislative achievement under the Articles of Confederation was the establishment of
   (A) a bicameral legislature
   (B) a system for orderly settlement of the West
   (C) general postwar prosperity
   (D) long-term sectional harmony
   (E) a termination date for the international slave trade

3. Alexander Hamilton disagreed with Thomas Jefferson's vision for the U.S. economy because
   (A) he esteemed the industrialization of England
   (B) he believed that the best economy included a mix of private and government control
   (C) he thought that wealthy financial interests should benefit from U.S. economic policies
   (D) he knew that swift action was necessary to rid the nation of its outstanding war debts
   (E) all of the above

GO ON TO THE NEXT PAGE.

4. "With malice toward none; with charity for all; with firmness in the right, as God gives us to see the right, let us strive on to finish the work we are in; to bind up the nation's wounds; to care for him who shall have borne the battle, and for his widow, and his orphan—to do all which may achieve and cherish a just and lasting peace, among ourselves, and with all nations."

   The words above were spoken by

   (A) President McKinley at the end of the Spanish-American War
   (B) President Wilson at the end of the First World War
   (C) President Polk following the War with Mexico
   (D) President Lincoln toward the end of the Civil War
   (E) President Lincoln at Gettysburg

5. After the Civil War, most freed slaves found work as

   (A) sharecroppers
   (B) factory workers
   (C) railroad workers
   (D) independent tradesmen
   (E) domestic servants

6. Propaganda created during World War I, like the poster below, was primarily concerned with

   (A) uniting a diverse population against the common enemy
   (B) denigrating French abuses of Belgian civilians
   (C) putting advertising executives to work
   (D) turning American sentiment against the Bolshevik Revolution in Russia
   (E) discouraging women from getting involved in the war effort

The Art Archive/Ellen Tweedy.

GO ON TO THE NEXT PAGE.

7. The 1954 Supreme Court case that ruled racially segregated school systems "inherently unequal" was
   (A) *Dred Scott v. Sanford*
   (B) *Brown v. Board of Education*
   (C) *Plessy v. Ferguson*
   (D) *Bakke v. State of California*
   (E) *Buck v. Bell*

8. All of the following are associated with globalization EXCEPT
   (A) multinational corporations
   (B) nation-state boundaries becoming obsolete
   (C) the fear of pandemic illnesses
   (D) spread of environmental pollution
   (E) income taxes

9. The principal motivation for drafting the Bill of Rights was the desire to
   (A) test the new process of amendment described in the Constitution
   (B) strengthen the power of the federal government
   (C) restore to the states the powers they had enjoyed under the Articles of Confederation
   (D) clarify the federal relationship among the states
   (E) protect rights not specified in the Constitution

TABLE 8.2 Number of Church Congregations by Denomination, 1780 and 1860

Denomination	Number of Congregations 1780	Number of Congregations 1860	Increased roughly by a factor of:
Anglican/Episcopalian	406	2,100	5
Baptist	457	12,150	26
Catholic	50	2,500	50
Congregational	742	2,200	3
Lutheran	240	2,100	9
Methodist	50	20,000	400
Presbyterian	495	6,400	13

10. What caused the occurrence revealed in the table above?
   (A) The decline of parental influence on the lives of their adult children
   (B) The Second Great Awakening
   (C) The rise of sentimentalism
   (D) The Era of Good Feeling
   (E) An economic depression following the War of 1812

GO ON TO THE NEXT PAGE.

11. President Lincoln suspended *habeas corpus* during the Civil War to
    (A) assure that civil liberties would be protected
    (B) demoralize the South
    (C) stop disloyal activities such as protests against the draft
    (D) encourage enlistment in the Union Army for the duration of the war
    (E) make it easier to set a quota for volunteers from the states

12. Which of the following jobs was NOT generally available to women at the end of the nineteenth century?
    (A) Domestic servant
    (B) Telephone operator
    (C) Teacher
    (D) Lawyer
    (E) Factory worker in the textile industry

13. Upton Sinclair's novel *The Jungle* helped bring about
    (A) antitrust legislation
    (B) the Meat Inspection and Pure Food and Drug Acts
    (C) the Mann Act
    (D) a strengthening of the power of urban political machines
    (E) the Panic of 1907

14. Which event did NOT influence U.S. entry into World War I?
    (A) Woodrow Wilson's aggressive foreign policy
    (B) The sinking of the *Lusitania*
    (C) Economic ties with Great Britain
    (D) German U-boat attacks on trans-Atlantic merchant ships
    (E) The Zimmerman telegram

15. Which of the following contributed most to the American victory in the Revolution?
    (A) Support from Amerindians
    (B) The British failure to capture Philadelphia
    (C) French military and financial assistance
    (D) Support from Loyalists
    (E) A major American victory at Bunker Hill

16. *Marbury v. Madison* (1803) is significant for establishing the principle of
    (A) equal access by any citizen to federal courts
    (B) due process of law
    (C) judicial review
    (D) the sanctity of contracts
    (E) the supremacy of the executive over the judicial branch

17. The major cause of death for Civil War soldiers was
    (A) wounds received in formal combat
    (B) poor quality food
    (C) sniper attacks
    (D) riots
    (E) disease and infection

GO ON TO THE NEXT PAGE.

18. "We demand that big business give the people a square deal; in return we must insist that when anyone engaged in big business honestly endeavors to do right he shall himself be given a square deal."

    This quotation summarizes the position held toward big business by which of the following politicians?

    (A) William McKinley
    (B) Eugene V. Debs
    (C) Theodore Roosevelt
    (D) William Jennings Bryan
    (E) Franklin D. Roosevelt

19. The National Origins Act of 1924

    (A) limited immigration to the United States
    (B) funded genealogical research
    (C) encouraged immigration to the United States in large groups
    (D) called for a recording of the populations of ethnic groups in the United States
    (E) sought to combat a resurgent Ku Klux Klan

20. *The Grapes of Wrath* and Okies are most directly associated with

    (A) movies during the depression
    (B) the Dust Bowl
    (C) efforts to end the depression
    (D) the urban workers' crisis
    (E) life in small towns

21. Those who responded most enthusiastically to Betty Friedan's *The Feminine Mystique* were

    (A) African American day workers
    (B) immigrant women
    (C) white, college-educated, middle-class women
    (D) college-educated African American women
    (E) blue-collar women of all ethnic groups

22. "When I looked around the ship too, and saw a large furnace or copper boiling, and a multitude of black people of every description chained together, every one of their countenances expressing dejection and sorrow, I no longer doubted of my fate . . . we continued to undergo more hardships than I can now relate; hardships which are inseparable from this accursed trade."

    This quote describes

    (A) the predicament of a Chesapeake indentured servant
    (B) the middle passage
    (C) the experience of conquered Pequot Indians
    (D) the travails of an unwilling female worker in Lowell
    (E) a black Loyalist during the Revolutionary War

23. In the early 1800s the federal government promoted economic growth through all of the following EXCEPT

    (A) enabling the active circulation of information through the U.S. Postal Service
    (B) protecting inventors' possible profits from their innovations through patent laws
    (C) using foreign tariffs to protect domestic industry from overseas competition
    (D) surveying public lands and opening territories for settlement
    (E) outlawing corporations

GO ON TO THE NEXT PAGE.

24. Each of the following was an example of the grassroots efforts in the civil rights movements EXCEPT
    (A) the decision to desegregate the schools
    (B) the Montgomery bus boycott
    (C) the lunch counter sit-ins
    (D) the freedom rides
    (E) SNCC and CORE voter registration efforts

25. The Bush doctrine is best defined as
    (A) government surveillance of citizens
    (B) the preemptive use of military force
    (C) a justification for torture
    (D) diplomatic cooperation with non-allies
    (E) independent isolationism

26. A result of the First Great Awakening was
    (A) a decline in the importance of higher education
    (B) an increased admiration for the growing business community
    (C) an increase in intolerance
    (D) a consolidation of churches
    (E) the growth of a democratic spirit

27. All of the following led to the Revolutionary War EXCEPT
    (A) virtual representation
    (B) Townshend Acts
    (C) *Common Sense*
    (D) the Treaty of Paris
    (E) Stamp Act

28. "The equal share that every citizen has in the liberty, and the possible share he may have in the government of our country, make it necessary that our ladies should be qualified to a certain degree by a peculiar and suitable education, to concur in instructing their sons in the principles of liberty and government."

    The above quote reflects the ideals of
    (A) second-wave feminism
    (B) the temperance movement
    (C) Progressivism
    (D) Republican motherhood
    (E) the cult of domesticity

29. President Andrew Jackson's main argument for destroying the national bank was that the
    (A) bank had not been successful at stabilizing the currency
    (B) bank was not able to influence credit in a satisfactory manner
    (C) government was forced to play too large a role in managing the bank
    (D) bank was a monopoly that benefited only a few owners, some of whom were foreigners
    (E) bank was powerless to keep inflationary policies of wildcat banks in check

GO ON TO THE NEXT PAGE.

30. During the Civil War, which of the following was a disadvantage for the North in comparison to the South?
    (A) Lincoln's difficulty in finding a general of the caliber of Lee
    (B) Population numbers
    (C) Capacity for industrial output
    (D) Amount of railroad track
    (E) Davis being a more capable president than Lincoln

31. Southerners responded to the end of slavery with
    (A) Black Codes
    (B) the Freedman's Bureau
    (C) an Ordinance of Nullification
    (D) the impeachment of President Andrew Johnson
    (E) the Civil Rights Act of 1866

32. Which of the following was NOT true of the nineteenth-century urban political machine?
    (A) It mediated between constituents and an unfeeling city bureaucracy.
    (B) It acted as a social service agency, providing assistance in times of trouble.
    (C) It kept new immigrants from taking jobs from native-born Americans.
    (D) It was one of the most democratic American institutions.
    (E) It was an integrating force, cutting across lines of race, ethnicity, and class.

33. The Niagara Movement led to
    (A) more public schools
    (B) the NAACP
    (C) the Tuskegee Institute
    (D) the Back-to-Africa Movement
    (E) the expansion of resort cities as tourist destinations

34. Which of the following is correct about the Scopes trial?
    (A) John Scopes was found not guilty.
    (B) The American Civil Liberties Union challenged the constitutionality of the trial.
    (C) William Jennings Bryan was the public defender in the trial.
    (D) Clarence Darrow defended the right to teach evolution in schools.
    (E) Scopes was a scapegoat because of his ethnic background.

35. "So first of all let me assert my firm belief that the only thing we have to fear . . . is fear itself . . . nameless, unreasoning, unjustified terror which paralyzes needed efforts to convert retreat into advance."

    These words were spoken in a moment of national crisis by
    (A) Woodrow Wilson
    (B) Herbert Hoover
    (C) Franklin Roosevelt
    (D) Harry Truman
    (E) Dwight D. Eisenhower

GO ON TO THE NEXT PAGE.

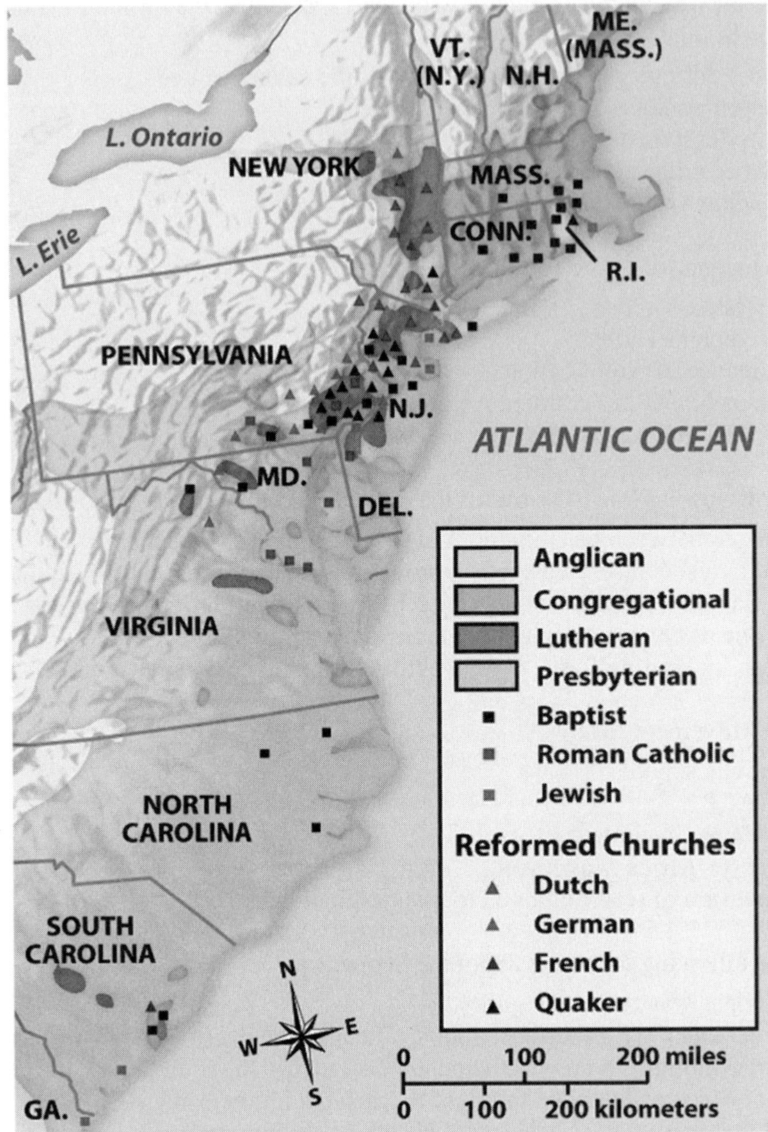

36. According to the map above, the colonies most inclined toward religious toleration were
   (A) the Carolinas and Delaware
   (B) Massachusetts, Connecticut, and New Hampshire
   (C) New York, New Jersey, and Pennsylvania
   (D) Virginia, North Carolina, and Maryland
   (E) North Carolina, Rhode Island, and Massachusetts

37. A result of the Loyalists' exodus during and after the Revolution was that
   (A) the leadership class had to be totally replaced
   (B) merchant entrepreneurs were replaced by property-owning traditionalists
   (C) their land was confiscated and divided among the landless
   (D) Patriot merchants replaced Tories at the top of the economic ladder
   (E) the number of slaves declined dramatically as the Loyalist took their slaves with them

GO ON TO THE NEXT PAGE.

38. The Philadelphia Convention's creation of the most democratic government in the world at the time was ironic because most of the delegates to the convention were
    (A) artisans
    (B) yeoman farmers
    (C) slaveholders
    (D) tenants
    (E) wealthy men

39. In the first quarter of the nineteenth century
    (A) there was a shift in public policy that encouraged business
    (B) western farmers became wealthy
    (C) property rights of farmers were protected from encroaching business ventures
    (D) government stayed out of the daily lives of Americans
    (E) the concept of eminent domain was not yet in existence

40. The slavery discussion at the time of the Missouri Compromise involved
    (A) northern justification for the widespread acceptance of abolitionism
    (B) preserving the existing balance of power between North and South in the Senate
    (C) sectional disagreements but no real talk of abolition
    (D) a basic difference of opinion regarding slavery as a moral evil
    (E) only constitutional arguments for the continuation of slavery

41. Which of the following is a true statement about the Indian Removal Act?
    (A) Some Cherokee Indians promoted it.
    (B) It eliminated the Seminole Indians from Florida.
    (C) It was precipitated by Black Hawk's War.
    (D) Congress passed it despite much public outcry.
    (E) John Marshall upheld the act in *Worcester v. Georgia*.

42. Which of the following is an example of America being a welcoming place for immigrants?
    (A) The Alien and Sedition Acts
    (B) Minstrel shows
    (C) German-language shop signs
    (D) Temperance reformers
    (E) The Whig Party

43. The biggest deterrent to industrialization in the South was
    (A) its increased immigration
    (B) its dependence on slavery
    (C) absence of an entrepreneurial class
    (D) lack of raw materials
    (E) its need for labor

44. "New" immigration patterns in the early twentieth century reflected the growing emigration from
    (A) southern and eastern Europe
    (B) north and central Europe
    (C) the British Isles
    (D) the eastern shores of Asia
    (E) Central and South America

GO ON TO THE NEXT PAGE.

45. Which of the following was true for middle-class families in the late nineteenth century?
    (A) Abortion and dissemination of birth control methods aided in the move toward smaller families.
    (B) Being an unmarried young adult was frowned upon.
    (C) Attitudes toward child rearing changed as children were indulged and remained dependent on their parents longer than they had previously.
    (D) Husbands and wives both worked in the home, thereby strengthening family ties.
    (E) With housework made easier due to new labor-saving devices, women pursued careers outside the home.

46. The group least affected by national Progressive Era reforms was
    (A) women
    (B) big business owners
    (C) railroad workers
    (D) African Americans
    (E) consumers

47. Which of the following is NOT an aspect of the 1960s antiwar movement?
    (A) Burning draft cards
    (B) Civil disobedience
    (C) Protesting university contracts
    (D) Robert Kennedy's assassination
    (E) Students for a Democratic Society

48. Two of Richard Nixon's most significant foreign policy successes were
    (A) SALT I and restoring relations with Communist China
    (B) invading Cambodia and Vietnamization
    (C) détente and My Lai
    (D) the Tet offensive and the two China policy
    (E) the Nixon Doctrine and invading Cambodia

49. Which of the following is true of child-rearing practices in colonial America?
    (A) Children's formal education was deemed very important.
    (B) Much emphasis was placed on children's cultural pursuits.
    (C) There was little time for idleness and amusement.
    (D) Children had chores to do, but they were sheltered from the really strenuous work.
    (E) Children were raised to be free thinkers and to challenge authority.

50. French colonists developed a better relationship with the Indians than did either the English or the Spanish because the French
    (A) did not try to convert the Native Americans to Christianity
    (B) respected Indian values, did not use natives for forced labor, and tried to keep alcohol away from them
    (C) supported the Iroquois in their move to consolidate fur trapping under their control
    (D) supported the Native Americans in their quest to free themselves from the Dutch
    (E) did not spread disease to the native peoples

GO ON TO THE NEXT PAGE.

51. During the early nineteenth century, the United States government alleviated an economic challenge for northwestern farmers by supporting the development of

(A) crop rotation
(B) irrigation
(C) the Western Confederacy
(D) the cotton gin
(E) turnpikes and canals

Library of Congress.

52. Which of the following reform movements most likely generated the lithograph depicted above?

(A) The woman's movement
(B) The temperance movement
(C) The public education movement
(D) The anti-prostitution movement
(E) The civil rights movement

53. The turning point in the Civil War was the battle at

(A) Bull Run
(B) Antietam
(C) Fredericksburg
(D) Chancellorsville
(E) Gettysburg

GO ON TO THE NEXT PAGE.

Minneapolis Tribune (1901).

THE PHILIPPINES: **"What yer got?"**
CUBA: **"Pie."**
THE PHILIPPINES: **"Where'd yer git it?"**
CUBA: **"Mah Uncle Sam gin it to me; any maybe ef you was half way decent he' gin you some."**

54. Considering the cartoon and caption above, which of the following foreign policies best suits how Americans felt about Cubans and Filipinos?
    (A) White Man's Burden
    (B) Big-stick policy
    (C) Pan Americanism
    (D) Watchful waiting
    (E) Isolationism

55. The goal of the Seneca Falls convention of 1848 was finally achieved with
    (A) equal pay for equal work laws
    (B) the Seventeenth Amendment
    (C) the Eighteenth Amendment
    (D) women's suffrage
    (E) equal treatment for women in the work force

56. In *Schenck v. United States*, the Supreme Court ruled that
    (A) civilians cannot be tried in military courts if a civilian court is available
    (B) restrictions on habeas corpus during wartime are legal
    (C) speech may be restricted when it represents a clear and present danger
    (D) civilians may not attempt to negotiate with foreign nations
    (E) during wartime, a person may be detained on suspicion

GO ON TO THE NEXT PAGE.

57. The greatest civil rights abuse during World War II was
   (A) the mistreatment of women industrial workers
   (B) the internment of Japanese Americans
   (C) discrimination against German Americans
   (D) the lack of benefits for families with breadwinners fighting in the war
   (E) Jim Crow segregation

58. Which of the following Axis nations did the United States help rebuild economically after World War II, to make it a bulwark against communism during the Cold War?
   (A) Bulgaria
   (B) East Germany
   (C) Austria
   (D) Japan
   (E) China

59. Harry Truman's actions during the railroad and coal strikes during the early postwar period
   (A) alienated the American people
   (B) galvanized the Democratic coalition
   (C) split the Republican Party
   (D) were a total failure
   (E) alienated labor

60. The Immigration Act of 1965
   (A) led to "Operation Wetback"
   (B) was stimulated by the *bracero* program
   (C) ended a century of discriminatory immigration policies
   (D) allowed for a new wave of immigration from southern and eastern Europe
   (E) ushered in a backlash by the Ku Klux Klan

61. Why was America's international ally during the Revolutionary War—France—an unlikely partner?
   (A) France was a devoutly Quaker nation.
   (B) France was a weak nation of loosely-joined republics.
   (C) France was normally neutral in international affairs.
   (D) France was a Roman Catholic monarchy.
   (E) France's African colonies could have been jeopardized by joining the American cause.

62. Which aspect of Alexander Hamilton's financial program, as it was implemented, was most disliked by the inhabitants of western Pennsylvania?
   (A) The protective tariff
   (B) The excise tax
   (C) Bank of the United States
   (D) The revenue tariff
   (E) His insistence that there should be a national debt

GO ON TO THE NEXT PAGE.

63. The practical reality of the *Dred Scott* decision was that
   (A) popular sovereignty was the most practical solution to the slavery controversy
   (B) Congress had the constitutional right to limit slavery in the territories
   (C) slavery could exist only if the residents of an area wanted it
   (D) slavery could exist everywhere in the nation
   (E) it temporarily lessened the animosity between the North and the South

64. Which of the following indicates a failure of Radical Reconstruction?
   (A) Freedmen's schools
   (B) The Fourteenth Amendment
   (C) Rights for married women
   (D) Ending of the Black Codes
   (E) Sharecropping

65. Urbanization became inevitable in the United States because of
   (A) the Panic of 1873
   (B) declining farm prices
   (C) the influx of immigrants
   (D) industrialism
   (E) the Panic of 1893

66. Who likely would be the most vocal opponent of the 1873 Comstock Law, which prohibited the mailing of birth control devices and information?
   (A) Carrie Chapman Catt
   (B) Frederick Douglass
   (C) Margaret Sanger
   (D) Robert LaFollette
   (E) Oliver Wendell Holmes

67. The Haymarket incident in 1886
   (A) led to an eight-hour day for the McCormick reaper workers
   (B) led to an increase in respect for unions
   (C) led to the downfall of the Knights of Labor
   (D) was an incident in which the police showed great restraint
   (E) had leaders who were pardoned by the courts

68. "Expansion westward with its new opportunities . . . furnish[es] the forces dominating American character . . . coarseness and strength combined with acuteness and inquisitiveness; that practical, inventive turn of mind, . . . that restless nervous energy; that dominant individualism, . . . and withal that buoyancy and exuberance which comes with freedom . . . [the] frontier did indeed furnish . . . a gate of escape from the bondage of the past."

   This passage was most likely written by
   (A) Alfred Thayer Mahan
   (B) Frederick Jackson Turner
   (C) Theodore Roosevelt
   (D) Albert Beveridge
   (E) Mark Twain

GO ON TO THE NEXT PAGE.

69. Which of the following is a true statement that created the most controversy in the United States at the end of the Spanish-American War?
    (A) Spain refused to grant Cuban independence.
    (B) England was ready to annex Guam.
    (C) There was a tremendous battle in the American press over acquisition of the Philippines.
    (D) Japan was eyeing Hawaii for expansion.
    (E) A border dispute was simmering between British Guiana and Venezuela.

70. The first action Franklin Roosevelt took to alleviate the Great Depression was to
    (A) end Prohibition
    (B) declare a bank holiday that allowed only sound banks to reopen
    (C) put people to work in the WPA
    (D) give states money for relief
    (E) open up soup kitchens to feed the poor

71. The Truman administration avoided the immediate threat of a postwar depression partially through
    (A) the GI Bill
    (B) containment
    (C) the Point Four Program
    (D) the Marshall Plan
    (E) the Berlin Airlift

72. Which of the following is true of post–World War II America?
    (A) City life flourished at the expense of the suburbs.
    (B) Americans enjoyed the highest standard of living in the world.
    (C) For the first time in American history, most African Americans and Spanish-speaking immigrants enjoyed a middle-class standard of living.
    (D) Youthful rebelliousness replaced consensus.
    (E) Women who had worked for the war effort were pleased to have only their household duties to attend to.

"I'm Mrs. Edward M. Barnes. Where do I live?"

73. The 1954 *New Yorker* cartoon is a humorous reflection on all of the following EXCEPT
    (A) Levittown
    (B) the stifling uniformity of suburban life
    (C) the 1950s preoccupation with conformity
    (D) white flight
    (E) the movement to the Sunbelt

74. Ronald Reagan cut federal spending programs by shifting the cost to
    (A) state and local governments
    (B) wealthy taxpayers
    (C) industry
    (D) unions
    (E) faith-based initiatives

75. The Montreal Protocol, the UN Earth Summit, the Basel Convention, *Silent Spring,* and the Kyoto Accord all pertain to
    (A) nuclear nonproliferation
    (B) weapons of mass destruction
    (C) the HIV/AIDS epidemic
    (D) a new world order after the fall of the Soviet Union
    (E) environmental issues

76. The sectionalism that eventually broke out into civil war had its beginnings in the
    (A) issue of statehood for Missouri
    (B) Mexican War
    (C) patterns of colonial settlement
    (D) Articles of Confederation
    (E) nullification movement in South Carolina

GO ON TO THE NEXT PAGE.

77. Reconstruction ended mostly because
    (A) African American government leaders in the South were incompetent
    (B) the North lost interest in the cause
    (C) the Democratic party lost its political base in the South
    (D) the Northern government had achieved all it had planned
    (E) the South acquiesced to an egalitarian society for blacks and whites

78. Which of these statements about the Vietnam War is NOT true?
    (A) It was the first televised war.
    (B) President Lyndon Johnson chose to escalate rather than withdraw troops.
    (C) Ho Chi Minh's death changed the entire course of the war.
    (D) The United States sprayed the herbicide known as Agent Orange knowing the possible birth defects and health risks it posed.
    (E) Vietnamization was a concept utilized by President Nixon.

79. The most explosive educational issue of the 1970s was
    (A) equal opportunity for African Americans in apprenticeships
    (B) busing to secure racial integration
    (C) equal access for women athletes
    (D) ending discrimination against women in admission to colleges and military institutions
    (E) bilingual education

80. The Moral Majority favored
    (A) the Equal Rights Amendment
    (B) a ban on abortion
    (C) welfare payments for single mothers
    (D) instituting court-mandated busing
    (E) no prayer in public schools

STOP

END OF SECTION I

UNITED STATES HISTORY
SECTION II

Part A
Document-Based Questions
(Suggested Writing Time—45 minutes)
Percent of Section II score—45

Directions: The following question requires you to construct a coherent essay that integrates your interpretation of Documents A–H and your knowledge of the period referred to in the question. High scores are earned only by essays that cite key pieces of evidence from the documents and draw on outside knowledge of the period.

1. To what extent was Cherokee assimilation into mainstream American society and culture successful?

Use the documents and your knowledge of the era to construct your response.

GO ON TO THE NEXT PAGE.

Document A

Source: Comparison of Select Native and European Objects in Susquehannock Burial Sites, 1575–1750.

Time	Site	No. of Graves	Stone Celts	Iron Axes	Iron Knives	Iron Hoes	Stone Points	Brass Points	Whole Guns	Native Pots	Brass Kettles	Native Pipes	Kaolin Pipes
1575–1600	Schultz	222	0	5	7	1	68	0	0	210	1	2	0
				2%	3%	<1%	31%			95%	<1%	1%	
1645–1665	Strickler	307	1	53	136	41	68	102	36	169	145	130	12
			<1%	17%	44%	13%	22%	33%	12%	55%	47%	42%	4%
1690–1750	Conestoga Town	69	0	24	74	3	3	11	9	0	42	9	37
				35%	100%	4%	4%	16%	13%		61%	13%	54%

GO ON TO THE NEXT PAGE.

Document B

Source: U.S. Population Density in 1803 and the Louisiana Purchase.

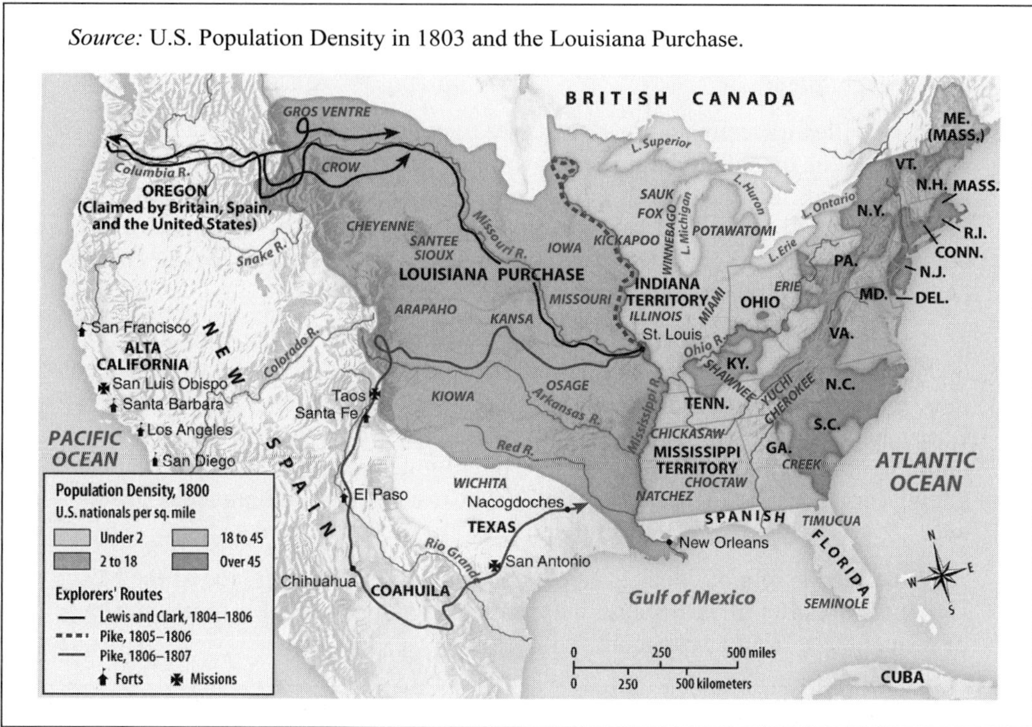

Document C

Source: Thomas Jefferson, Letter to Governor William H. Harrison, 1803.

Dear Sir,

. . . Our system is to live in perpetual peace with the Indians, to cultivate an affectionate attachment to them, by everything just and liberal which we can do for them within the bounds of reason, and by giving them effectual protection against wrongs from our own people . . . our settlements will gradually circumscribe and approach the Indians, and they will in time either incorporate with us as citizens of the United States, or remove beyond the Mississippi. The former is certainly the termination of their history most happy for themselves; but, in the whole course of this, it is essential to cultivate their love. As to their fear, we presume that our strength and their weakness is now so visible that they must see we have only to shut our hand to crush them, and that all our liberalities to them proceed from motives of pure humanity only. Should any tribe be foolhardy enough to take up the hatchet at any time, the seizing the whole country of that tribe, and driving them across the Mississippi, as the only condition of peace, would be an example to others, and a furtherance of our final consolidation.

GO ON TO THE NEXT PAGE.

Document D

Source: Cherokee Women Petition, June 30, 1818.

Beloved Children,

We have called a meeting among ourselves to consult on the different points now before the council, relating to our national affairs. We have heard with painful feelings that the bounds of the land we now possess are to be drawn into very narrow limits. The land was given to us by the Great Spirit above as our common right, to raise our children upon, & to make support for our rising generations . . . we therefore claim the right of the soil.

. . . Our Father the President advised us to become farmers, to manufacture our own clothes, & to have our children instructed. To this advice we have attended in every thing as far as we were able . . . Some of our children have become Christians. We have missionary schools among us. We have heard the gospel in our nation. We have become civilized & enlightened, & are in hopes that in a few years our nation will be prepared for instruction in other branches of sciences & arts, which are both useful and necessary in a civilized society.

. . . Now the thought of being compelled to remove to the other side of the Mississippi is dreadful to us, because it appears to us that we, by this removal, shall be brought to a savage state again.

GO ON TO THE NEXT PAGE.

Document E

Source: Andrew Jackson, First Annual Message to Congress, 1829.

The condition and ulterior destiny of the Indian tribes within the limits of some of our States have become objects of much interest and importance. It has long been the policy of Government to introduce among them the arts of civilization, in the hope of gradually reclaiming them from a wandering life. This policy has, however, been coupled with another wholly incompatible with its success. Professing a desire to civilize and settle them, we have at the same time lost no opportunity to purchase their lands and thrust them farther into the wilderness. By this means they have not only been kept in a wandering state, but been led to look upon us as unjust and indifferent to their fate. Thus, though lavish in its expenditures upon the subject, Government has constantly defeated its own policy, and the Indians in general, receding farther and farther to the west, have retained their savage habits. A portion, however, of the Southern tribes, having mingled much with the whites and made some progress in the arts of civilized life, have lately attempted to erect an independent government within the limits of Georgia and Alabama. These States, claiming to be the only sovereigns within their territories, extended their laws over the Indians, which induced the latter to call upon the United States for protection.

Our conduct toward these people is deeply interesting to our national character. Their present condition, contrasted with what they once were, makes a most powerful appeal to our sympathies. It is too late to inquire whether it was just in the United States to include them and their territory within the bounds of new States, whose limits they could control . . . But the people of those States and of every State, actuated by feelings of justice and a regard for our national honor, submit to you the interesting question whether something can not be done, consistently with the rights of the States, to preserve this much-injured race . . .

As a means of effecting this end I suggest for your consideration the propriety of setting apart an ample district west of the Mississippi, and without the limits of any State or Territory now formed, to be guaranteed to the Indian tribes as long as they shall occupy it, each tribe having a distinct control over the portion designated for its use. There they may be secured in the enjoyment of governments of their own choice, subject to no other control from the United States than such as may be necessary to preserve peace on the frontier and between the several tribes. There the benevolent may endeavor to teach them the arts of civilization, and, by promoting union and harmony among them, to raise up an interesting commonwealth, destined to perpetuate the race and to attest the humanity and justice of this Government.

GO ON TO THE NEXT PAGE.

Document F

Source: Senator Theodore Frelinghuysen, Speech, 1830.

It is alleged, that the Indians cannot flourish in the neighborhood of a white population—that whole tribes have disappeared under the influence of the propinquity . . .

Sir, had we devoted the same care to elevate their moral condition, that we have to degrade them, the removal of the Indians would not now seek for an apology in the suggestions of humanity. But I ask, as to the matter of fact, how stands the account? Wherever a fair experiment has been made, the Indians have readily yielded to the influences of moral cultivation. Yes, Sir, they flourish under this culture, and rise in the scale of being. They have shown themselves to be highly susceptible of improvement, and the ferocious feelings and habits of the savage are soothed and reformed by the mild charities of religion. They can very soon be taught to understand and appreciate the blessings of civilization and regular government . . .

And, Sir, weigh a moment the considerations that address us on behalf of the Cherokees especially. Prompted and encouraged by our counsels, they have in good earnest resolved to become men, rational, educated, Christian men; and they have succeeded to our most sanguine hopes. They have established a regular constitution of civil government, republican in its principles. Wise and beneficent laws are enacted. The people acknowledge their authority, and feel their obligation. A printing press, conducted by one of the nation, circulates a weekly newspaper, printed partly in English, and partly in the Cherokee language. Schools flourish in many of their settlements. Christian temples, to the God of the Bible, are frequented by respectful, devout, and many sincere worshipers. God, as we believe, has many people among them, whom he regards as the "apple of his eye." They have become better neighbors to Georgia. They made no complaints during the lapse of fifty years, when the tribes were a horde of ruthless, licentious and drunken savages; when no law controlled them; when the only judge was their will, and their avenger the tomahawk.

GO ON TO THE NEXT PAGE.

Document G

Source: Chief John Ross, Memorial Protest of the Cherokee Nation, 1836.

To the Senate and the House of Representatives

Washington City 21st June, 1836

The undersigned representatives of the Cherokee nation, east of the river Mississippi, impelled by duty, would respectfully submit, for the consideration of your honorable body, the following statement of facts: It will be seen, from the numerous subsisting treaties between the Cherokee nation and the United States, that from the earliest existence of this Government, the United States, in Congress assembled, received the Cherokee and their nation Into favor and protection; and that the chiefs and warriors, for themselves and all parts of the Cherokee nation, acknowledged themselves and the said Cherokee nation to be under the protection of the United States of America . . . The Cherokees were happy and prosperous under the scrupulous observance of treaty stipulations by the Government of the United States, and from the fostering hand extended over them, they made rapid advances In civilization, morals, and in the arts and sciences. Little did they anticipate that when taught to think and feel as the American citizen, and to have with him a common interest, they were to be despoiled by their guardian, to become strangers and wanderers in the land of their fathers, forced to return to the savage life, and to seek a new home in the wilds of the far west, and that without their consent.

GO ON TO THE NEXT PAGE.

Document H

Source: Major Ridge, A Cherokee Chief, ca. 1838.

Library of Congress.

END OF DOCUMENTS FOR QUESTION 1

UNITED STATES HISTORY
SECTION II

Part B and Part C
Free-Response Questions
(Suggested total planning and writing time—70 minutes)
Percent of Section II score—55

Part B

Directions: Choose ONE question from this part. You are advised to spend 5 minutes planning and 30 minutes writing your answer. Cite relevant historical evidence in support of your generalizations and present your arguments clearly and logically.

2. "The growth and prosperity of the emerging society of a free colonial British America . . . were achieved as a result of slave labor." Assess the validity of this statement.

3. Analyze the military, economic, and political reasons why the Union won the Civil War.

GO ON TO THE NEXT PAGE.

Part C

Directions: Choose ONE question from this part. You are advised to spend 5 minutes planning and 30 minutes writing your answer. Cite relevant historical evidence in support of your generalizations and present your arguments clearly and logically.

4. Discuss the extent to which progressives achieved reform in THREE of the following four areas between the years 1900 and 1920.

   Workers' rights

   Women's rights

   The political process

   African American rights

5. Evaluate the ways in which the year 1968 may be one of the most significant years in modern American history.

STOP

END OF EXAM

Answer Key for Practice Exam 1

Answers for Section I: Multiple-Choice Questions

1. D	21. C	41. A	61. D
2. B	22. B	42. C	62. D
3. E	23. E	43. B	63. D
4. D	24. A	44. A	64. E
5. A	25. B	45. C	65. D
6. A	26. E	46. D	66. C
7. B	27. D	47. D	67. C
8. E	28. D	48. A	68. B
9. E	29. D	49. C	69. C
10. B	30. A	50. B	70. B
11. C	31. A	51. E	71. A
12. D	32. C	52. B	72. B
13. B	33. B	53. E	73. E
14. A	34. D	54. A	74. A
15. C	35. C	55. D	75. E
16. C	36. C	56. C	76. C
17. E	37. D	57. B	77. B
18. C	38. E	58. D	78. C
19. A	39. A	59. E	79. B
20. B	40. B	60. C	80. B

1. **Answer (D) followed mercantilist policies.** While the other answers refer to one or two of the three nations' colonial entities, only D applies to all. English, Spanish, and French leaders all used their colonies to increase their national wealth and to raise revenue for further expansion and wars. (*America's History,* Seventh Edition, Chapters 1–3, pp. 35–36, 44–45, and 76–77)

2. **Answer (B) a system for orderly settlement of the West.** Under the Articles, U.S. leaders had a unicameral legislature and had a hard time economically in the postwar years. But the Land Ordinances of 1787 were a notable achievement, especially considering the overlapping land claims of many of the original thirteen states in the Old Northwest region. (*America's History,* Seventh Edition, Chapter 6, pp. 189–191)

3. **Answer (E) all of the above.** Hamilton, the first secretary of the treasury, had many reasons for his economic proposals and policies, most of which were opposed by Jefferson, the first secretary of state, who envisioned a nation made up of gentleman farmers. Hamilton is credited with putting the United States on a firm economic footing; all of the reasons given are correct. Note: while it's unlikely that you will see an "all of the above" question on the AP Exam, you may encounter them on regular tests, and questions with similar wordings do appear on the AP Exam. (*America's History,* Seventh Edition, Chapter 7, pp. 204–208)

4. **Answer (D) President Lincoln toward the end of the Civil War.** These words are from Lincoln's Second Inaugural Address, spoken just a few weeks before his assassination and as the Civil War was ending. Note his reference to "a just and lasting peace **among ourselves**"—these words are the key clue to the answer. The speech is not quoted directly in the textbook, but relevant background information can be found. (*America's History,* Seventh Edition, Chapter 14, pp. 452–459)

5. **Answer (A) sharecroppers.** Although in theory the freedmen had rights and citizenship, in practice the economic situation most found themselves in—sharecropping—was little different from slavery. (*America's History,* Seventh Edition, Chapter 15, pp. 473–479)

6. **Answer (A) uniting a diverse population against the common enemy.** Because the United States had experienced such an extraordinary influx of immigration in the decades preceding World War I, leaders were concerned that some of these newer Americans wouldn't support the war effort (particularly German Americans and Irish Americans). The gorilla in the picture represents Germany, not France or Russia, and the woman represents Lady Liberty. Note the burned remnants of European cities in the background. Political cartoonists of the period often used gorilla imagery to represent peoples who were perceived of as being racially inferior. (*America's History,* Seventh Edition, Chapter 24, pp. 766–767)

7. **Answer (B) *Brown v. Board of Education.*** This case overturned the 1896 case *Plessy v. Ferguson* that had allowed for "separate but equal" facilities and schools for African Americans. The NAACP spent decades mounting a legal challenge to Plessy and finally prevailed in 1954. (*America's History,* Seventh Edition, Chapter 27, pp. 859–861)

8. **Answer (E) income taxes.** Individual earners' income taxes are not directly tied to the economic trends of globalization. (*America's History,* Seventh Edition, Chapter 31, pp. 976–981)

9. **Answer (E) protect rights not specified in the Constitution.** While Madison and the other framers initially thought that a Bill of Rights was unnecessary in the Constitution since most states' constitutions had such protections, they were convinced by the concerns raised by Antifederalists during the ratification debates. The first ten amendments, otherwise known as the Bill of Rights, were ratified by 1791. (*America's History,* Seventh Edition, Chapter 7, p. 204)

10. **Answer (B) The Second Great Awakening.** Statistics-driven questions like this tend to be fairly straightforward if you read the tables carefully. The left-hand column of denominations indicates that this is a religious history question; the only response that refers to a religious occurrence is B. (*America's History,* Seventh Edition, Chapter 8, pp. 259–262)

11. **Answer (C) stop disloyal activities such as protests against the draft.** A writ of habeas corpus (literally "you shall have the body" in Latin) is a law meant to protect citizens from being dragged into court without stated cause or process. Lincoln suspended this constitutional protection to preserve security during wartime, especially since many in the North opposed conscription (the draft). (*America's History,* Seventh Edition, Chapter 14, p. 440)

12. **Answer (D) Lawyer.** Many occupations during the Gilded Age were circumscribed by gender. Women could find work as teachers, nurses, factory workers, domestic servants, and in some office jobs such as low-level clerks and telephone operators, but the field of law was one of many that were unattainable for them. (*America's History,* Seventh Edition, Chapter 17, pp. 537–540)

13. **Answer (B) the Meat Inspection and Pure Food and Drug Acts.** *The Jungle* repulsed many Americans, including President Theodore Roosevelt, with its descriptions of how food was processed in America's factories. Roosevelt helped to secure passage of these two important laws that protected consumers. (*America's History,* Seventh Edition, Chapter 19, p. 610)

14. **Answer (A) Woodrow Wilson's aggressive foreign policy.** In the first two years of the war, 1914–1916, Wilson worked hard to maintain American neutrality. The events mentioned in responses B, C, D, and E all contributed to the eventual entry of the United States into the conflict in 1917. Wilson's foreign policy can be understood as idealistic—see the Fourteen Points—but is rarely described as aggressive. (*America's History,* Seventh Edition, Chapter 21, pp. 667–671)

15. **Answer (C) French military and financial assistance.** Although their assistance to the upstart colonists bankrupted France and eventually led to its own revolution in 1789, the French were able to attain some revenge on their long-time foes by supporting American independence. Loyalists (D) and most Native Americans (A) supported the British during the war. (*America's History,* Seventh Edition, Chapter 6, pp. 178–181)

16. **Answer (C) judicial review.** John Marshall is the Chief Justice credited with establishing the precedent of judicial review with the Court's decision in this case. This means that the Supreme Court has "the province and duty" to determine if a passed law is constitutional. (*America's History,* Seventh Edition, Chapter 7, pp. 217–218)

17. **Answer (E) disease and infection.** Despite practices implemented by the U.S. Sanitary Commission and the heroic efforts of thousands of volunteer nurses, Civil War soldiers were nearly twice as likely to die from disease and infection as from combat. (*America's History,* Seventh Edition, Chapter 14, pp. 441–442)

18. **Answer (C) Theodore Roosevelt.** This quote epitomizes Theodore Roosevelt's pragmatic approach to checking the power of big corporations. He saw it as his duty to determine the difference between "good" and "bad" trusts, and to go after those he saw as bad. (*America's History,* Seventh Edition, Chapter 20, pp. 637–638)

19. **Answer (A) limited immigration to the United States.** After decades of extraordinarily high immigration, Americans turned inward during the 1920s, closing the door to new immigrants (particularly from perceived inferior regions) through this and other restrictions. (*America's History,* Seventh Edition, Chapter 22, pp. 693–694)

20. **Answer (B) the Dust Bowl.** The environmental devastation of the Great Plains led thousands of Americans from Dust Bowl states like Oklahoma to seek greener pastures further west, especially in California. Steinbeck's novel depicts such an exodus. (*America's History,* Seventh Edition, See Chapter 23, pp. 743–744)

21. **Answer (C) white, college-educated, middle-class women.** Friedan wrote of the alienation and purposelessness of women's lives in the suburbs, where all of their efforts went into maintaining happy households for their husbands and children. The *Feminine Mystique* helped to inspire what historians refer to as "second wave feminism" in the 1960s. (*America's History,* Seventh Edition, Chapter 28, p. 889)

22. **Answer (B) the middle passage.** This term refers to the experience of Africans who were taken from their homes by force, put on ships, and brought across the Atlantic to lives of bondage in the colonies. This particular quote is from the published narrative of Olaudah Equiano, who eventually gained his freedom, married a British woman, and became an early abolitionist. (*America's History,* Seventh Edition, Chapter 3, pp. 84–86 and 88)

23. **Answer (E) outlawing corporations.** On the contrary, both the Supreme Court and state courts consistently upheld the rights of corporations at the same time that legislatures were supporting patent laws, the U.S. Postal Service, the construction of roads and canals, and other measures that facilitated economic development. (*America's History,* Seventh Edition, Chapter 8, pp. 238–242)

24. **Answer (A) the decision to desegregate the schools.** All of the other events listed represent "bottom-up" efforts to ensure civil rights for African Americans. It took the "top-down" Supreme Court decision in *Brown v. Board of Education* to desegregate the schools in 1954 (but as explained above in question 7, the NAACP was responsible for bringing the case to court in the first place). (*America's History,* Seventh Edition, Chapter 27, pp. 859–866)

25. **Answer (B) the preemptive use of military force.** While the other responses list aspects of President George W. Bush's War on Terror following the September 11, 2001 attacks, the Bush doctrine is a specific foreign policy approach that policymakers within the Bush cabinet promoted to justify going to war against Saddam Hussein in Iraq, even though there was no imminent threat to the United States. (*America's History,* Seventh Edition, Chapter 31, p. 999)

26. **Answer (E) the growth of a democratic spirit.** The Great Awakening was a religious movement that affected many aspects of American life—but none of the first four answers apply. Because preachers stressed the individual's relationship with God, the Great Awakening inspired Americans of all classes to question authority—not only in matters of religion, ultimately. (*America's History,* Seventh Edition, Chapter 4, pp. 121–124)

27. **Answer (D) the Treaty of Paris.** Wars typically *end* with treaties, so answer D should stand out as the exception. All of the other items contributed to the growing antagonism between the American colonies and the British authorities. (*America's History,* Seventh Edition, Chapter 5, especially pp. 149–151 and 163–165)

28. **Answer (D) Republican motherhood.** Even if you have not seen this specific quote before, you should be able to identify the key ideals of Republican motherhood—the idea that in a Republic, women had the important role of educating their sons to be well-informed citizens. (*America's History,* Seventh Edition, See Chapter 8, p. 246)

29. **Answer (D) bank was a monopoly that benefited only a few owners, some of whom were foreigners.** In Jackson's view, the Constitution did not allow for a national bank, and he gained the ardent support of working men throughout the country who distrusted elite moneyed interests. (*America's History,* Seventh Edition, Chapter 10, pp. 313–314)

30. **Answer (A) Lincoln's difficulty in finding a general of the caliber of Lee.** Military leadership was a real problem for Lincoln in the early years of the war. The North, however, did enjoy many other advantages, including a larger population, more industrialization and railroads, and a more effective president in Abraham Lincoln than the Confederacy's Jefferson Davis. (*America's History,* Seventh Edition, Chapter 14, pp. 435–437)

31. **Answer (A) Black Codes.** Years of brutal war embittered southerners; they were not prepared to accept the reality of slavery's end and passed Black Codes in order to maintain their legally sanctioned racial superiority over blacks. (*America's History,* Seventh Edition, Chapter 15, p. 464)

32. **Answer (C) It kept new immigrants from taking jobs from native-born Americans.** On the contrary, bosses and their operatives often found jobs for new immigrants in return for their political support. (*America's History,* Seventh Edition, Chapter 19, pp. 607–609)

33. **Answer (B) the NAACP.** W.E.B. DuBois and William Monroe Trotter called a meeting of African American leaders at Niagara on the Canadian side of the border and wrote a set of principles that coalesced into the founding of the National Association for the Advancement of Colored People. (*America's History,* Seventh Edition, Chapter 20, p. 642)

34. **Answer (D) Clarence Darrow defended the right to teach evolution in schools.** This question is tricky because you need to read the other answers carefully to discern the inaccuracies. For example, for response B, the ACLU did not challenge the constitutionality of the trial—it challenged the constitutionality of the Tennessee law that forbade the teaching of evolution in the schools. This is one of the few non–Supreme Court cases in U.S. history that is important to comprehend, particularly in the context of the traditional-versus-modern values debate of 1920s America. (*America's History,* Seventh Edition, Chapter 22, pp. 692–693)

35. **Answer (C) Franklin Roosevelt.** Found in one of the most important political speeches of twentieth-century American history, this quotation is from Franklin Roosevelt's inaugural address, delivered in 1933 as he sought to reassure Americans battered by three years of the Great Depression. The speech is not quoted in *America's History,* but Roosevelt's agenda can be discerned in its words. (*America's History,* Seventh Edition, Chapter 23, pp. 723–725)

36. **Answer (C) New York, New Jersey, and Pennsylvania.** These Mid-Atlantic colonies were the most tolerant of different religions and attracted settlers from many different European places and classes. Pennsylvania was guided by William Penn's Quaker beliefs and his Frame of Government that ensured religious freedom. (*America's History,* Seventh Edition, Chapters 3 and 4, pp. 76, 113, and 115)

37. **Answer (D) Patriot merchants replaced Tories at the top of the economic ladder.** In fact, many Patriots were already members of the economic elite before the war began, but around 100,000 Loyalists (also called monarchists) fled, leaving behind property and riches. The republican Patriots who replaced the Loyalist elite tended to invest in new ventures and thus helped to take the American economy in a new direction. (*America's History,* Seventh Edition, Chapter 6, pp. 187 and 189)

38. **Answer (E) wealthy men.** Merchants, lawyers, and slaveholding planters made up most of the delegates to the Constitutional Convention in the summer of 1787. (*America's History,* Seventh Edition, Chapter 6, pp. 193–195)

39. **Answer (A) there was a shift in public policy that encouraged business.** Both the federal government and states sought measures to facilitate the development of a market economy (see answers to questions 3 and 23, above). (*America's History,* Seventh Edition, Chapters 8 and 9, pp. 241–242 and 273–280)

40. **Answer (B) preserving the existing balance of power between North and South in the Senate.** The Missouri Compromise was made in 1820 and set a pattern for compromises to maintain the slave/free state balance in the Senate up to the Civil War. This was a time of rapid inclusion of new states into the Union, so it was, unfortunately for lawmakers, a recurring challenge. (*America's History,* Seventh Edition, Chapter 8, pp. 256–258)

41. **Answer (A) Some Cherokee Indians promoted it.** This is another question that requires careful reading of the incorrect answers. The Act did not move the Seminoles from Florida; it was not a response to Black Hawk's War, it faced strong opposition, and it was contested, not upheld, by Chief Justice Marshall in *Worcester v. Georgia.* But it is in fact true that some Cherokee leaders did support their forced migration west. (*America's History,* Seventh Edition, Chapter 10, pp. 315, 318–319)

42. **Answer (C) German-language shop signs.** Efforts that American business owners made to welcome customers of any ethnic background shows how economic interests have served to break down ethnic divisions among Americans. German and Irish immigrants came in significant numbers between 1840 and 1860, stirring up nativist sentiment and hatred against newcomers, particularly when jobs were scarce. (*America's History,* Seventh Edition, see Chapter 11, pp. 343–344)

43. **Answer (B) its dependence on slavery.** Because the southern planter elites prospered on the export of cotton, they saw little need to facilitate industrialization. (*America's History,* Seventh Edition, Chapter 12, pp. 379–380)

44. **Answer (A) southern and eastern Europe.** By the time nineteenth-century Americans had adjusted to German and Irish immigration (see question 42), they faced an influx of immigrants from Italy, Greece, Austria-Hungary, Russia, and other eastern and southern European states. This is referred to as the "new" immigration to distinguish it from the earlier wave of Germans and Irish. (This term can be confusing since there has been yet another wave of immigration from Latin America, Asia, Africa, and other regions since 1965). (*America's History,* Seventh Edition, Chapter 17, pp. 545–546)

45. **Answer (C) Attitudes toward child rearing changed as children were indulged and remained dependent on their parents longer than they had previously.** Americans began to have smaller families once the motivation to breed a bevy of farmhands was no longer a priority. (*America's History,* Seventh Edition, Chapter 18, pp. 560–561)

46. **Answer (D) African Americans.** The first two decades of the twentieth century saw unprecedented reforms for American women, consumers, workers, and citizens, but African Americans saw little improvement in their political, social, and economic status. It would take the civil rights movement of the 1950s and 1960s to effect real change. (*America's History,* Seventh Edition, Chapter 20, pp. 641–644 and 648–649)

47. **Answer (D) Robert Kennedy's assassination.** Robert Kennedy became a vocal opponent of the war in Vietnam when he ran for the Democratic nomination for president in 1968. On the night he won the California primary, Kennedy was killed by Palestinian Sirhan Sirhan, whose motives had nothing to do with the war. (*America's History,* Seventh Edition, Chapter 28, pp. 894–899)

48. **Answer (A) SALT I and restoring relations with Communist China.** To answer this kind of question correctly you must be sure that both parts of the answer are correct. In this case, only response A offers two correct examples of Nixon's foreign policy achievements. (*America's History,* Seventh Edition, Chapter 28, pp. 906–911)

49. **Answer (C) There was little time for idleness and amusement.** Although children were highly esteemed by New England families, and parents fretted over what land they would be able to bequeath to their children, there was no time for anyone to be idle. (*America's History,* Seventh Edition, Chapter 4, pp. 106–108)

50. **Answer (B) respected Indian values, did not use natives for forced labor, and tried to keep alcohol away from them.** Like their European counterparts, French colonists did spread disease and attempted to convert Indians to Christianity. But they also accommodated Indians and their ways in order to coexist relatively peacefully—a

necessity, perhaps, since the French were so greatly outnumbered by Indians in the regions they settled. (*America's History,* Seventh Edition, Chapter 2, pp. 42–47)

51. **Answer (E) turnpikes and canals.** This is yet another question that addresses the important economic developments of the early national period. While railroads would emerge by the 1840s as the most essential form of transport for American farmers and merchants, in early decades of the Republic, roads and canals formed essential connections between farmers and markets. (*America's History,* Seventh Edition, Chapter 9, pp. 285–286)

52. **Answer (B) The temperance movement.** The lithograph depicted in the question can be found in your textbook on p. 297. It is titled "The Drunkard's Progress: From the First Glass to the Grave." Supporters of temperance saw alcohol as a destructive element to society and sought to outlaw it, a generations-long effort that led to the Eighteenth Amendment's ratification in 1919, outlawing all "intoxicating liquors." (*America's History,* Seventh Edition, See Chapter 9, p. 297)

53. **Answer (E) Gettysburg.** Military history does not get a lot of attention from AP test developers, but it is important for you to remember that Gettysburg on the eastern front, along with Grant's victory at Vicksburg on the western front, was the turning point of the Civil War. Although the South would fight on for nearly two more years, the tide turned in favor of the Union after July 1863. (*America's History,* Seventh Edition, Chapter 14, pp. 447–448)

54. **Answer (A) White Man's Burden.** This is the title of a poem by British poet Rudyard Kipling, who wrote it about American imperialism following the Spanish-American War. The cartoon reflects attitudes of racial superiority that many white Americans had toward nonwhite populations at the turn of the twentieth century. (*America's History,* Seventh Edition, Chapter 21, pp. 656–661)

55. **Answer (D) women's suffrage.** This was achieved with passage of the Nineteenth Amendment, ratified in 1920. Take care to remember the Progressive amendments that allowed for the collection of a national income tax (XVI), provided for the direct election of senators (XVII), prohibited the sale of alcohol (XVIII), and gave women the vote (XIX). (*America's History,* Seventh Edition, Chapter 11, pp. 356–357)

56. **Answer (C) speech may be restricted when it represents a clear and present danger.** Schenck was a socialist imprisoned for distributing pamphlets that questioned American involvement in World War I. Dissent during wartime has been suppressed repeatedly throughout American history, and in this case even the Supreme Court agreed that at certain times, security interests superseded individual rights. (*America's History,* Seventh Edition, Chapter 21, p. 674)

57. **Answer (B) the internment of Japanese Americans.** You may think that this question asks you to make a value judgment about civil rights abuses—Japanese internment versus persistent racial segregation of black Americans—but read the question carefully. Jim Crow segregation existed during World War II, but it had begun during Reconstruction. Japanese internment is the only response that addresses a decision made during World War II, which is why it is the best answer. (*America's History,* Seventh Edition, Chapter 24, pp. 770–773)

58. **Answer (D) Japan.** Although the United States and Japan were enemies during World War II, priorities changed when the war was over, and communism, not fascism, became the main threat to American security. In addition to Japan, the United States helped to rebuild the devastated economies of western Europe through the Marshall Plan. (*America's History,* Seventh Edition, Chapter 25, p. 794)

59. **Answer (E) alienated labor.** Unions traditionally supported Democrats and enjoyed their last period of significant influence during the 1930s under Franklin Roosevelt's presidency. But in the postwar period, Truman took a harder line against union demands, damaging his support among Democratic-leaning union voters. (*America's History,* Seventh Edition, Chapter 26, pp. 824–825)

60. **Answer (C) ended a century of discriminatory immigration policies.** Perhaps no other law passed during Johnson's Great Society initiative has had greater impact on American society than this reopening of "the golden door" for aspiring immigrants (these words come from the Emma Lazarus poem inscribed on the base of the Statue of Liberty). (*America's History,* Seventh Edition, Chapter 28, pp. 886–887)

61. **Answer (D) France was a Roman Catholic monarchy.** The French were not motivated by ideology when they chose to support American independence: they sought to damage their traditional foe, the British, and were able to make vital contributions to the Patriot cause. (*America's History,* Seventh Edition, Chapter 6, p. 178)

62. **Answer (D) The revenue tariff.** This tariff led to the Whiskey Rebellion in Pennsylvania by farmers who resented the new tax. (*America's History,* Seventh Edition, Chapter 7, pp. 206–208)

63. **Answer (D) slavery could exist everywhere in the nation.** Chief Justice Roger B. Taney sought to end the slavery debate once and for all, ruling that Congress could not restrict slavery anywhere in the country. The decision only further inflamed both sides in the politically tumultuous 1850s. (*America's History,* Seventh Edition, Chapter 13, p. 422)

64. **Answer (E) Sharecropping.** All of the other answers refer to successes of Reconstruction; widespread sharecropping by Reconstruction's end was a decided failure to those who had hoped for real political and economic equality for freedmen. (*America's History,* Seventh Edition, Chapter 15, pp. 473, 476–479)

65. **Answer (D) industrialism.** Industrialization accelerated in the late nineteenth century, helping to transform the United States from a majority rural population to a majority urban population by 1920. (*America's History,* Seventh Edition, Chapter 19, pp. 592–594)

66. **Answer (C) Margaret Sanger.** Sanger was an outspoken supporter of birth control and family planning during the Progressive era; the Comstock Law outlawed birth control devices. This question asks you to apply your knowledge of Sanger by predicting her reaction to a historical event, a useful skill to cultivate for the AP Exam. (*America's History,* Seventh Edition, Chapter 18, p. 560 for the Comstock Law; Chapter 22, pp. 685–686 for Sanger)

67. **Answer (C) led to the downfall of the Knights of Labor.** The association of the Knights of Labor with anarchist violence damaged the national reputation of the Knights of Labor. On that day in Chicago in May 1886, anarchists threw a bomb that killed several police, disrupting what was meant to be a peaceful protest meeting on behalf of McCormick reaper workers. It was an unfortunate episode and a setback for progress on reasonable working conditions for American workers. (*America's History,* Seventh Edition, Chapter 17, p. 552)

68. **Answer (B) Frederick Jackson Turner.** Turner's 1893 thesis, "The Significance of the Frontier in American History," argued that the presence of a frontier was integral to the development of American identity. With the closing of the western frontier by the 1890s, Turner argued that Americans would need to seek other frontiers to pursue their interests. Although he is not mentioned specifically in *America's History,* Seventh Edition, Turner does appear frequently on the AP Exam and is important to recognize.

69. **Answer (C) There was a tremendous battle in the American press over acquisition of the Philippines.** Americans went to war with Spain over Cuba; they hadn't anticipated acquiring the Philippines. The public debate that ensued over what to do with the Philippines pitted supporters of the spoils of war against those who thought it a very bad idea to annex 8 million Filipinos into the nation. (*America's History,* Seventh Edition, Chapter 21, pp. 656–659)

70. **Answer (B) declare a bank holiday that allowed only sound banks to reopen.** The unstable banking system was enfeebling the entire U.S. economy; Roosevelt and his advisors recognized that it had to be stabilized. The Emergency Banking Act allowed for banks to be reopened if the Treasury Department verified that their reserves were in good shape, thus restoring faith in those banks and the system overall. (*America's History,* Seventh Edition, Chapter 23, pp. 724–725)

71. **Answer (A) the GI Bill.** Officially known as the Serviceman's Readjustment Act of 1944, the GI bill sent millions of American veterans to college instead of leaving them on their own to look for work. As a result, by the 1950s the American workforce was the best educated in the world. (*America's History,* Seventh Edition, Chapter 26, pp. 823–824)

72. **Answer (B) Americans enjoyed the highest standard of living in the world.** By 1960, fully 62 percent of Americans owned their own home, and income inequality sharply declined. African Americans and newer immigrants still faced challenging economic conditions, growth of the suburbs exploded, and although some women were dissatisfied and some elements of society such as the Beats criticized the materialism and vacuity of mainstream culture, the best answer here is B. (*America's History,* Seventh Edition, Chapter 26, pp. 823–824)

73. **Answer (E) the movement to the Sunbelt.** The demographic change that saw increases in southern and western states while populations in the Northeast and Midwest declined certainly was a phenomenon of the post–World War II era, but it is not represented in this cartoon, which clearly speaks to the conformity of suburban life. (*America's History,* Seventh Edition, Chapter 26, pp. 833–837)

74. **Answer (A) state and local governments.** Some Republicans like Newt Gingrich referred to this as "devolution" to the states. The philosophical intent was to empower governments closer to their populations to make more of the decisions that affected their citizens' lives rather than mandating costly nationwide programs. In general, Republicans since the 1930s have called for smaller federal government. (*America's History,* Seventh Edition, Chapter 30, pp. 956–957 and 960–961)

75. **Answer (E) environmental issues.** While you might not recognize all of the items in a list question like this—the Kyoto treaty is not mentioned in *America's History,* Seventh Edition, for example—you are likely to recall at least one or two items that signal environmentalism here. *Silent Spring* by Rachel Carson was published in the early 1960s and raised the alarm of how DDT and other chemicals were affecting plants, animals, and the natural world. (*America's History,* Seventh Edition, Chapter 29, pp. 917–918)

76. **Answer (C) patterns of colonial settlement.** Many historians now agree that the roots of sectionalism in the United States go back to before it existed as a country. From the seventeenth century onward, southern colonies were "slave societies": their economies depended wholly on the existence of slave labor. Northern and Mid-Atlantic colonies were "societies with slaves": slavery existed there, but it was not an essential to those economies. (*America's History,* Seventh Edition, Chapter 3, pp. 84–94)

77. **Answer (B) the North lost interest in the cause.** This was, unfortunately, true: as national attention turned westward, the project of integrating former slaves fully into citizenship and economic opportunity was cut short. It was not due to the incompetence of

African American politicians, nor to any achievement of egalitarian goals; and the Democratic Party retained its hold on the South for a century to come. (*America's History,* Seventh Edition, Chapter 15, pp. 483–487)

78. **Answer (C) Ho Chi Minh's death changed the entire course of the war.** Although Ho Chi Minh died in 1969, the war dragged on, violently; the Viet Cong continued with their cause. All of the other statements are true. (*America's History,* Seventh Edition, Chapter 28, pp. 890–895)

79. **Answer (B) busing to secure racial integration.** Note the word *explosive*: it connotes violent division. While all of the answers refer to controversies in American education in the 1970s and thereafter, the forced busing of students, particularly in struggling cities like Boston, caused fear and anger in both white and black families affected by the changes. (*America's History,* Seventh Edition, Chapter 29, p. 929)

80. **Answer (B) a ban on abortion.** In the 1980s and 1990s, abortion was one of the most divisive issues in the "culture wars." As a conservative Christian political action committee, the Moral Majority would have opposed all of the other policies listed, and they worked hard to fight legal abortion. (*America's History,* Seventh Edition, Chapters 30 and 31, pp. 954, 958, 968, 988–989)

Answers for Section II

Part A: Document Based-Question

1. To what extent was Cherokee assimilation into mainstream American society and culture successful?

This DBQ examines the response of the Cherokee Indians to the inexorable spread of European-American population and culture. The documents suggest a more complex perspective than the simplistic victimization story told in the past. You may want to invoke the concept of agency (the power to act) to emphasize choices the Cherokees made as they adjusted to changing conditions. Ultimately, the question asks you to determine whether or not assimilation was a successful choice. You should address the issue of Indian removal and consider why the Cherokees weren't simply left alone, since they were playing by the rules. Giving up their cultures and traditions did not, in the end, protect them from their ultimate fate: removal from their ancestral lands.

Documents A and B reflect how native peoples' environment changed following the incursions of European-Americans and how they adapted. Document C, an 1803 letter from Thomas Jefferson, states an either/or situation: Indians could "incorporate with us as citizens of the United States, or remove beyond the Mississippi." Document D shows that these Cherokee women have faithfully abided by assimilation policies, and they express concern that being moved would reduce them to a "savage state again," and Document H depicts an assimilated Cherokee man, John Ridge, who protests strongly against removal in Document G. Document F echoes the concerns from the Cherokee women and opposes removal on the basis of the Cherokees' successful assimilation. Document E, from President Jackson, lays out his justification for removal.

Outside information should include the two Supreme Court cases on this matter, *Cherokee Nation v. Georgia* and *Worcester v. Georgia,* the latter of which upheld Cherokee sovereignty, but which President Jackson chose to ignore. Drawing connections to other assimilation policies, such as the Dawes Severalty Act and the Indian boarding schools that came later in the nineteenth century, is best.

To review the assimilation and removal policies that affected the Cherokees and other eastern tribes in the antebellum period, see Chapter 10.

Parts B and C: Free-Response Questions

2. "The growth and prosperity of the emerging society of a free colonial British America . . . were achieved as a result of slave labor." Assess the validity of this statement.

This statement points to one of the great ironies of American history. You may argue that slavery was essential to the wealth and growth of the colonies by emphasizing the following:

- The plantation elite and their prominence in colonial assemblies, such as Virginia's House of Burgesses
- The dependence of southern colonial economies on slavery
- The lifestyle of the southern gentry
- Northern colonists' participation in the slave trade

You might choose to disagree with the statement by emphasizing developments in the New England and Mid-Atlantic colonies, where slavery existed but was not essential to those economies:

- New England town meetings
- Religious diversity/tolerance in the Mid-Atlantic colonies
- Yeoman farmers/free labor

Sophisticated answers will note the differences among the three colonial regions regarding the practice of slavery and the extent to which it affected prosperity and growth.

3. Analyze the military, economic, and political reasons why the Union won the Civil War.

The best answers to this question will recognize some of the advantages the South had—unity of cause, stronger military leadership—while emphasizing the North's abundant resources. Note that this question gives you a solid organizational structure. Each set of reasons (military, economic, political) can get its own brief paragraph. Some of the reasons the Union won are listed below:

Military:

- Industrial production of weapons
- Industrial production of soldiers' rations, uniforms, and other supplies
- More railroads for the transport of material and men
- A larger male population from which to draw their soldiers

Economic:

- Access to capital
- More factories
- A diversified economy more durable to disruption

Political:

- Abraham Lincoln's leadership
- An established Constitution
- Recognition as a legitimate nation on the world stage

4. Discuss the extent to which Progressives achieved reform in THREE of the following four areas between the years 1900 and 1920:

Workers' rights
Women's rights
The political process
African American rights

In answering this question, you may want to contrast areas in which there was quite a lot of progress—workers' and women's rights, and the political process—with African American rights. But it is also responsible to point to significant activism by Ida B. Wells, W.E.B. DuBois, and others who laid the groundwork for future reforms. You may also choose to emphasize the many inequities that existed in American society even after the wave of Progressive reform subsided by 1920. Below are some notable achievements of each item above:

Workers' rights:

- *Muller v. Oregon* limits women's work hours
- Antitrust legislation
- Theodore Roosevelt's resolution of the 1902 coal strike
- Workplace reforms after the 1911 Triangle Shirtwaist fire

Women's rights:

- Right to vote (Nineteenth Amendment)
- Margaret Sanger and birth control
- Settlement house support for women and families
- Activism of women's clubs

The political process:

- Direct election of senators (Eighteenth Amendment)
- Recall
- Referendum

African American rights:

- Ida Wells's public crusade against lynching
- W.E.B. Du Bois, the Niagara Movement, founding of the NAACP

5. Evaluate the ways in which the year 1968 may be one of the most significant years in modern American history.

Some or all of the following events should be discussed in your response:

- Assassination of Martin Luther King Jr.
- Urban riots
- Report of the Kerner Commission
- Civil Rights Act of 1968
- Tet Offensive

- Largest draft call in the history of the Vietnam war
- Lyndon Johnson chooses not to run for President again
- Assassination of Robert Kennedy
- Eugene McCarthy's presidential candidacy
- Democratic National Convention's "police riot" in Chicago
- White backlash and George Wallace's presidential candidacy
- Campus unrest—e.g., Columbia University
- Women's Liberation Movement emerges

PRACTICE EXAM 2

UNITED STATES HISTORY
SECTION I

Multiple-Choice Questions
(Time—55 minutes)
Number of Questions—80

Directions: Each of the questions or incomplete statements below is followed by five suggested answers or completions. Select the one that is best in each case.

1. Which of the following best characterizes the purpose of British mercantilist policy in the colonies?

   (A) To develop the colonies' industrial base
   (B) To exploit colonial resources for the benefit of Britain
   (C) To foster democracy and self-government in the New World
   (D) To establish British military bases in the New World
   (E) To create a new nation to which those who were persecuted at home, such as the Puritans, could be sent

2. "Make the best of this new government—say it is composed of anything but inspiration—You ought to be extremely cautious, watchful, jealous of your liberty; for, instead of securing your rights, you may lose them forever. If this new government will not come up to the expectation of the people, and they shall be disappointed, their liberty will be lost, and tyranny must and will arise."

   This statement was most likely said by

   (A) a member of Parliament
   (B) an Antifederalist
   (C) a Confederate
   (D) an abolitionist
   (E) a Patriot

3. The Monroe Doctrine of 1823 asserted that

   (A) individuals who wrote "false or malicious" claims against the government could be imprisoned
   (B) each slave would be counted as three-fifths of a person
   (C) the Supreme Court had the authority to declare laws unconstitutional
   (D) any European interference in the Americas would be seen as a hostility to the United States
   (E) slavery would be banned in all territories within the Louisiana Purchase above the 36° 30' latitude line

GO ON TO THE NEXT PAGE.

4. The New Deal's most significant legacy is that it
   (A) saved the nation's institutions from extinction
   (B) expanded federal presence both in the economy and peoples' lives
   (C) made the United States the largest creditor nation in the world
   (D) ended the Jazz Age
   (E) began a Republican dynasty that lasted nearly three decades

5. The GI Bill provided
   (A) education, job training, medical care, pensions, and mortgage loans to veterans
   (B) entertainment for the troops
   (C) higher pay for soldiers
   (D) transportation home for wounded soldiers
   (E) free housing for veterans of both World War I and World War II

6. "The woman took the tiny clod of dirt and placed it in the middle of the great sea turtle's back. Then the woman began to walk in a circle around it, moving in the direction that the sun goes. The earth began to grow. When the earth was big enough, she planted the roots she had clutched between her fingers when she fell from the Sky-World. Thus the plants grew on the earth."

   From the Iroquois myth above, historians can reasonably conclude that
   (A) Iroquois women faced exploitation and abuse
   (B) Indians believed in renewal after the destruction of the smallpox epidemics
   (C) agriculture was important to woodland tribes like the Iroquois
   (D) tobacco became an important cash crop as Indians became implicated in colonial European commerce
   (E) European potatoes became an important part of the Indian diet during the Columbian Exchange

7. Which of the following correctly characterizes the political experience of the colonists after the Seven Years' (French and Indian) War?
   (A) The colonists had not yet experienced anything that could be classified as representative government.
   (B) The colonists seemed most comfortable waiting for directives from the king.
   (C) The colonists were accustomed to a significant degree of local self-government.
   (D) Smaller colonies looked to Massachusetts and Virginia for political leadership.
   (E) The colonists enjoyed direct representation in Parliament.

8. Initially, Thomas Jefferson was conflicted over the Louisiana Purchase because
   (A) he felt the Constitution did not specifically authorize such action
   (B) war with Spain might occur
   (C) he believed that the purchase was not a fair deal for France
   (D) the Federalists supported it
   (E) slavery would have to be permitted in the new territories

9. Which of the following statements is true about Amendments 13 to 20 of the Constitution of the United States?
   (A) The amendments reflected Americans' growing fear of a strong centralized government
   (B) Earlier constitutional protections were eviscerated by the new amendments
   (C) Generally speaking, the amendments sought to correct perceived errors in the Bill of Rights
   (D) The amendments marked a new era of both stronger federal regulations and protections
   (E) The amendments had little impact on the lives of most Americans

GO ON TO THE NEXT PAGE.

10. Woodrow Wilson's Fourteen Points incorporated all of the following EXCEPT
    (A) open diplomacy
    (B) freedom of the seas
    (C) support for imperialist authority
    (D) creation of an international organization to preserve the peace and security of its members
    (E) national self-determination

IMMIGRATION BY DECADE

Year	Number	Immigrants during this Decade as a Percentage of Total Population	Year	Number	Immigrants during this Decade as a Percentage of Total Population
1821–1830	151,824	1.6	1921–1930	4,107,209	3.9
1831–1840	599,125	4.6	1931–1940	528,431	0.4
1841–1850	1,713,251	10.0	1941–1950	1,035,039	0.7
1851–1860	2,598,214	11.2	1951–1960	2,515,479	1.6
1861–1870	2,314,824	7.4	1961–1970	3,321,677	1.8
1871–1880	2,812,191	7.1	1971–1980	4,493,000	2.2
1881–1890	5,246,613	10.5	1981–1990	7,338,000	3.0
1891–1900	3,687,546	5.8	1991–2000	9,095,083	3.7
1901–1910	8,795,386	11.6	**Total**	**32,433,918**	
1911–1920	5,735,811	6.2			
Total	**33,654,785**		1821–2000	**GRAND TOTAL**	**66,088,703**

Sources: U.S. Bureau of the Census, *Historical Statistics of the United States, Colonial Times to 1970* (1975), part 1, 105–106; *Statistical Abstract of the United States, 2001*.

11. According to the chart above, immigration had the greatest impact on American society
    (A) between 1921 and 1930
    (B) between 1881 and 1890
    (C) between 1851 and 1860
    (D) between 1861 and 1870
    (E) between 1901 and 1910

12. Which of the following is true about life in the United States during the Cold War?
    (A) Fearful of too powerful a government, the public insisted on decreasing the power of the president.
    (B) Tension over communism abroad fostered a period of domestic repression and fear at home.
    (C) Intent on protecting itself from communism within its own government at home, the United States banned covert operations abroad.
    (D) Fearing socialism, Congress cut back on Social Security and unemployment insurance.
    (E) The cost of countering communism was so great that the American standard of living declined in the postwar period.

13 Which of the following was NOT an element of Lyndon Johnson's Great Society?
    (A) Civil rights legislation
    (B) Education initiatives
    (C) Health-care reform
    (D) Poverty programs
    (E) Counterculture

GO ON TO THE NEXT PAGE.

"Civilization begins at home"

Library of Congress.

14. The cartoonist who created the above image was most likely
    - (A) critiquing the Ku Klux Klan's influence during the Grant administration
    - (B) pushing for a U.S. invasion of the Philippines
    - (C) decrying Japanese abuses during the Bataan Death March
    - (D) protesting U.S. annexation of the Philippines
    - (E) promoting the expansion of American liberties around the world

15. In *Muller v. Oregon,* the Supreme Court agreed with Progressive reformers who asserted that
    - (A) African Americans should receive equal pay for equal work
    - (B) child labor under the age of fourteen should be prohibited
    - (C) the federal government had no interest in regulating occupational safety
    - (D) female workers required special rules and protections on the job
    - (E) the railroads were exploiting farmers

16. The Marshall Plan
    - (A) helped to rebuild European economies
    - (B) emphasized the destruction of Communist economies
    - (C) had no benefit to American companies
    - (D) led to the Korean War
    - (E) was a failure

17. One way in which William Penn's colony was distinctive was that it
    - (A) required membership in the Puritan church
    - (B) negotiated fairly with Indians
    - (C) based its economy solely on tobacco
    - (D) was devoted to the Anglican Church
    - (E) violently seized land from Indians

GO ON TO THE NEXT PAGE.

18. Although suffrage requirements varied from colony to colony, all eighteenth-century voting laws included a
    (A) property qualification
    (B) education qualification
    (C) gender qualification
    (D) slave-ownership qualification
    (E) religious qualification

19. Which of the following quotations best embodies the viewpoint presented in Thomas Paine's *Common Sense*?
    (A) "A government of our own is our natural right . . . TIS TIME TO PART."
    (B) "It was the best of times. It was the worst of times."
    (C) "The right to levy internal taxes was never supposed to be in Parliament as we are not represented there."
    (D) "The exercise of [Parliamentary] authority is not perfectly constitutional in respect to the colonies."
    (E) "We hold these truths to be self-evident, that all men are created equal."

20. The antebellum reform movement was, in large part, precipitated by
    (A) national government initiatives
    (B) a religious revival movement
    (C) state government initiatives
    (D) an economic recession
    (E) nativist pressures

21. Which of the following religious movements originated in the United States?
    (A) Mormonism
    (B) Puritanism
    (C) Presbyterianism
    (D) Unitarianism
    (E) Catholicism

22. Which provision of the 1954 Geneva Accords was never realized?
    (A) Free elections for a united Vietnam in 1956
    (B) French withdrawal of troops in the north
    (C) Partitioning of Vietnam
    (D) Establishment of a demarcation line at the seventeenth parallel
    (E) Unification of North and South Vietnam

23. One result of the postwar housing boom was
    (A) Levittown
    (B) urbanization
    (C) the Sunbelt
    (D) "half down and ten years to pay"
    (E) "the Affluent Society"

GO ON TO THE NEXT PAGE.

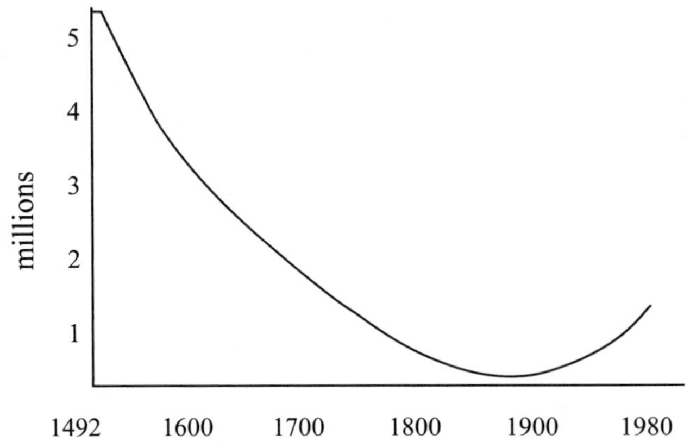

American Indian Population Decline and Recovery in the United States Area, 1492–1980

24. What was the most significant cause of the situation shown on the graph above between 1492 and 1700?
    (A) European warfare
    (B) Native American wars over territory
    (C) Disease
    (D) Famine
    (E) Religious wars

25. Andrew Jackson supported all of the following EXCEPT
    (A) Indian removal
    (B) the right of states to nullify federal laws
    (C) the removal of federal deposits from the Bank of the United States
    (D) use of the presidential veto power
    (E) annexation of new territory

26. Emerson's idea of personal improvement through spiritual awareness and self-discipline contradicted the fundamental principles of
    (A) transcendentalism
    (B) the Second Great Awakening
    (C) predestination
    (D) deism
    (E) Unitarianism

27. One result of the Enrollment Act of 1863 was
    (A) rioting in New York City
    (B) a fairer draft system was set up in the South than in the North
    (C) the elimination of the inequities of service
    (D) a system for punishing draft dodgers
    (E) an end to the exemption fee

GO ON TO THE NEXT PAGE.

28. *Plessy v. Ferguson* (1896) was significant because
    (A) it established the precedent of "separate but equal" facilities in the South
    (B) the Supreme Court declared that Congress could not restrict slavery
    (C) it decreed that the courts, not the president, would determine between good and bad trusts
    (D) the Supreme Court upheld the legality of restricting workers' workday hours
    (E) it protected each citizen's right to "due process"

29. "[The power to conquer and create colonies] is not among the express powers granted in the Constitution. This power our forefathers and their descendants loathed and abhorred . . . The power to conquer alien peoples and hold them in subjugation is nowhere implied as necessary for the accomplishment of the purposes declared by the Constitution."

    Which statement concerning the quote above is true?
    (A) The author is referring to America's occupation of Cuba.
    (B) Alfred T. Mahan and Teddy Roosevelt shared the author's sentiments.
    (C) The author is an anti-imperialist.
    (D) The author is a late-nineteenth-century proponent of the ideology of Manifest Destiny.
    (E) The author believes the United States has the duty to serve as a global policeman protecting democracy and free markets in fledgling nations.

30. America's entry into World War I
    (A) confirmed one of the most important shifts of power in the twentieth century
    (B) came as a huge surprise to Europe
    (C) was the first time the United States fought a European nation
    (D) allowed England and France to send their troops home
    (E) was the first time American soldiers fought on foreign soil

31. Which of the following is true about how social groups were influenced by the New Deal?
    (A) New Deal programs treated women and men equally.
    (B) Discrimination was not allowed in New Deal programs.
    (C) African Americans outside the South shifted their voting patterns away from the party of Lincoln.
    (D) Mexican Americans increasingly clung to their heritage and refused to Americanize.
    (E) The New Deal strengthened the Dawes Act to help the Indians.

32. What is one reason why the New England colonies developed differently from the Chesapeake colonies?
    (A) New England settlers rejected the institution of slavery.
    (B) The New England colonies were run by corporations.
    (C) Religion was a much more important force in shaping New England society than it was in shaping Chesapeake society.
    (D) The migrants who chose to settle in New England were generally younger than those who settled in the Chesapeake.
    (E) Relations with Native Americans were much more peaceful in New England.

GO ON TO THE NEXT PAGE.

33. Which of the following was true of the United States Constitution as adopted at the Constitutional Convention in September 1787?
    (A) It was built on a series of compromises.
    (B) It included a Bill of Rights.
    (C) It was a revised version of the English Constitution.
    (D) It exactly reflected Madison's proposed Virginia Plan.
    (E) It included a presidential cabinet.

34. Which of the following was most responsible for encouraging the growth of domestic markets in the first half of the nineteenth century?
    (A) An increase in the number of large factories
    (B) Better transportation networks
    (C) The national bank's loan policy
    (D) The national government's economic subsidies
    (E) Increased farm production

35. The Know-Nothing party was created in opposition to
    (A) women's rights advocates
    (B) nativists
    (C) Irish and German immigrants
    (D) abolitionists
    (E) supporters of the Mexican War

36. Which of the following did NOT support slavery?
    (A) Southern churches
    (B) Southern white non-slaveholders
    (C) Free blacks
    (D) The U.S. Constitution
    (E) Quakers

37. In the first half of the nineteenth century, American manufacturers' main advantage over the British mills was that they had
    (A) cheaper shipping
    (B) lower interest rates
    (C) more natural resources
    (D) a ready supply of cheap labor
    (E) a longer history of success

38. During the Civil War, both sides financed their cause through
    (A) income taxes
    (B) creating a national banking system
    (C) taxing exports
    (D) confiscation of personal property
    (E) issuing paper money

39. The Union general considered the most ruthless by southerners was
    (A) Ulysses S. Grant
    (B) William T. Sherman
    (C) Stonewall Jackson
    (D) George McClellan
    (E) Robert Scott

GO ON TO THE NEXT PAGE.

40. As a result of the Spanish-American War, Spain relinquished to the United States control of Cuba, Puerto Rico, and which of the following?
    (A) Alaska
    (B) Hawaii
    (C) The Panama Canal Zone
    (D) Guam
    (E) The Philippines

41. President Franklin Roosevelt differed from President Herbert Hoover in his
    (A) commitment to maintaining the nation's basic institutions
    (B) belief in the basic morality of a balanced budget
    (C) belief in the value of hard work, cooperation, and sacrifice
    (D) personal charisma and willingness to experiment
    (E) acceptance of the Reconstruction Finance Corporation

42. During the Age of Exploration, the Columbian Exchange trade routes shifted from the
    (A) Atlantic to the Pacific Ocean
    (B) Atlantic to the Indian Ocean
    (C) Mediterranean Sea to the Atlantic Ocean
    (D) Indian to the Atlantic Ocean
    (E) Mediterranean Sea to the Indian Ocean

43. An example of mercantilism is
    (A) The Proclamation of 1763
    (B) The Navigation Acts
    (C) The Dominion of New England
    (D) Leisler's Rebellion
    (E) The Albany Plan

44. "By the rude bridge that arched the flood,
    Their flag to April's breeze unfurled,
    Here once the embattled farmers stood,
    And fired the shot heard 'round the world."
    To which event do the preceding words of Ralph Waldo Emerson refer?
    (A) The Boston Massacre
    (B) The Boston Tea Party
    (C) Shays's Rebellion
    (D) The Battles of Lexington and Concord
    (E) The Battle of Saratoga

45. The notion of slavery as a "necessary evil" and a "positive good" was supported by which idea?
    (A) In a slave country, every free man is an aristocrat.
    (B) Slavery gave whites the psychological satisfaction of knowing they ranked above blacks.
    (C) Slavery allowed a civilized lifestyle for whites and provided tutelage for genetically inferior blacks.
    (D) Whites educated and Christianized slaves in return for their labor and loyalty.
    (E) Slavery was an economic necessity that promoted greater economic opportunity for all white people.

GO ON TO THE NEXT PAGE.

46. The South was unable to convince England to enter the Civil War on her behalf largely because
    (A) England no longer needed Southern cotton
    (B) of the increased importance of the American merchant marine
    (C) England's agriculture was self-sufficient
    (D) the English public was indifferent to the war
    (E) the South was winning militarily during the first three years of the war

47. William Randolph Hearst's and Joseph Pulitzer's sensationalist style of reporting was known as
    (A) scandal sheet copy
    (B) star exposure
    (C) paparazzi coverage
    (D) human interest writing
    (E) yellow journalism

48. Which of the following made the growth of skyscrapers possible?
    (A) The development of steel girders, plate glass, and elevators
    (B) Government subsidies to contractors who would build them
    (C) Architects competing for the "Form Follows Function Award"
    (D) The newly built system of canals that connected cities to sources for building materials
    (E) Innovations in light-weight aluminum construction

49. "You shall not crucify mankind on a cross of gold," is a line from a speech given by
    (A) William Jennings Bryan at the 1896 Democratic Nominating Convention
    (B) William McKinley from his home in Canton, Ohio
    (C) Marcus Hanna when he nominated McKinley for president
    (D) Grover Cleveland when he spoke against the Sherman Silver Purchase Act
    (E) Benjamin Harrison in his presidential campaign in 1888

50. Industrialism and urbanization changed middle-class family life in all of the following ways EXCEPT
    (A) families became smaller
    (B) separate spheres emerged for husbands and wives
    (C) the family home became a sanctuary from the outside world
    (D) home schooling increased
    (E) families took advantage of outside services for things they once did at home

51. A key leader of the Progressives who pushed for the rights of referendum and recall was
    (A) Robert La Follette
    (B) Joseph Cannon
    (C) William Howard Taft
    (D) Theodore Roosevelt
    (E) Robert Wagner

52. One great irony of America's involvement in World War I was that it fought for democracy
    (A) side-by-side with Communists in 1918
    (B) while supporting a monarchy
    (C) with a Jim Crow army
    (D) with airplanes against a cavalry
    (E) even though many Americans couldn't vote

GO ON TO THE NEXT PAGE.

53. Three dominant features of the 1950s suburban nation were
    (A) nightclubs, immigration, and subways
    (B) houses, cars, and children
    (C) trains, buses, and skyscrapers
    (D) air conditioning, public schools, and desegregation
    (E) hippies, sexual liberation, and protests

54. President Eisenhower's promotion of the civil rights movement involved
    (A) initiating the construction of a national interstate system
    (B) publicly supporting the Greensboro sit-in
    (C) sending troops into Little Rock, Arkansas
    (D) attending the Bretton Woods Conference
    (E) privately supporting the *Brown v. Board of Education* decision

55. The Declaration of Independence did all of the following EXCEPT
    (A) appeal to the philosophy of natural rights
    (B) call for the abolition of the slave trade
    (C) officially end the colonies' political ties to Britain
    (D) accuse George III of tyranny
    (E) assert the right of the thirteen United States to declare war

56. Both Shays's Rebellion and the Whiskey Rebellions were
    (A) slave revolts
    (B) insurrections over the Alien and Sedition Acts
    (C) spontaneous uprisings regarding United States foreign policy
    (D) tax revolts
    (E) Embargo Act protests

57. The terms of the Treaty of Guadalupe-Hidalgo ending the Mexican War included all of the following EXCEPT
    (A) giving the United States present-day California, New Mexico, Arizona, Nevada, and Utah
    (B) acceptance of the United States' annexation of Texas
    (C) the banning of slavery from all territory ceded to the United States
    (D) a guarantee of liberty, property and rights to male citizens of the ceded area
    (E) United States payment of $15 million for all of the ceded land from Mexico

58. The Emancipation Proclamation stated that
    (A) slaves in the seceded states would be freed
    (B) slaves in the border states would be freed
    (C) all slaves in the United States would be freed
    (D) all fugitive slaves and all slaves captured by the Union Army were forever free
    (E) the Union Army was authorized to confiscate all property, including slaves, used to support the rebellion

GO ON TO THE NEXT PAGE.

59. "Possibly our efforts slightly modified the worst conditions, but they still remained intolerable, and the fourth summer the situation became for me absolutely desperate when I realized in a moment of panic that my delicate little nephew for whom I was guardian could not be with me at Hull-House at all unless the sickening odors were reduced."

Who is the most likely author of the sentence above?

(A) Jane Addams
(B) Alice Paul
(C) Elizabeth Cady Stanton
(D) Sojourner Truth
(E) Rose Schneiderman

60. The administrations of President Lincoln during the Civil War and President Wilson during World War I both

(A) created huge bureaucracies to help with the war effort
(B) had the unquestioned loyalty of the American people
(C) limited individual liberties
(D) put great confidence in their generals
(E) had weak cabinets

61. The "new immigrants" who entered the United States from 1880–1920

(A) found adjustment to the new country easier than earlier groups
(B) often lived among their own ethnic groups and had their own institutions
(C) came from Asia and Eastern Europe
(D) were welcomed much more graciously than were the Irish in 1840
(E) mostly settled on Midwestern farms

62. The concept that championed black literature and cultural identity in the midst of white society was known as the

(A) Harlem Renaissance
(B) Jazz Age
(C) Lost Generation
(D) Back-to-Africa movement
(E) Black-Is-Beautiful movement

63. Franklin Roosevelt's Good Neighbor policy

(A) renounced the use of military force and armed intervention in Latin America
(B) promised "all aid short of war" to Great Britain
(C) created "lend-lease"
(D) improved economic relations with Canada
(E) asserted that all states must recognize the laws of other states

64. Which of the following was NOT agreed to at Yalta?

(A) The division of Germany into four occupation zones
(B) The establishment of the United Nations
(C) The determination that the Soviets would have a sphere of influence in Eastern Europe
(D) Dropping the atomic bomb on Japan
(E) The United States, France, England, China, and the Soviet Union becoming permanent members of the Security Council

GO ON TO THE NEXT PAGE.

65. The Gulf of Tonkin Resolution
   (A) stated that America would support the anti-Communist Diem regime in South Vietnam
   (B) declared that "we are not going to send American boys . . . thousands of miles away . . . to do what Asian boys ought to do for themselves"
   (C) outlined the plans for bombing Hanoi with a nuclear weapon
   (D) gave Congressional approval for using Agent Orange in the jungles of Vietnam
   (E) authorized the president to take any action necessary to prevent further aggression in Vietnam

66. In 1968, the American Indian Movement was organized to protest all of the following EXCEPT
   (A) an unemployment rate ten times worse than the national average
   (B) inadequate housing
   (C) the highest disease rates in the nation
   (D) the least access to education in the country
   (E) the Indian Removal Act

67. Of the following, who would most likely become a Federalist?
   (A) A yeoman farmer in Kentucky
   (B) A tenant in Ohio Territory
   (C) A Shaysite in western Massachusetts
   (D) A Tennessee squatter
   (E) A Pennsylvania merchant

68. The Compromise of 1850 included all of the following EXCEPT
   (A) admittance of California as a free state
   (B) a strong fugitive slave law
   (C) popular sovereignty in the Mexican cession
   (D) abolition of the slave trade in Washington, D.C.
   (E) a constitutional amendment that would permanently balance power between slave and free states

69. In the slave-based colonial societies of the South
   (A) only about 5 to 10 percent of the population dominated the republican institutions
   (B) small landowners were the heart of the community
   (C) the culture was more egalitarian than that of the northern colonies
   (D) relationships between poor whites and freed blacks were encouraged
   (E) nearly everyone owned at least several slaves

70. The Thirteenth Amendment
   (A) balanced the power between the North and the South in the Senate
   (B) protected citizens through *habeas corpus*
   (C) prohibited slavery throughout the United States
   (D) granted citizenship to slaves freed by the Emancipation Proclamation
   (E) made secession from the Union illegal

GO ON TO THE NEXT PAGE.

71. The Freedman's Bureau was
    (A) founded by ex-Confederate states to help rebuild the South
    (B) instituted by private citizens to help former slaves
    (C) part of Lincoln's Ten Percent Plan
    (D) created by Congress to help ex-slaves adjust to freedom and secure their basic civil rights
    (E) an organization established to help southern whites deal with the problem of freed slaves

72. To encourage business enterprise, the national government provided railroad companies with
    (A) land grants and incorporation
    (B) subsidies and business advice
    (C) entrepreneurial assistance
    (D) discounted steel for their rails
    (E) tax breaks and business advice

73. The last great Indian "battle" was a massacre of Sioux Indians
    (A) known as the Great Northern War
    (B) in Mesa Verde
    (C) in Oklahoma
    (D) at Wounded Knee
    (E) at Little Big Horn

74. The Haymarket incident in 1886
    (A) led to an eight-hour day for the McCormick reaper workers
    (B) led to the downfall of the Knights of Labor
    (C) led to an increase in respect for unions
    (D) was an incident in which the police showed great restraint
    (E) had leaders who were pardoned by the courts

75. Booker T. Washington's Atlanta Compromise suggested that
    (A) accommodation would lead to black economic progress, which would lead to political and civil rights
    (B) quotas would be set for admission of African Americans into white schools
    (C) African Americans would fight for their place in society peacefully
    (D) blacks would stop rioting if they were given voting rights
    (E) the NAACP would thereafter settle discrimination situations

76. Which of the following is NOT a contribution of the Progressives?
    (A) Presidential leadership was important again.
    (B) Government took on a new role in the nation's life.
    (C) A radical ideology began that would last for thirty years.
    (D) The foundation for twentieth-century social and economic policy was laid.
    (E) The federal government was expanded in service to a cautious and pragmatic approach to the nation's problems.

GO ON TO THE NEXT PAGE.

77. Franklin Roosevelt's initial response to the Supreme Court's declaring the NRA, the AAA, and other New Deal legislation unconstitutional was to
    (A) ask Congress to impeach several justices
    (B) attempt to pack the Courts with his own men
    (C) change those parts of the legislation the courts found objectionable
    (D) ignore it and move on making sure subsequent laws were worded more carefully
    (E) threaten the justices with removal from office if they did not comply with his program

78. The most significant impact of the Korean War was that, throughout the remainder of the Cold War,
    (A) even in peacetime, the United States kept a standing army activated
    (B) military expenditures were drastically cut
    (C) American involvement in Asia decreased
    (D) Congress held a tight rein on the president so there would be no more undeclared wars
    (E) the American economy continually flirted with recession

79. Many historians consider Kennedy's greatest foreign policy blunder to be the
    (A) Cuban Missile Crisis
    (B) building of the Berlin Wall
    (C) Bay of Pigs invasion
    (D) Alliance for Progress
    (E) Bretton Woods system

80. Which of the following is NOT representative of the Carter administration?
    (A) American boycott of the Moscow Olympics
    (B) The Iranian hostage affair
    (C) The Camp David accords
    (D) Creation of the Office of Human Rights in the State Department
    (E) A stable, prosperous economy

STOP

END OF SECTION I

UNITED STATES HISTORY
SECTION II

Part A
Document-Based Question
(Suggested Writing Time—45 minutes)
Percent of Section II score—45

Directions: The following question requires you to construct a coherent essay that integrates your interpretation of Documents A–I and your knowledge of the period referred to in the question. High scores are earned only by essays that cite key pieces of evidence from the documents and draw on outside knowledge of the period.

1. At the Yalta Conference in February 1945, the United States and the Soviet Union agreed to recognize their separate spheres of influence. In what ways did the United States implement foreign policies in response to the breakdown in relations with the Soviet Union?

Use the documents and your knowledge of the era to construct your response.

GO ON TO THE NEXT PAGE.

Document A

Source: Library of Congress Prints and Photographs Division.

Prime Minister Winston Churchill, President Franklin D. Roosevelt, and Marshal Joseph Stalin at the palace in Yalta, February 1945.

Library of Congress, Prints and Photographs Division.

Document B

Source: Arthur Vandenburg, Speech to the Senate in Support of the United Nations (1945).

The San Francisco Charter may not succeed in its God-blessed purposes. Personally, I think it will. World War No. 3 is too horrible to contemplate. It clearly threatens the end of civilization. Here is our chance to try to stop this disaster before it starts; and here is a formula which, in its initial operation at the San Francisco Conference, has proved that it can work in harmonizing controversies among fifty nations of this world.

GO ON TO THE NEXT PAGE.

Document C

Source: Winston Churchill, The Sinews of Peace Speech at Westminster College (1946).

If the population of the English-speaking Commonwealths be added to that of the United States with all that such co-operation implies in the air, on the sea, all over the globe and in science and in industry, and in moral force, there will be no quivering, precarious balance of power to offer its temptation to ambition or adventure. On the contrary, there will be an overwhelming assurance of security. If we adhere faithfully to the Charter of the United Nations and walk forward in sedate and sober strength seeking no one's land or treasure, seeking to lay no arbitrary control upon the thoughts of men; if all British moral and material forces and convictions are joined with your own in fraternal association, the high-roads of the future will be clear, not only for us but for all, not only for our time, but for a century to come.

Document D

Source: Nikolai Novikov, Soviet Ambassador to the United States, Telegram (1946).

The political support that the United States provides for England is very often manifested in the international events of the postwar period. At recent international conferences the United States and England have closely coordinated their policies, especially in cases when they had to oppose the policy of the Soviet Union.

Document E

Source: Harry S. Truman, The Truman Doctrine (1947).

One of the primary objectives of the foreign policy of the United States is the creation of conditions in which we and other nations will be able to work out a way of life free from coercion.... To ensure the peaceful development of nations, free from coercion, the United States has taken a leading part in establishing the United Nations. The United Nations is designed to make possible lasting freedom and independence for all its members. We shall not realize our objectives, however, unless we are willing to help free peoples to maintain their free institutions and their national integrity against aggressive movements that seek to impose upon them totalitarian regimes. . . .

GO ON TO THE NEXT PAGE.

Document F

Source: NSC-68: United States Objectives and Programs for National Security (1950).

For the time being, the United States possesses a marked atomic superiority over the Soviet Union which, together with the potential capabilities of the United States and other free countries in other forces and weapons, inhibits aggressive Soviet action. This provides an opportunity for the United States, in cooperation with other free countries, to launch a build-up of strength which will support a firm policy directed to the frustration of the Kremlin design.

Document G

Source: Douglas MacArthur, Farewell Address to Congress (1951).

Through these past 50 years, the Chinese people have thus become militarized in their concepts and in their ideals. They now constitute excellent soldiers with competent staffs and commanders. This has produced a new and dominant power in Asia which for its own purposes is allied with Soviet Russia, but which in its own concepts and methods has become aggressively imperialistic, with a lust for expansion and increased power normal to this type of imperialism.

Document H

Source: Memorandum of a Conversation among Secretary of State John Foster Dulles, British Foreign Minister Selwyn Lloyd, and French Foreign Minister Christian Pineau (1956).

Lloyd: We don't think the United States realizes the importance that France and the UK attach to the Suez…We are risking all of our influence in that part of the world. We are willing to do all in our power not to use force, but Nasser surely will go farther and farther…Russia is in back of him. The chief of all navigation in the Canal Zone now is a Russian. We risk Russian domination of the whole area. The temporizing tactics of the U.S. alarm us. We will play the game in the Security Council but we will not get bogged down in procedure.

Document I

Source: Robert S. McNamara, "Actions Recommended for Vietnam" (1966).

In essence, we find ourselves…no better, and if anything worse off. This important war must be fought and won by the Vietnamese themselves. We have known this from the beginning. But the discouraging truth is that, as was the case in 1961 and 1963 and 1965, we have not found the formula, the catalyst, for training and inspiring them into effective action.

END OF DOCUMENTS FOR QUESTION 1

UNITED STATES HISTORY
SECTION II

Part B and Part C
Free-Response Questions
(Suggested total planning and writing time—70 minutes)
Percent of Section II score—55

Part B

Directions: Choose ONE question from this part. You are advised to spend 5 minutes planning and 30 minutes writing your answer. Cite relevant historical evidence in support of your generalizations and present your arguments clearly and logically.

2. Compare and contrast the economic, political, and cultural developments of TWO of the following colonial empires in America:

   Spain
   Great Britain
   France
   The Netherlands

3. How and why did transportation improvements spark economic growth between 1800 and 1860?

Part C

Directions: Choose ONE question from this part. You are advised to spend 5 minutes planning and 30 minutes writing your answer. Cite relevant historical evidence in support of your generalizations and present your arguments clearly and logically.

4. "It is impossible to understand American attitudes and values without examining the influence of the frontier." Assess the validity of this statement.

5. To what extent did the United States' acquisition of overseas territories represent the desire to spread democratic institutions?

STOP

END OF EXAM

Answer Key for Practice Exam 2

Answers for Section I: Multiple-Choice Questions

1. B	21. A	41. D	61. B
2. B	22. A	42. C	62. A
3. D	23. A	43. B	63. A
4. B	24. C	44. D	64. D
5. A	25. B	45. C	65. E
6. C	26. C	46. A	66. E
7. C	27. A	47. E	67. E
8. A	28. A	48. A	68. E
9. D	29. C	49. A	69. A
10. C	30. A	50. D	70. C
11. E	31. C	51. A	71. D
12. B	32. C	52. C	72. A
13. E	33. A	53. B	73. D
14. D	34. B	54. C	74. B
15. D	35. C	55. B	75. A
16. A	36. E	56. D	76. C
17. B	37. C	57. C	77. B
18. A	38. E	58. A	78. A
19. A	39. B	59. A	79. C
20. B	40. E	60. C	80. E

1. **Answer (B) To exploit colonial resources for the benefit of Britain.** This is essentially the definition of mercantilism: it's a set of policies to regulate colonial economies to benefit the mother country—in this case, Great Britain. All of the European colonial powers used it to amass wealth: that way they could fight wars to win more territory. (*America's History,* Seventh Edition, Chapter 3, pp. 76–77)

2. **Answer (B) an Antifederalist.** Clues are "this new government," and "tyranny must and will arise." These words were said by Virginian Patriot Patrick Henry—most famous for the words "Give me liberty, or give me death!"—who opposed the strong federal government the 1787 Constitution proposed. (*America's History,* Seventh Edition, Chapter 6, pp. 198–199)

3. **Answer (D) any European interference in the Americas would be seen as a hostility to the United States.** Written by Secretary of State John Q. Adams and delivered by James Monroe, the Doctrine was a warning to European powers and served to shape American foreign policy in Latin America for nearly a century—Teddy Roosevelt would add his own spin to it during his presidency (1901–1908). (*America's History,* Seventh Edition, Chapter 7, p. 232)

4. **Answer (B) expanded federal presence in both the economy and peoples' lives.** None of the other answers are credible: American institutions had not been close to extinction; the United States did not become the world's largest creditor nation as a result; the Jazz Age was a cultural phenomenon; and the largely popular New Deal was the work of Democrats, not Republicans. As your textbook authors explain, while its effectiveness continues to be debated, the New Deal undoubtedly changed American expectations of their government. (*America's History,* Seventh Edition, Chapter 23, pp. 723–725, 728)

5. **Answer (A) education, job training, medical care, pensions, and mortgage loans to veterans.** The GI Bill was credited with alleviating the kind of economic recession that occurred in the immediate aftermath of World War I, and it caused the United States workforce to become the best educated in the world in the 1950s and 1960s. (*America's History,* Seventh Edition, Chapter 24, p. 763 and Chapter 26, pp. 823–824)

6. **Answer (C) agriculture was important to tribes like the Iroquois.** This is a "skill" question: what can be known from this primary source? The correct answer assumes the least: farming was clearly important to a people who told myths such as the one excerpted in the question. (*America's History,* Seventh Edition, Chapter 2, p. 45 has more information about the Iroquois)

7. **Answer (C) The colonists were accustomed to a significant degree of local self-government.** From colonial assemblies to town meetings to the communication and travel challenges the British faced in ruling colonists an ocean away, the British colonists managed their affairs quite independently for generations. One British official referred to their strategy as "salutary [beneficial] neglect." (*America's History,* Seventh Edition, Chapter 4, pp. 124–127)

8. **Answer (A) he felt the Constitution did not specifically authorize such action.** Like many presidents before and after him, Jefferson encountered challenges and opportunities during his presidency that challenged his previously stated political positions. One of these was his stance as a strict constructionalist of the Constitution—he had opposed Alexander Hamilton's plan for a national bank in the early 1790s on the grounds that it was not specifically permitted in the Constitution. (*America's History,* Seventh Edition, Chapter 7, p. 220)

9. **Answer (D) The amendments marked a new era of both stronger federal regulations and protections.** Amendments 13–20 encompass both Reconstruction and Progressive Era reforms, from the abolition of slavery and the protection of citizenship rights to the direct election of senators, prohibition, and extending suffrage to women. (*America's History,* Seventh Edition, Chapters 15 and 20)

10. **Answer (C) support for imperialist authority.** On the contrary, Wilson believed that European imperial competition was largely to blame for the start of World War I, and his proposal for national self-determination was a direct challenge to European imperial authority. The other answers are all included among the principles articulated in the Fourteen Points. (*America's History,* Seventh Edition, Chapter 21, p. 678)

11. **Answer (E) 1901 to 1910.** The significant figure to notice is not the total number of immigrants, since the American population grows so rapidly from the 1820s to the year 2000. The figure that is important is the percentage of immigrants as a percentage of the total population of the United States. The first decade of the twentieth century thus saw the most significant demographic impact of immigration, at 11.6 percent of total population. (*America's History,* Seventh Edition, Chapter 17, pp. 544–549)

12. **Answer (B) Tension over communism abroad fostered a period of domestic repression and fear at home.** During the Cold War, the government—especially

the presidency—became more powerful, and the CIA engaged in covert operations around the world. Despite continued investment in the social safety net, the American standard of living rose overall—although poverty and discrimination persisted for many. (*America's History,* Seventh Edition, Chapter 25, pp. 801–806 and Chapter 26, pp. 820–821)

13. **Answer (E) Counterculture.** The Great Society was Johnson's term for the program of legislation he pursued to help alleviate the suffering of poverty, hunger, and inequality in America. The counterculture of the 1960s was not a government program—it arose from mostly young Americans as an alternative to the materialistic, militaristic, and conformist aspects of Cold War America. (*America's History,* Seventh Edition, Chapters 27 and 28, pp. 868, 885–888)

14. **Answer (D) protesting U.S. annexation of the Philippines.** The three important symbols of this cartoon are the map of the Philippines, Lady Liberty, and the tragic background image of an African American being lynched—a horror at the turn of the century. The juxtaposition of these symbols suggest that the cartoonist believed the United States had problems of its own to address before it could consider annexing additional territory. (*America's History,* Seventh Edition, Chapter 21, pp. 656–659)

15. **Answer (D) female workers required special rules and protections on the job.** This was an important triumph in the Progressives' and unions' ongoing efforts to make workplaces safer. Some feminists objected to the premise of *Muller v. Oregon,* however, because it relied on the perceived weaknesses of the female gender. (*America's History,* Seventh Edition, Chapter 20, p. 641)

16. **Answer (A) helped to rebuild European economies.** It also helped American businesses and promoted capitalism and free markets in contrast to the Communist economic policies pursued by the Soviet Union and its satellites. (*America's History,* Seventh Edition, Chapter 25, pp. 790–791)

17. **Answer (B) negotiated fairly with Indians.** It was also a religiously tolerant colony with a diverse economy. Penn's approach to governing was influenced greatly by his Quaker faith. (*America's History,* Seventh Edition, Chapter 3, pp. 75–76)

18. **Answer (A) property qualification.** This requirement was based in British tradition. Although the Revolution brought more "middling men" into state governments compared with the colonial assemblies, it wasn't until the late 1820s when all taxpaying men began to enjoy the citizenship rights of voting and holding office. (*America's History,* Seventh Edition, Chapter 6, p. 184)

19. **Answer (A) "A government of our own is our natural right . . . TIS TIME TO PART."** Answer B is the only quote that does not come from a revolutionary-era document: it is the opening line from Charles Dickens' *A Tale of Two Cities.* Response E should be recognizable as language from the Declaration of Independence. Clues in answer A that point to Paine's *Common Sense* are the appeal to natural rights, and the urgency of the message to separate from Great Britain. Paine's pamphlet helped to galvanize colonial sentiment for revolution in the winter of 1775–1776, leading to the writing and signing of the Declaration of Independence in July 1776. (*America's History,* Seventh Edition, Chapter 5, pp. 164–166)

20. **Answer (B) a religious revival movement.** It was the Second Great Awakening that inspired many of the reform movements of the early 1800s, including temperance and abolitionism. But middle-class reformers were also inspired negatively, by economic changes and a growing sense of disorder in cities. Historians call the efforts by ministers and lay people the "Benevolent Empire." (*America's History,* Seventh Edition, Chapter 9, pp. 293–296)

21. **Answer (A) Mormonism.** The Church of Latter-day Saints was founded in upstate New York by Joseph Smith, inspired in part by the Second Great Awakening. The *Book of Mormon* was published in 1830. The other denominations listed all had European origins. (*America's History,* Seventh Edition, Chapter 11, pp. 339–341)

22. **Answer (A) Free elections for a united Vietnam in 1956.** The United States was largely responsible for this failure: Eisenhower's diplomats rejected the accords, and the CIA helped to establish the pro-American government of Ngo Dinh Diem in the southern portion of Vietnam to challenge Ho Chi Minh. (*America's History,* Seventh Edition, Chapter 25, p. 809)

23. **Answer (A) Levittown.** Levittowns were developments of identical houses that became a symbol of the wave of suburban growth in the postwar period. The Sunbelt refers to the shift in population and political power from the north to southern and western states around the same time. "Housing boom" are the words that point to Levittown, since it refers to housing development. (*America's History,* Seventh Edition, Chapter 26, p. 829)

24. **Answer (C) Disease.** Although warfare, famine, and religious strife all contributed to demographic disaster for American Indians, disease was far and away the most significant cause. Europeans, Asians, and Africans had interacted for centuries prior to contact with American peoples, which gave them the opportunity to build up immunity to diseases their populations had been exposed to for many generations. (*America's History,* Seventh Edition, Chapter 1, pp. 27, 30)

25. **Answer (B) the right of states to nullify federal laws.** This is one of those cases when a president has seen fit to adjust his previously held political positions when faced with challenges while in office. Although as a Democrat Jackson was more states-rights oriented, as president he responded decisively when South Carolina tried to nullify the Tariff of 1828, encouraging Congress to pass the Force Bill in 1833 to reign in South Carolina's unconstitutional act (declaring a federal law null). (*America's History,* Seventh Edition, Chapter 10, pp. 311–313)

26. **Answer (C) predestination.** Emerson conceived of the American idea of transcendentalism, a way of thinking coming out of his Unitarian faith that portrayed man as a "radically free" individual who should seek knowledge of the eternal through communion with nature, not social traditions and dogma. (*America's History,* Seventh Edition, Chapter 11, pp. 332–333)

27. **Answer (A) rioting in New York City.** One of many acts of dissent during the Civil War, working-class men in New York and elsewhere took to the streets to protest forced conscription. Because many viewed the war as a brutal effort to eliminate slavery, tragically, many of the protesters took out their anger on African American New Yorkers, even attacking an African American orphanage. (*America's History,* Seventh Edition, Chapter 14, pp. 439–441)

28. **Answer (A) it established the precedent of "separate but equal" facilities in the South.** *Plessy v. Ferguson* upheld segregation as the law of the land for generations, until the decision in *Brown v. Board of Education* overturned it in 1954. (*America's History,* Seventh Edition, Chapter 20, p. 635)

29. **Answer (C) The author is an anti-imperialist.** This statement was made following the Spanish-American War, as President McKinley decided what to do about the Philippines. Although the "splendid little war" of 1898 generated a wave of patriotic sentiment, to many Americans the concept of acquiring the Philippines as a colony was abhorrent. (*America's History,* Seventh Edition, Chapter 21, pp. 654–656)

30. **Answer (A) confirmed one of the most important shifts of power in the twentieth century.** Of course, the United States had fought European powers many times, from the Revolution onward; U.S. involvement did not surprise Europeans, but what it did signify was the global power shift from the imperial nations and empires of Europe to the United States, a shift that would be complete by 1945 and the end of World War II. (*America's History,* Seventh Edition, Chapter 21, pp. 667–671)

31. **Answer (C) African Americans outside the South shifted their voting patterns away from the party of Lincoln.** This marked a significant shift in voting patterns: after all, the Democratic Party was the party of "lost cause" apologists and white racists in the South since Reconstruction, while the Republican Party freed the slaves. But Franklin Roosevelt's New Deal caused working Americans of all racial backgrounds to believe that the Democratic Party cared more about their concerns than the Republican Party did. (*America's History,* Seventh Edition, Chapter 23, pp. 737–738)

32. **Answer (C) Religion was a much more important force in shaping New England society than it was in shaping Chesapeake society.** Because of their strong faith and establishment of public political and legal practices upon Puritan principles, New England communities developed quite differently from the slavery-dependent colonies in the Chesapeake. Violence and disorganization plagued Jamestown and other Virginia settlements for many years. (*America's History,* Seventh Edition, Chapter 2, pp. 49–51)

33. **Answer (A) It was built on a series of compromises.** There was no Bill of Rights or presidential cabinet in the original Constitution; establishing these were the first two orders of business Congress took on after the Constitution was ratified. Compromises balancing the interests of small and large states, as well as slave and free states, shaped the way the constitutional system would operate. (*America's History,* Seventh Edition, Chapter 6, pp. 193–198)

34. **Answer (B) Better transportation networks.** The main challenge for farmers and merchants was getting products from place to place: the interior of the country was difficult to penetrate. The federal government and many states built roads and dug canals (such as the epic Erie Canal in upstate New York) to facilitate commerce and the new market economy. (*America's History,* Seventh Edition, Chapter 9, pp. 283–289)

35. **Answer (C) Irish and German immigrants.** They were called the American Party officially, but their xenophobic platform of anti-immigrant sentiment was kept secret. The party arose in response to the large number of new immigrants from Ireland and Germany in the 1830s and 1840s. (*America's History,* Seventh Edition, Chapter 15, p. 420)

36. **Answer (E) Quakers.** The Quakers were America's first abolitionists, publically opposing the institution of slavery on moral grounds beginning in the eighteenth century. (*America's History,* Seventh Edition, Chapter 11, pp. 348–352)

37. **Answer (C) more natural resources.** The answer to this question reveals as much about Great Britain as it does about the young United States. Because the British lived on a small island nation with scant resources, they had to seek natural resources overseas in order to continue to industrialize. Americans had greater resources at their disposal but also felt compelled to expand—in their case, westward across the American continent rather than in distant continents. (*America's History,* Seventh Edition, Chapter 9, p. 277)

38. **Answer (E) issuing paper money.** In both cases but particularly in the South, the currency became extremely devalued as a result, and inflation wrecked havoc on the home front. (*America's History,* Seventh Edition, Chapter 14, pp. 443–446)

39. **Answer (B) William T. Sherman.** In justifying his destructive march through Georgia, Sherman explained that "[We] must make old and young, rich and poor, feel the hard hand of war." He eschewed traditional distinctions between the military and civilians, and southerners felt very bitter about the results. One could argue that a cost of this 'total war' military strategy was the resistance of white southerners to Reconstruction era policies. (*America's History,* Seventh Edition, Chapter 14, pp. 452–453, 456)

40. **Answer (E) The Philippines.** This island colony of Spain became the key problem for President McKinley once Spain was defeated, because Americans were sharply divided over what to do with it. Pro-imperialists thought that Americans should annex the islands, while anti-imperialists thought that it should be turned over to the Filipinos themselves. (*America's History,* Seventh Edition, Chapter 21, pp. 656–659)

41. **Answer (D) personal charisma and willingness to experiment.** By the end of his presidency and in the depths of the Great Depression, Hoover had begun to promote policies such as major public works projects that departed from the Republican philosophy of limited government. Yet these were not enough to alleviate widespread economic disaster. Roosevelt appropriated many of these policies and sold them more successfully through the program he called a New Deal for Americans, and he used mass media such as the radio to connect with Americans on a personal level. Roosevelt was more of a pragmatist than an ideologue, and he was willing to change course when a given policy didn't work. (*America's History,* Seventh Edition, Chapter 23, pp. 720–724)

42. **Answer (C) Mediterranean Sea to the Atlantic Ocean.** European merchants had long sailed the Mediterranean seeking purveyors of goods from Africa and Asia. Once they figured out the trade winds and currents of the Atlantic Ocean, trade routes shifted there and launched an unprecedented era of interaction known as the Columbian Exchange in which goods, peoples, animals, and disease circulated around the Atlantic basin. (*America's History,* Seventh Edition, Chapter 1, pp. 30–32)

43. **Answer (B) the Navigation Acts.** These acts of Parliament specifically promoted mercantilist policies because they sought to amass wealth in Great Britain and keep the colonies in a dependent economic position. (*America's History,* Seventh Edition, Chapter 3, pp. 76–77, 98–99)

44. **Answer (D) The Battles of Lexington and Concord.** These lines from Emerson's ode to the revolutionaries have been widely quoted, but perhaps you are not familiar with them. If you encounter a primary source excerpt on the AP test that you have not read in class, don't panic: just read carefully and look for clues. In this case, the words "April," "embattled farmers," and "shot heard round the world" point you to these opening moments of the Revolutionary War. (*America's History,* Seventh Edition, Chapter 5, p. 163 on Lexington/Concord, and Chapter 11, pp. 332–335, on Emerson)

45. **Answer (C) Slavery allowed a civilized lifestyle for whites and provided tutelage for genetically inferior blacks.** In the antebellum South, in response to the abolitionists' attacks on slavery starting in the 1830s, there was a shift in the southern defense of slavery. Jefferson and his generation of slaveholders tended to view the institution as a 'necessary evil,' but by the 1830s, the defense had intensified. Slavery was now a 'positive good' that both protected the perceived inferior race of slaves while allowing for the gentility and advancement of southern whites. (*America's History,* Seventh Edition, Chapter 12, pp. 371–373)

46. **Answer (A) England no longer needed Southern cotton.** When trouble brewed in the United States in the 1850s, British merchants stockpiled cotton and began to seek new sources from Egypt and India. This is one of the ways the American Civil War had a global impact. (*America's History,* Seventh Edition, Chapter 14, p. 443)

47. **Answer (E) yellow journalism.** The term refers to the cheap paper upon which such newspapers were printed but came to be associated with tabloid-style, attention-grabbing reporting that sometimes relied on innuendo and rumor rather than responsibly reported facts. (*America's History,* Seventh Edition, Chapter 19, pp. 604–605)

48. **Answer (A) The development of steel girders, plate glass, and elevators.** These were the innovations that made the vertical development of American cities possible, and it was a race to great heights sparked by corporate competition, profits, and the growth of the American steel industry (which also facilitated the rapid construction of railroad tracks in the decades following the Civil War). (*America's History,* Seventh Edition, Chapter 19, pp. 593–594)

49. **Answer (A) William Jennings Bryan at the 1896 Democratic Nominating Convention.** This is one of the classic American political speeches and addressed American farmers' populist interest in switching from a gold to silver currency standard. Most farmers were debtors, which meant that 'cheaper' currency would make it easier for them to pay their bills. The transition to a silver standard did not occur in the 1890s, but its prominence as a political issue speaks to the economic crisis that affected Americans in that difficult decade. (*America's History,* Seventh Edition, Chapter 20, pp. 632–635)

50. **Answer (D) home schooling increased.** On the contrary, it was this era that saw the spread of compulsory public education for all American children. But it is true that families became smaller; the home began to be seen as a sanctuary; and families could purchase many consumer products that used to be homemade. (*America's History,* Seventh Edition, Chapter 18, pp. 560–562)

51. **Answer (A) Robert La Follette.** Progressive reformers in state houses, city governments, the state level, and in new social agencies and services all had an impact on the way government worked; their efforts grew to a groundswell especially in the years 1901–1919. La Follette of Wisconsin advocated for the direct referendum in order to make the political process more democratic. (*America's History,* Seventh Edition, Chapter 20, p. 642)

52. **Answer (C) with a Jim Crow army.** American regiments in World War I were segregated by race, and black soldiers were not permitted to serve as officers. Despite these obstacles, over 400,000 African American soldiers served bravely. (*America's History,* Seventh Edition, Chapter 21, p. 671)

53. **Answer (B) houses, cars, and children.** The baby boom caused a huge demographic shift towards large families in the postwar years. Certain government policies such as the GI Bill facilitated the rapid growth of housing developments to fit all of these families; the chosen mode of transportation in the 1950s was automobiles. Another iconic aspect of 1950s life was the television set. (*America's History,* Seventh Edition, Chapter 26, pp. 825–827)

54. **Answer (C) sending troops into Little Rock, Arkansas.** President Eisenhower reluctantly upheld *Brown v. Board of Education* by sending in support only when the situation escalated to violence. Eisenhower's record on civil rights is not generally remembered as one of his presidency's strengths. (*America's History,* Seventh Edition, Chapter 27, pp. 860–861)

55. **Answer (B) call for the abolition of the slave trade.** In an early draft of the Declaration, Jefferson blamed the existence of slavery in the colonies among George III's long list of misdeeds, but members of the Second Continental Congress had that reference excised before signing the Declaration. The 1787 Constitution did, however, include a provision that called for the slave trade's abolishment exactly twenty years after ratification. (*America's History,* Seventh Edition, Chapter 5, pp. 165–167)

56. **Answer (D) tax revolts.** Shays's Rebellion in western Massachusetts was launched by farmers who felt that the Boston State House represented the interests of bankers and merchants in the eastern part of the state and ignored the economic desperation of farmers (many of them veterans) in the challenging years following the Revolution. The Whiskey Rebellion occurred during Washington's presidency in reaction against Hamilton's taxation policies. (*America's History,* Seventh Edition, Chapters 6–7, pp. 191–193, 208)

57. **Answer (C) the banning of slavery from all territory ceded to the United States.** Although antislavery Democrats and conscience Whigs in the North objected to the War with Mexico because of its potential to upset the slave/free balance of national power, the Treaty that ended the war had no provision to ban slavery in the acquired regions. Pennsylvania congressman David Wilmot tried to have a Proviso passed that would have banned slavery, but it did not pass. (*America's History,* Seventh Edition, Chapter 13, p. 408)

58. **Answer (A) slaves in the seceded states would be freed.** Lincoln could have abolished slavery in the border states, but he chose not to, given the tenuousness of the border states' support for the Union cause. In part, the Proclamation was a military strategy intended to disorder southern society, but it is momentous for its significant step on the road to slavery's end in the United States. That end came with ratification of the Thirteenth Amendment at the end of the Civil War. (*America's History,* Seventh Edition, Chapter 14, pp. 446–447)

59. **Answer (A) Jane Addams.** The key clue here is "Hull House," the settlement house in Chicago that Addams founded and ran to minister to the needs of the immigrant, poverty-stricken neighborhoods. Answers B, C, and D are the names of prominent feminist activists; Rose Schneiderman was a labor activist and socialist. (*America's History,* Seventh Edition, Chapter 19, pp. 612–614)

60. **Answer (C) limited individual liberties.** Lincoln suspended habeas corpus and permitted the military's expulsion of Ohio dissenter Clement Vallangdigham; Wilson compelled national unity during World War I through the Committee on Public Information, the Espionage Act of 1917, and the Sedition Act of 1918. The other answers to this question address qualities of one but not both of these war efforts; for example, Wilson indeed created a vast bureaucracy to support the war effort, while Lincoln did not. (*America's History,* Seventh Edition, Chapters 15 and 21, pp. 440, 673–674)

61. **Answer (B) often lived among their own ethnic groups and had their own institutions.** Despite maintaining their own traditions and ways, most immigrant families succumbed to the inevitable process of assimilation within a generation or two. (*America's History,* Seventh Edition, Chapter 19, pp. 594–600)

62. **Answer (A) Harlem Renaissance.** The Great Migration was the demographic movement of African Americans from the South to northern cities in pursuit of industrial jobs during and after World War I. As African American neighborhoods like Harlem in New York City grew, so too did a flowering of culture known as the Harlem Renaissance. Some of the most prominent writers and artists of the movement were Zora Neale Hurston, Jacob Lawrence, Langston Hughes, and Jean Toomer. (*America's History,* Seventh Edition, Chapter 22, p. 698)

63. **Answer (A) renounced the use of military force and armed intervention in Latin America.** From the war with Mexico to the Spanish-American War to Roosevelt's usurpation of Panama, the United States had done more than its share of meddling in the affairs of its Latin American neighbors. Its right to do so was first asserted in 1823 by President James Monroe. In the 1930s, President Roosevelt forged a new course

of cooperation, the "Good Neighbor" policy, which is not described in *America's History,* Seventh Edition, but is nevertheless an important bit of foreign policy history to remember.

64. **Answer (D) Dropping the atomic bomb on Japan.** The Manhattan Project, or building of atomic bombs, was such a state secret that even Vice President Truman didn't know about it until he became president in April of 1945 after Roosevelt's death. Roosevelt did not inform his allies, Stalin and Churchill, either, but at Yalta they did discuss strategies to end the conflict, the establishment of a United Nations, and what to do with Germany and its territories once unconditional surrender had been achieved. (*America's History,* Seventh Edition, Chapter 24, p. 782)

65. **Answer (E) authorized the preident to take any action necessary to prevent further aggression in Vietnam.** The Congress's approval of the Gulf of Tonkin resolution was the closest it ever got to an official declaration of war. In fact, the U.S. Congress hasn't made a formal declaration of war since 1941, during World War II, despite its numerous military actions in the seven decades since then. (*America's History,* Seventh Edition, Chapter 28, p. 891)

66. **Answer (E) the Indian Removal Act.** The Removal Act of 1830 was not on the list of grievances by Indian activists in the 1960s; in the intervening 130 years, countless other injustices and abuses had occurred, and conditions on Indian reservations were dire, including staggering unemployment, rampant alcoholism, and inadequate schooling, housing, and health care. (*America's History,* Seventh Edition, Chapter 27, pp. 877–878)

67. **Answer (E) a Pennsylvania merchant.** Merchants and bankers generally supported a stronger federal government and Secretary of the Treasury Alexander Hamilton's economic policies because instability was bad for business. Only a strong central government could put the United States on the path to economic growth, and the Federalist party supported such policies. (*America's History,* Seventh Edition, Chapters 6 and 7, pp. 198, 204, 208, 225)

68. **Answer (E) a constitutional amendment that would permanently balance power between slave and free states.** No constitutional amendment like this was ever passed. The Compromise of 1850 was a series of laws passed when the large territory called California applied for statehood. Its provisions, the most controversial of which was the fugitive slave law, were meant to appease both sides of the slavery divide, but it largely worsened relations between slave and free states. (*America's History,* Seventh Edition, Chapter 13, pp. 415–417)

69. **Answer (A) only about 5 to 10 percent of the population dominated the republican institutions.** The white planter elite wielded unlimited power over their slaves, and held the lion's share of political power in the colonies. It was anything but an egalitarian society. It is not true that "nearly everyone had at least several slaves"; but on the eve of Revolution in the Chesapeake, 60 percent of white families did have at least one slave. (*America's History,* Seventh Edition, Chapter 3, pp. 92–93)

70. **Answer (C) prohibited slavery throughout the United States.** See response to question 58, above, on the Emancipation Proclamation, for the difference between these two measures. This was the first of the three Reconstruction amendments that abolished slavery and asserted citizenship rights. (*America's History,* Seventh Edition, Chapter 14, p. 453)

71. **Answer (D) created by Congress to help ex-slaves adjust to freedom and secure their basic civil rights.** Passed along with the Civil Rights Act in 1866, the Freedman's Bureau did a lot of good for former slaves in the South, but not nearly enough. (*America's History,* Seventh Edition, Chapter 15, p. 466)

72. **Answer (A) land grants and incorporation.** There weren't any corporate taxes to speak of in the nineteenth century, so governments had to be creative in rewarding enterprise. The railroad companies amassed enormous wealth and opportunity through the property they received from the federal government. (*America's History,* Seventh Edition, Chapter 16, pp. 494–495)

73. **Answer (D) at Wounded Knee.** This massacre was caused by U.S. officials' misunderstanding of the plains Indians' Ghost Dance movement, a spiritual movement begun in the late 1880s that sought a return of the buffalo and the exit of white Americans. Fearing it was a call to war, the U.S. army overreacted in 1890 at Wounded Knee Creek, killing more than 150 Lakota, including women and children. (*America's History,* Seventh Edition, Chapter 16, pp. 519–520, 522)

74. **Answer (B) led to the downfall of the Knights of Labor.** When anarchists joined a labor protest in Chicago in May 1886, and police attempted to disperse the crowd, a bomb was thrown, the police overreacted, and the general public recoiled against the senseless violence. It was a public relations disaster for the nascent labor movement and the Knights of Labor in particular. (*America's History,* Seventh Edition, Chapter 17, p. 552)

75. **Answer (A) accommodation would lead to black economic progress, which would lead to political and civil rights.** Booker T. Washington's ideas contrasted sharply with W.E.B. Du Bois, who advocated a more proactive approach to eradicating inequality. The founding of the NAACP came out of Du Bois' efforts, not Washington's. (*America's History,* Seventh Edition, Chapter 18, pp. 562–563)

76. **Answer (C) A radical ideology began that would last for thirty years.** Although progressives of all kinds sought active responses to the challenges of the modern world, they were not all radicals. It was not a coherent ideology, and furthermore it did not last for thirty years. The 1920s marked a conservative backlash against change, although the tide would turn yet again in the 1930s. (*America's History,* Seventh Edition, Chapter 20, pp. 648–650)

77. **Answer (B) attempt to pack the Courts with his own men.** Roosevelt's "court-packing" scheme is generally explained as executive branch overreach. Furthermore, it did not really work. But Roosevelt felt he had a mandate from the people to alleviate economic pain, and he was impatient with the Supreme Court for putting an end to some of them. (*America's History,* Seventh Edition, Chapter 23, pp. 733–735)

78. **Answer (A) even in peacetime, the United States kept a standing army activated.** This marked a departure from traditions extending back to George Washington, but it was justified on the grounds that the United Sates faced unprecedented dangers in the Cold War. (*America's History,* Seventh Edition, Chapter 25, pp. 795–797)

79. **Answer (C) Bay of Pigs invasion.** The invasion was a botched CIA attempt to overthrow Communist Fidel Castro. The Cuban Missile crisis was related, but it cannot be considered a blunder since Kennedy was ultimately able to resolve the conflict peaceably. (*America's History,* Seventh Edition, Chapter 25, pp. 811–813)

80. **Answer (E) A stable, prosperous economy.** Carter took office amidst widespread economic troubles—the worst economy since the Great Depression. He also faced intractable foreign relations debacles, such as the Iranian hostage crisis, and thus was defeated by Republican Ronald Reagan in the 1980 election. (*America's History,* Seventh Edition, See Chapter 29, pp. 925–926)

Answers for Section II

Part A: Document-Based Question

1. **At the Yalta Conference in February 1945, the United States and the Soviet Union agreed to recognize their separate spheres of influence. In what ways did the United States implement foreign policies in response to the breakdown in relations with the Soviet Union?**

   This document-based question requires you to consider how Documents A–I fit into the larger context of American actions regarding the Soviet Union. The documents illustrate the complexity of the early Cold War, beginning with America's search for allies to contain the spread of Soviet imperialism and ending with its engagement of war in Vietnam. They also reveal a distinction between the high-minded intentions of Yalta, with the establishment of a United Nations that could be instrumental in "harmonizing controversies" (Vandenburg, Document B), and the anxious division that emerged between American and Soviet leaders.

   Document A, a photograph of FDR, Stalin, and Churchill at Yalta in 1945, reveals the tension of the momentous meeting, the strains of World War II, and Roosevelt's poor health; he would die of a stroke just two months later. Documents B and C indicate the subtle shift from the traditional American isolationist impulses to more interventionist policies after World War II. Documents C, D, E, and F illustrate (1) the move toward multilateral alliances in the face of the perceived Soviet threat, and (2) the development of active preparation for potential military action. Documents G, H, and I raise the problems of fissures in America's NATO alliance and indicate the United States' increasing tendency to shoulder the burdens of actual conflict alone.

   Successful responses will describe the evolution of the Cold War, assess the impact of the Cold War on domestic institutions, and explain the effectiveness of Cold War alliances and policies. Outside information to bring in should include some discussion of the development of atomic weapons by the Soviet Union, the degree to which postwar culture was shaped by international fears and competition, the Korean War, and the impact of the Vietnam War on the United States and the world. Your assessment should ultimately determine whether or not the fears that shaped American policy were justified, based on what was known at the time and what is now known about how events turned out.

   To review these events, consult the coverage in Chapter 25 and Chapter 28 of the escalation, fighting, and end of the Vietnam War.

Parts B and C: Free-Response Questions

2. **Compare and contrast the economic, political, and cultural developments of TWO of the following colonial empires in America:**

   Spain

   Great Britain

   France

   The Netherlands

   This compare-and-contrast question gives you the opportunity to choose the two empires you are best equipped to explain. Again, this type of question should lend itself to an obvious organizational structure. You should point out both similarities and differences. Below are some comparative points in provided categories of economic, political, and cultural (religious) developments. See Chapters 1 and 2 to review the colonial empires.

Economic:

- The Spanish sought gold and silver.
- The English sought wealth through cash crops and trade.
- The French colonists engaged in the fur trade.
- The Dutch focused on trade.

Political:

- The French and Spanish used missionaries to help organize and maintain authority.
- English colonists were given a great deal of autonomy and self-governance.

Cultural:

- The Spanish forced American Indians to convert to Catholicism.
- French missionaries (Jesuits, known as Black Robes) were respectful of Indian spiritual practices.
- The French and Dutch both struggled to get enough settlers to the Americas.
- The English did not attempt forced conversions but sought to remove Indians from lands they desired for cultivation; northern colonies were community-, religion-, and family-oriented, while Chesapeake colonies were focused on profit.
- Disease devastated Indian tribes that came into contact with Europeans, causing social unrest and weakening resistance.

3. **How and why did transportation improvements spark economic growth between 1800 and 1860?**

An analytical way to respond to this is to discuss both transportation improvements and other policies that facilitated the rise of a market economy.

Transportation improvements included:

- National Road and other roads
- Charters for turnpike companies
- The Erie Canal and other canals
- Steamships
- Early railroads

Other policies that facilitated the "Capitalist Commonwealth":

- Hamilton's financial policies, including the First Bank of the United States
- State-chartered banks
- The U.S. Patent Office
- Rights given for private enterprise
- Legal protections for corporate charters and eminent domain for transportation

To review this topic, see Chapter 8.

4. **"It is impossible to understand American attitudes and values without examining the influence of the frontier." Assess the validity of this statement.**

For the strongest response you ought to have mentioned Frederick Jackson Turner's thesis on the vanishing frontier by name; ideally, you will have addressed both sides of the argument. Here are some ideas that support and refute the statement:

Agree: The West has had a profound impact on American attitudes and values, for good reason.

- Frederick Jackson Turner's thesis
- Safety valve for social expansion
- Democratization—land available for those willing to work it (mention Homestead Act and other incentives)
- "Rugged individualism"

Disagree: Many aspects of the story of the West are mythical and not rooted in historical realities.

- Turner's thesis was an overstatement that ignored the presence of Native Americans.
- Immigrants from colonial times onward already possessed rugged individualism or they could not have settled America.
- Immigrants left repressive regimes at home for more democracy and economic opportunity in the United States.
- The safety valve was a myth: mention Molly Maguires, race riots, strikes, Chinese exclusion.
- Rugged individualism of the West is a myth, as its settlement would have been impossible without the actions of the federal government (incentive acts, railroad land grants, roads and dams built, Indian Wars fought by the Army that made white settlement possible)

See Chapter 16 of America's History *for an overview of trans-Mississippi settlement.*

5. **To what extent have the United States' international interventions from 1898 to the present represented the desire to spread democratic institutions?**

Remember to take a stand somewhere along the spectrum of "did" to "did not" represent the desire to spread democracy. Below are some examples to support each end of the spectrum, and you may choose to complicate the issue by mentioning items from each category.

Examples supporting Americans' desire to spread democracy:

- Assisting Cubans with their independence from Spain
- Wilson's Fourteen Points
- U.S. involvement in World War I
- FDR's Good Neighbor policy in Latin America
- Lend-lease
- U.S. involvement in World War II

- Cold War policies such as the Marshall Plan and the Berlin airlift
- Korean and Vietnam wars
- Both Iraq wars
- Afghanistan War/Taliban

Examples to support a foreign policy tradition of self-interest:

- Retention of the Philippines, Guam, and Puerto Rico following the Spanish-American War
- Open Door policy in Asia
- Refusing to join the League of Nations
- CIA covert operations during the Cold War
- Korean and Vietnam wars

Text Credits

Page 36, Question 7. Miguel Leon-Portilla. "The Broken Spears." Copyright © 1962, 1990 by Miguel Leon-Portilla. Expanded and Updated Edition © 1992 by Miguel Leon-Portilla. Reprinted by permission of Beacon Press, Boston.

Page 61, Question 14. Thomas Grimke. "Give me a host of educated pious mothers and sisters . . ." Reprinted by permission by Columbia University Press.

Page 63, Document C. Dr. Benjamin Rush. Niles: "Address to the People of the United States," Philadelphia, 1787," as reprinted from *The Annals of America,* Copyright © 1976, 2003 Encyclopedia Brittanica, Inc., 85–88.

Page 87, Document D. Alexis de Tocqueville, "Education of Young Women in The United States," 1840, from *Democracy in America* by Alexis de Tocqueville, translated by Henry Reeve, copyright © 1945 and renewed 1973 by Alfred A. Knopf, a division of Random House, Inc. Used by permission of Alfred A. Knopf, a division of Random House 209–210.

Page 131, Document G. Henry Pratt Fairchild, *The Melting Pot Mistake*, 1926; *The Meltin-Pot Mistake*, Boston, 1926: "The Duty of America," as reprinted from *The Annals of America*, Vol. 15 Copyright © 1976, 2003 Encyclopedia Brittanica, Inc.

Page 153, Document A. Rexford. G. Tugwell, excerpt from "Design for Government" from *The Battle for Democracy* (New York: Columbia University Press, 1935), 12-16. Copyright 1935 by Columbia University Press. Reprinted with permission of the publisher.

Page 153, Document C. Mary Ross, "Why Social Security?" 1936; Social Security Board Publication No. 15: Why Social Security?, Washington, 1937, SS1.2: So 1/2, as reprinted from *The Annals of America,* Vol. 15 Copyright © 1976, 2003 (Encyclopedia Brittanica, Inc., 1968), 471–474.

Page 154, Document D. Norman Thomas, "What Was the New Deal?" 1936; Reprinted with permission of Scribner, an imprint of Simon & Schuster Adult Publishing Group from *After the New Deal, What?* By Norman Thomas. Copyright © 1936 by Norman Thomas; copyright renewed © 1963 by Norman Thomas, pp. 16–25. All rights reserved.

Page 154, Document E. Odette Keun, "TVA in Foreign Eyes," 1937. *A Foreigner Looks at the TVA,* New York, 1937, pp. 75–84.

Page 154, Document F. Alfred Hayes/Earl Robinson, "Joe Hill," 1938; As reprinted by Hal Leonard Vol. 15 © 1976, 2003, 515–516.

Page 155, Document H. Robert A. Taft, "New Problems of Government," *Speech to the Institute of Public Affairs,* University of Virginia, 1939; A Republican Program, Cleveland, 1939, pp 21–34, as reprinted in *The Annals of America,* Vol. 15, © Copyright 1976, 2003 Encyclopedia Britannica, Inc., 571-574.

Page 170, Question 1. Excerpt from "Silent Spring" by Rachel Carson. Copyright © 1962 by Rachel L. Carson, renewed 1990 by Roger Christie. Reprinted by permission of Houghton Mifflin Harcourt Publishing Company. All rights reserved.

Page 174, Document A. Barry Commoner, "The First Law of Ecology: Everything is Connected to Everything Else," 1971; From *The Closing Circle: Nature, Man & Technology* by Barry Commoner. Copyright © 1971 by Barry Commoner. Reprinted by permission of Alfred A. Knopf, Inc., as reprinted in Robert Griffith, *Major Problems in American History Since 1945,* (New York: D.C. Heath 1992).

Page 175, Document C. James G.Watt, *Interview with U.S. News and World Report* on Economic Development and the Environment, 1981; "Interview with James G. Watt, Secretary of the Interior." Copyright 1981, U.S. News and World Report.

Page 247, Document C. Winston Churchill, The Sinews of Peace Speech at Westminster College (1946); VSD, March 15, 1946: "Alliance of English-Speaking People," as reprinted in *The Annals of America,* Vol. 16 Copyright © 1976, 2003, Encyclopedia Brittanica, Inc., 365–369.

Page 247, Document D. Nikolai Novikov, "Soviet Ambassador to the United States, Telegram (1946)." Reprinted by permission Cold War International History Project. **www.cwihp.org**